STUDIES IN EVANGELICAL HISTORY AND THOUGHT

Communion in the Spirit

The Holy Spirit as the Bond of Union in the Theology of Jonathan Edwards

STUDIES IN EVANGELICAL HISTORY AND THOUGHT

A full listing of titles in this series
appears at the end of this book

STUDIES IN EVANGELICAL HISTORY AND THOUGHT

Communion in the Spirit

The Holy Spirit as the Bond of Union in the Theology of Jonathan Edwards

Robert W. Caldwell III

Wipf & Stock
PUBLISHERS
Eugene, Oregon

Wipf and Stock Publishers
199 W 8th Ave, Suite 3
Eugene, OR 97401

Communion in the Spirit
The Holy Spirit as the Bond of Union in the Theology of Jonathan Edwards
By Caldwell, Robert W., III
Copyright©2006 Paternoster
ISBN 13: 978-1-55635-238-6
ISBN 10: 1-55635-238-7
Publication date 1/31/2007
Previously published by Paternoster, 2006

This Edition Published by Wipf and Stock Publishers
by arrangement with Paternoster

Paternoster
9 Holdom Avenue
Bletchley
Milton Keyes, MK1 1QR
Great Britain

STUDIES IN EVANGELICAL HISTORY AND THOUGHT

Series Preface

The Evangelical movement has been marked by its union of four emphases: on the Bible, on the cross of Christ, on conversion as the entry to the Christian life and on the responsibility of the believer to be active. The present series is designed to publish scholarly studies of any aspect of this movement in Britain or overseas. Its volumes include social analysis as well as exploration of Evangelical ideas. The books in the series consider aspects of the movement shaped by the Evangelical Revival of the eighteenth century, when the impetus to mission began to turn the popular Protestantism of the British Isles and North America into a global phenomenon. The series aims to reap some of the rich harvest of academic research about those who, over the centuries, have believed that they had a gospel to tell to the nations.

Series Editors

David Bebbington, Professor of History, University of Stirling, Stirling, Scotland, UK

John H.Y. Briggs, Senior Research Fellow in Ecclesiastical History and Director of the Centre for Baptist History and Heritage, Regent's Park College, Oxford, UK

Timothy Larsen, Professor of Theology, Wheaton College, Illinois, USA

Mark A. Noll, McManis Professor of Christian Thought, Wheaton College, Wheaton, Illinois, USA

Ian M. Randall, Deputy Principal and Lecturer in Church History and Spirituality, Spurgeon's College, London, UK, and a Senior Research Fellow, International Baptist Theological Seminary, Prague, Czech Republic

For my wife, Lisa
Proverbs 18:22

Contents

	Preface	xiii
	Acknowledgements	xv
	Introduction	
	The Holy Spirit as the Bond of Union in the Theology of Jonathan Edwards	1
I.1	Focus of Our Study	4
I.2	Importance of Our Study	8
I.3	Outline of Our Study	13

Part I – Behind the Scenes: The Trinity and the Immanent Spirit

	Chapter 1	
	Trinity: Jonathan Edwards's Trinitarianism	19
1.1	Explorations of Divinity: The Ontological Setting of Edwards's Trinitarianism	20
1.2	Outlines of the Immanent Trinity: Edwards's "Discourse on the Trinity"	28
1.3	The Augustinian "Flavor" of Edwards' Trinitarianism	33
	Chapter 2	
	Pneumatology: The Holy Spirit as the Bond of Union of the Immanent Trinity	41
2.1	The Immanent Spirit and the Shape of Union	42
2.2	Facets of Divine Love: The Spirit as God's Holiness, Excellency, Happiness, Fullness, and Grace	49
2.2.1	*Holiness*	50

2.2.2	*Excellency*	50
2.2.3	*Happiness*	51
2.2.4	*Fullness*	51
2.2.5	*Grace*	52
2.2.6	*Communication, Communion and Participation*	54

Part II – Setting the Stage: Bridges to Creation and Redemption

Chapter 3
The Trinitarian Plan of Creation and Redemption — 59

3.1	Outward Bound: God's Diffusive Disposition, the Covenant of Redemption, and the Holy Spirit	60
3.1.1	*God's Communicative Disposition*	61
3.1.2	*The Continuity of God's Immanent and Economic Activity*	63
3.1.3	*The Covenant of Redemption*	65
3.2	Anthropology: The Receivers of Communicated Divine Glory	68
3.3	Segue: The Fall and the Loss of the Supernatural Image	71

Chapter 4
Christology: The Holy Spirit as the Bond of Union of Christ's Two Natures — 74

4.1	The Redemptive Plan of the Incarnate Christ	77
4.1.1	*The Necessity of the Incarnation*	77
4.1.2	*The Necessity of the Incarnation Post Creation*	80
4.2	The Spirit as the Bond of Union of the *Unio Personalis*	83
4.2.1	*Exegetical Arguments*	87
4.2.2	*Theological Arguments*	89
4.2.3	*Christ's Knowledge and Edwards's Reformed Christological Language*	93
4.3	Concluding Remarks	96

Part III – Acts in the Drama of Redemption: The Spirit and the Stages of the Christian Life

Chapter 5
Regeneration and Justification: The Holy Spirit as the Bond of the Christian's Union with Christ — 101

5.1	"Grace After a Principle of Nature:" The Holy Spirit's Union with the Saint	102
5.1.1	*The Movement of the Spirit into the Soul: Illumination and Infusion*	104
5.1.2	*The Movement of the Spirit in the Soul: The Nature of Grace*	108
5.1.3	*The Movement of the Spirit in the Soul: Grace "After a Principle of Nature"*	111
5.1.4	*The Nature of the Pneumatological Union: A Compatiblist Model*	118
5.2	Faith as a "Union of Soul to Christ as Savior:" The Saint's Union with Christ	120
5.2.1	*The Spirit's Indwelling as the Logical Ground of the Salvation Process*	121
5.2.2	*Faith and Its Relation to Divine Love*	126
5.2.3	*Faith as an Act of Union with Christ*	130
5.3	The "Real" and the "Legal:" Union with Christ and Justification	133

Chapter 6
Sanctification: The Holy Spirit as the Bond of Union in the Christian Life — 138

6.1	Personal Sanctification: The Holy Spirit and the Nature of Christian Experience	141
6.1.1	*Spiritual Sight: The Foundation of Christian Experience*	142
6.2	Ecclesial Sanctification: The Holy Spirit as the Bond of Union in the Church	155
6.2.1	*The Holy Spirit among the Ecclesial Community*	157

Part IV – Finale: The Spirit and the Christian's Glorification

Chapter 7
Glorification: The Holy Spirit as the Bond of Union in Heaven   169

7.1	A Brief History of Heaven	170
7.1.1	*Heaven's Creation: Imagining Heaven's Place and Original Inhabitants*	170
7.1.2	*Heaven and the History of Redemption*	173
7.1.3	*Heaven's First Period: From Creation to Christ's Ascension*	174
7.1.4	*Heaven's Second Period: From Christ's Ascension to the Consummation*	175
7.1.5	*The Church Triumphant and the Beatific Vision*	177
7.2	Heaven is a World of Union: Heaven's Third Period from the Consummation to Eternity	182
7.2.1	*Heaven: The Place of Love*	184
7.2.2	*Heaven, Union with Christ, and the Object of Love*	186
7.2.3	*Heaven and the Eternal Progress of Love and Union*	189

Chapter 8
Conclusion   194

8.1	The Spirit and Spiritual Union in Edwards's Theology	196
8.2	The Spirit as the Bond of Union and the Structure of Edwards's Theology	198
8.3	Postscript: Sarah Edwards on Being "Lost in God"	200

Bibliography   203

Name and Subject Index   209

Preface

Jonathan Edwards (1703-1758), the colonial American pastor and theologian, is well known for his life-long fascination with the nature of religious experience. What is not well-known is the fact that this fascination was part of a wider theological vision he pursued throughout his life, a vision anchored in the bedrock of a trinitarian theology which prominently featured the doctrine of the Holy Spirit. Following Augustine's trinitarian insights, Edwards conceived of the Holy Spirit as the personal divine love of the Godhead, a love which binds the Father and Son together in a union of infinite affection and which can be communicated to the hearts of created beings. This study seeks to examine the continuities Edwards drew between the Holy Spirit's inner-trinitarian and economic operations. I argue that, in Edwards's theology, the Holy Spirit's activity as the bond of the trinitarian union between the Father and the Son is paradigmatic for all other holy unions in his theology. In the personal union of Christ's two natures, the mystical union believers have with Christ, and the union of fellowship that believers have with each other, the Holy Spirit works *ad extra* in a manner that is patterned after his inner-trinitarian work.

Our study will expose us to the major regions of Edwards's pneumatology. We first shall investigate Edwards's understanding of the Spirit as the third person of the Trinity, giving particular attention to the way Edwards understands the Spirit as the bond of union of the Godhead. From there, our investigation will turn to the Spirit's economic work in Edwards's theology where we will observe the parallels he envisioned between his immanent trinitarian work, and his work *ad extra*. Here the Spirit operates as the bond of union in redemption, uniting Christ's two natures, and uniting believers together in Christ. This study demonstrates the strong trinitarian shape of Edwards's theology of the spiritual life by highlighting the vital links between the believer's devotional life and the persons of the Trinity.

ACKNOWLEDGEMENTS

Many years went into the preparation and writing of this book which was originally my doctoral dissertation which I defended at Trinity Evangelical Divinity School in 2003. Many individuals aided in the effort. At Trinity, my doctoral advisor, Douglas Sweeney, truly modeled for me the characteristics of an outstanding academic mentor. Anyone who has been through the gauntlet of a doctoral dissertation knows that one not only needs direction and wisdom but (perhaps more importantly) encouragement to make it through the long months of seemingly fruitless labor. Doug provided me with these in abundance and much more, rendering my time in doctoral work a joy. I would also like to recognize the other members of my dissertation committee – Willem VanGemeren and Kevin J. Vanhoozer – who provided valuable support and insight toward the end of the doctoral process. Steven Studebaker, fellow Trinity alum and at the time a doctoral student at Marquette University, proved to be a stimulating conversation partner who helped sharpen my insights into Edwards's trinitarianism. It goes without saying that while these scholars challenged and shaped my thinking in the writing process, I take full responsibility for the text, including the errors and overstatements that may be found therein.

I would also like to recognize two administrators at Southwestern Baptist Theological Seminary in Fort Worth, Texas, for their encouragement and making room in my schedule to finish this project: Malcolm Yarnell, Assistant Dean of the Division of Theological Studies, and David Allen, Dean of the School of Theology. Andy Tooley assisted in the work on the index and in some much needed legwork in researching.

Lastly, I would like to recognize my best friend, my wife, Lisa, who stood beside me for many years supporting this project. Words cannot express my gratitude and love to her. Her patience is exemplary; her encouragement, priceless. I dedicate this book to her.

Robert W. Caldwell III
Southwestern Baptist Theological Seminary
August 2006

Introduction

The Holy Spirit as the Bond of Union in the Theology of Jonathan Edwards

> All divine communion, or communion of the creatures with God or with one another in God, seems to be by the Holy Ghost. 'Tis by this that believers have communion with Christ, and I suppose 'tis by this that the man Christ Jesus has communion with the eternal Logos. The Spirit of God is the bond of perfectness by which God, Jesus Christ, and the church are united together.[1]

Well known for his fiery sermon "Sinners in the Hands of an Angry God" as well as for his penetrating insights into the nature of the Christian's "religious affections," the colonial American pastor and theologian Jonathan Edwards (1703-1758) has remained a prominent fixture in the psyche of American Christianity since international attention was turned to his Northampton ministry in the mid 1730s.[2] Since then, countless individuals have looked to his writings as a well-spring of seemingly endless information. English-speaking Christians of many stripes have long prized Edwards for his piety, his theological acumen, and spiritual wisdom, a fact evinced by the multiple editions and reprints of his works that have come off the presses over the past

---

1 Jonathan Edwards, "Miscellanies" No. 487, in *The Works of Jonathan Edwards*, vol. 13, *The "Miscellanies" a-500*, ed. Thomas A. Schafer (New Haven: Yale University Press, 1994), 529-30. After initial citation, individual volumes in the Yale edition of Edwards's works will be indicated as *Works* followed by the volume and page numbers.

2 The religious revival that took place in Edwards's Northampton, Massachusetts congregation in the mid 1730s attracted the attention of Isaac Watts, the celebrated English hymn-writer, who published Edwards's account of it in 1737. See *A Faithful Narrative of the Surprising Work of God in the Conversion of Many Hundreds of Souls in Northampton*, in *The Works of Jonathan Edwards*, vol. 4, *The Great Awakening*, ed. C. C. Goen (New Haven: Yale University Press, 1972), 144-211; hereafter referred to as *A Faithful Narrative*. For further biographical accounts of Edwards's life, see George Marsden, *Jonathan Edwards: A Life* (New Haven: Yale, 2003); Iain H. Murray, *Jonathan Edwards: A New Biography* (Carlisle, Pa.: Banner of Truth, 1987); and Patricia J. Tracy, *Jonathan Edwards, Pastor: Religion and Society in Eighteenth-Century Northampton* (New York: Hill and Wang, 1979).

two and a half centuries.³ In the last fifty years, Edwards has attracted much attention in the American academy due primarily to the energetic leadership and provocative scholarship of Perry Miller in the 1940s through the early 60s.⁴ In the wake of Miller's work, a renaissance of Edwards scholarship flourished, which generated a succession of excellent studies on Edwards's life and thought,⁵ and also produced a new critical edition of his works.⁶ More recently, theologians and historians interested in historical theology have taken notice of Edwards, finding in him a sophisticated and intriguing dialogue partner on issues such as the doctrine of God, the Trinity, the nature of salvation, and religious pluralism.⁷ This rise of interest in Edwards as a

---

3   While Thomas Schafer's brief appendix, "Previous Publication of the 'Miscellanies'" (*Works*, 13:545-57) is a publication history of Edwards's "Miscellanies" notebooks, it contains an excellent overview of the major publications of Edwards's writings. For studies that examine the different ways Edwards shaped American Christianity, see Joseph A. Conforti, *Jonathan Edwards, Religious Tradition, and American Culture* (Chapel Hill: University of North Carolina Press, 1995); *Jonathan Edwards's Writings: Text, Context, Interpretation*, ed. Stephen J. Stein (Bloomington: Indiana University Press, 1996); *Edwards in Our Time: Jonathan Edwards and the Shaping of American Religion*, ed. Sang Hyun Lee and Allen C. Guelzo (Grand Rapids: Eerdmans, 1999); and Douglas A. Sweeney, *Nathaniel Taylor, New Haven Theology and the Legacy of Jonathan Edwards* (New York: Oxford, 2003).
4   See his intellectual biography of Edwards, *Jonathan Edwards* (New York: William Sloan Associates, 1949) as well his article, "The Rhetoric of Sensation," in *Errand Into the Wilderness* (Cambridge, Mass.: Belknap, 1964), 168-83.
5   Of the numerous studies on Edwards's thought in the generation after Miller's death, three of the most important are Conrad Cherry, *The Theology of Jonathan Edwards: A Reappraisal* (Garden City, N.Y.: Doubleday, 1966); Roland Delattre, *Beauty and Sensibility in the Thought of Jonathan Edwards: An Essay in Aesthetics and Theological Ethics* (New Haven: Yale University Press, 1968); and Sang Hyun Lee, *The Philosophical Theology of Jonathan Edwards*, (Princeton: Princeton University Press, 1988). Citations from Lee's book will be drawn from the expanded Princeton University Press edition (2000).
6   *The Works of Jonathan Edwards* (New Haven: Yale University Press, 1957 to date). There are currently twenty-three volumes published out of the projected twenty-six.
7   In addition to Sang Hyun Lee's, *Philosophical Theology of Jonathan Edwards*, see Robert W. Jenson, *America's Theologian: A Recommendation of Jonathan Edwards* (New York: Oxford, 1988); Anri Morimoto, *Jonathan Edwards and the Catholic Vision of Salvation* (University Park, Pa.: Penn State Press, 1995); Michael J. McClymond, *Encounters with God: An Approach to the Theology of Jonathan Edwards* (New York: Oxford, 1998); Stephen R. Holmes, *God of Grace and God of Glory: An Account of the Theology of Jonathan Edwards* (Grand Rapids: Eerdmans, 2000); Gerald R. McDermott, *Jonathan Edwards Confronts the Gods: Christian Theology, Enlightenment Religion, and Non-Christian Faiths* (New York: Oxford, 2000); Robert E. Brown, *Jonathan Edwards and the Bible* (Bloomington: Indiana University Press, 2002); Amy Plantinga Pauw, *The Supreme Harmony of All: The*

theologian is partially due, no doubt, to the greater accessibility of his works provided by the Yale edition, as well as the publication of his private theological notebooks, which show him "at work" as a theologian.[8] By 1994, M. X. Lesser documented over three thousand articles, essays, monographs, and dissertations which have been published on his life and thought.[9] Clearly, when it comes to the academy, Jonathan Edwards seems to have "arrived." Yet the question arises: is there anything else that can be mined from his writings?

While he is well-known for his insights on the nature of religious experience, it may come as a surprise to those not familiar with the inner mechanics of his theology that this life-long fascination was part of a wider theological vision he pursued throughout his life; a vision anchored in the bedrock of a trinitarian theology that prominently featured the doctrine of the Holy Spirit. As we shall see in the following study, Edwards conceived of the Holy Spirit as the personal divine love of the Godhead, a love which binds the Father and Son together in a union of infinite affection and which can be communicated to the hearts of created beings in such a way that they too can be united to God and participate in this divine affection. Thus, according to Edwards, to experience true religious affections is actually to partake of the divine nature (2 Pet 1:4) and to commune in the trinitarian society. The Trinity and Christian spirituality are deeply intertwined in his theology, and the common link between these two theological spheres is the Holy Spirit. Furthermore, Edwards makes it explicit throughout his theological reflections

---

Trinitarian Theology of Jonathan Edwards (Grand Rapids: Eerdmans, 2002); Stephen J. Nichols, *An Absolute Sort of Certainty: The Holy Spirit and the Apologetics of Jonathan Edwards* (Phillipsburg, NJ: Presbyterian and Reformed, 2003); William J. Danaher Jr., *The Trinitarian Ethics of Jonathan Edwards* (Louisville: Westminster John Knox Press, 2004); and *The Princeton Companion to Jonathan Edwards* ed. Sang Hyun Lee (Princeton: Princeton University Press, 2005).

8 Of the many scriptural, theological, and philosophical notebooks that Edwards kept, his main theological workshop was undoubtedly his "Miscellanies" notebooks, which occupies four volumes in the Yale edition (vols. 13, 18, 20, and 23). This notebook, which Edwards himself indexed, consists of a series of roughly 1400 theological essays, paragraphs, references, and quotations. Their value lies in the fact that we can trace his theological development by watching him take an idea, build upon it, and shape it through years of reflection.

9 See M. X. Lesser's two volumes on Edwards's bibliography: *Jonathan Edwards: A Reference Guide* (Boston: G. K. Hall & Co., 1981), and *Jonathan Edwards: An Annotated Bibliography, 1979-1993*, Bibliographies and Indexes in Religious Studies, number 30 (Westport, Conn.: Greenwood Press, 1994). For studies which canvas the prominent works done in the last decade, see Kenneth P. Minkema, "Jonathan Edwards in the Twentieth Century," *Journal of the Evangelical Theological Society* 47.4 (2004): 659-87, and Sean Michael Lucas, "Jonathan Edwards Between Church and Academy," in *The Legacy of Jonathan Edwards*, ed. D. G. Hart, Sean Michael Lucas, and Stephen J. Nichols (Grand Rapids: Baker Academic, 2003), 228-47.

that we are in error if we distinguish too sharply between the Spirit's immanent trinitarian life and his external activities in the work of redemption. In other words, the Spirit repeats his own immanent trinitarian activity within the elect in a finite way, catching them up into the current of divine love by uniting them to Christ, and enabling them to "participate" in the union, communion, and eternal life of the Trinity. Yet what does Edwards mean when he states that the Holy Spirit repeats himself in the elect? How do the saints participate in the divine nature? What, in short, does Edwards mean by union in his theology? In this study we will address these questions as we analyze a fundamental dynamic of Edwards's pneumatology, namely, that the Holy Spirit is the bond of union throughout his theology.

I.1 Focus of Our Study

Throughout the centuries Christian theologians have identified three different unions which are vitally important to Christian theology. The first, the inner-trinitarian union, is that union which obtains among the Father, Son, and Holy Spirit within the Godhead. Orthodox Christian theology strongly affirms and defends monotheism, while at the same time it acknowledges the profound mystery that though God is One, he has never been "alone." Through intensive reflection on the Scriptures, the church over the centuries has discerned that there mysteriously subsist three distinct persons within the Godhead, each of whom is infinitely and eternally God. The three are bound in an inexplicable union whereby they share a common essence (i.e., they are consubstantial with one another) and fully interpenetrate and coinhere each other (i.e., they share the property of perichoresis). Yet the fact that there are three persons in the Godhead neither threatens the divine unity nor Christianity's commitment to monotheism.[10] This mysterious inner-trinitarian union, which human reason can only faintly discern with the aid of special revelation, renders it possible for us to speak of the doctrine of the Trinity.

Equally fascinating and no less mysterious is the second union, known as the personal or *hypostatic* union. This union renders it possible for us to speak of the incarnation. Part of the wonder of the gospel lies in the miracle of Immanuel, or God with us (Isa 7:14; Matt 1:23). Orthodox Christians teach that God the Son, the second person of the Trinity, assumed a complete human nature into union with his own divine nature at the moment of the incarnation. Theologians refer to this union as the "personal" or *hypostatic* union (from the Greek word for person) because in it the divine person of God the Son is united

---

10 For more details on Edwards's trinitarianism see chapter one below. For a historical introduction to the doctrine of the Trinity, see Robert Letham, *The Holy Trinity: In Scripture, History, Theology, and Worship* (Phillipsburg, NJ: Presbyterian and Reformed, 2004).

to a complete human being, bringing about the "God-man," Jesus Christ.[11]

A third union, known as the mystical union, the *unio Christi,* or the Christian's union with Christ, seeks to articulate what the New Testament writers (especially the apostle Paul) meant by the fact that Christians individually and collectively are "in Christ." Paul writes that "if any man be *in Christ*, he is a new creature" (2 Cor 5:17).[12] Similarly, Jesus teaches in the parable of the vine and the branches that "He that abideth *in me*, and I in him, the same bringeth forth much fruit: for without me ye can do nothing" (John 15:5). It has often been recognized that in the Christian's union with Christ something more is indicated than merely a moral observance of Jesus' teachings. As the union of human marriage, from a theological point of view, is something more than either a legal document or an agreement between a man and a woman, so the church's union with Christ, also likened to human marriage (Eph 5:23, 32-33; Rev 21:2, 9), is something more than membership in a church, or a prayerful decision to follow Christ. The key question is what is the nature of this "something more?" As we shall see in the forthcoming chapters, Edwards had his own understanding of this union. For now we must recognize that whatever "union with Christ" is, it is something of vital interest to Christian theology for without it there is no salvation, no eternal life.[13]

Thus it is that the concept of union is of vital importance to Christian theology. Without it we would not be able to articulate the Trinity, the incarnation, or the nature of salvation as portrayed in the Scriptures. Christian theology, in short, would hardly be "Christian" were it not for a developed understanding of union.

When we turn to the writings of Jonathan Edwards, we find that he not only recognizes the centrality of these three unions, but he also sees a great degree of similarity between them. Early in his theological development, while he was a twenty-one year old tutor of undergraduates at Yale College (1725), he jotted down an intriguing note in his "Miscellanies" notebook on the nature of spiritual union. "What insight I have in the nature of minds," he writes in entry No. 184, "I am convinced that there is no guessing what kind of union and mixtion, by consciousness or otherwise, there may be between them." He does not specify the nature of his "insight," but he is certain that by it "all difficulty is removed in believing what the Scripture declares about spiritual unions - of the persons of the Trinity, of the two natures of Christ, of Christ and the minds

---

11 For more details on Edwards's christology, see chapter four. For an introduction to christology, see Donald Macleod, *The Person of Christ*, Contours of Christian Theology, ed. Gerald Bray (Downers Grove, Ill.: InterVarsity Press, 1998).
12 All Scripture citations, unless otherwise noted, will be taken from the King James Version to avoid any potential confusion with Edwards's own biblical citations.
13 For more details on Edwards's doctrine of the Christian's union with Christ, see chapter five.

of saints."[14] Clearly, his insight into the nature of minds enabled him to see a strong degree of continuity between these unions, tying them together in some way which he leaves unspecified.

Elsewhere we observe that the common denominator in each of these unions is the presence and agency of the Holy Spirit who unites persons together in a bond of divine love. As observed in the quote opening this chapter, Edwards writes that "All divine communion, or communion of the creatures with God or with one another in God, seems to be by the Holy Ghost." This includes the communion of the Father and the Son in the immanent Trinity, the communion "the man Christ Jesus has . . . with the eternal Logos," and the communion that believers have with Christ and with one another in Christ. "The Spirit of God is the bond of perfectness by which God, Jesus Christ, and the church are united together."[15] Similarly, in his *Treatise on Grace*, Edwards writes that "the holiness of God consist[s] in his love, especially in the perfect and intimate union and love there is between the Father and the Son. But the Spirit that proceeds from the Father and the Son is the bond of this union [of love between them], *as it is of all holy union* between the Father and the Son, and between God and the creature, and between the creatures among themselves."[16] It is in the person of the Holy Spirit where communion within God and with God obtains. He is the context and the medium of their divine fellowship.

The reason why Edwards can give such theological versatility to the Spirit, locating him as the agent of union throughout his theology, has to do not only with the fact that he understands the Spirit to be the eternal and infinite divine love of the Godhead, uniting the Father and the Son together, but also due to the fact that this divine love, who is the Spirit, is "repeatable" outside of the immanent Trinity within the creation. Dwelling in the hearts of the saints and angels, the Spirit repeats the love that he essentially is externally within the hearts of created beings. In distinguishing the Spirit's work in the hearts of the saint from the hearts of the unregenerate, Edwards writes that

> the Spirit of God in the souls of his saints exerts its own proper nature; that is to say, it communicates and exerts itself in the soul in those acts which are its proper, natural and essential acts in itself *ad intra*, or within the Deity from all eternity. The proper nature of the Spirit of God, the act which is its nature and wherein its being consists, is (as we have shown) divine love. Therefore the Holy Ghost influences the minds of the godly by living in the godly. . . . The Spirit of

---

14 Edwards, "Miscellanies" No. 184, in *Works*, 13:330.
15 Jonathan Edwards, "Miscellanies" No. 487, in *Works*, 13:529-30.
16 Jonathan Edwards, *Treatise on Grace*, in *The Works of Jonathan Edwards*, vol. 21, *Writings on the Trinity, Grace, and Faith*, ed. Sang Hyun Lee (New Haven: Yale University Press, 2003), 186, emphasis mine.

God operates in the minds of the godly by only being in them, uniting itself to their souls, and living in 'em and acting itself.[17]

Here Edwards appears to be saying that the Holy Spirit operates in godly souls in much the same manner as he does within the immanent Trinity; he "communicates and exerts" himself in the souls of the godly, "in those acts which are its proper, natural and essential acts in itself *ad intra*, or within the Deity from all eternity." Likewise, he operates in them as divine love, "uniting itself to their souls, and living in 'em and acting itself." From these somewhat cryptic statements emerges a larger pattern which we find throughout Edwards's theology: that the Holy Spirit's immanent ways within the Godhead are not to be too sharply distinguished from his economic ways in his work of redemption. There is, in other words, a great deal of continuity in the Spirit's *ad intra* and *ad extra* operations, a continuity that results in a substantial similarity between the inner-trinitarian, hypostatic, and mystical unions in Edwards's theology. This study will focus specifically on Edwards's understanding of these pneumatologically effected unions, noting the parallels between the immanent and economic trinities, and how this feature in his thought effects the shape of his theology.

Numerous theological questions arise at this point, which could direct our study down a number of different paths. What does Edwards mean exactly when he says that God communicates and repeats the fullness of his divine love externally? Is he teaching something akin to a doctrine of *theosis*? How can the Holy Spirit be the uniting agent of Christ's two natures? Does Edwards's formulation of the Holy Spirit as divine love threaten the personhood of the Spirit? As frustrating as these questions may be, more frustrating is the fact that Edwards does not explicitly answer many of them. As is well-known, his life was cut short right at the time he was planning to summarize his theology in several major treatises, so we are not left with any systematic theology to consult.[18] Furthermore, when he wrote on issues of spiritual union, we find

---

17 Edwards, "Miscellanies" No. 471, in *Works*, 13:513. Editor Thomas A. Schafer notes that Edwards most probably refers to "Miscellanies" Nos. 94 and 98 in his parenthetical note "as we have shown."

18 Shortly before the time of his sudden death (March, 1758), Edwards was beginning plans to write two "great works" on biblical theology. The first was to be a work he entitled a *History of the Work of Redemption*, which he envisioned would be "a body of divinity in an entire new method, being thrown into the form of a history; considering the affair of Christian Theology, as the whole of it." Edwards had preached a series of sermons on this topic in 1739, which is printed in *The Works of Jonathan Edwards*, vol. 9, *A History of the Work of Redemption*, ed. John F. Wilson (New Haven: Yale University Press, 1989), 111-528 (hereafter, *History of Redemption*). The other "great work" he entitled *The Harmony of the Old and New Testament*, which would consist of demonstrating the harmonies of the Testaments in three areas: prophecy, typology, and doctrine. See his Letter No. 230, "To the

him sticking closely to the language and categories of Scripture without offering substantial theological analyses. Nevertheless, Edwards does give us clues throughout his writings, enough so that by the end of our study we shall have a deeper understanding of how spiritual union operated in his theology, and how the Spirit is the agent of these unions.

Perhaps the best way to bring focus to our study of Edwards's pneumatology is to organize it around the following question: In the theology of Jonathan Edwards, what is the relationship between the Holy Spirit's immanent trinitarian activity and his economic operations in redemption? This question underscores the Holy Spirit's work as the bond of union in Edwards's theology in a way that will enable us to compare the immanent trinitarian activity of the Spirit with his economic operations, so that we may determine the similarities and differences between the Spirit's work in these two realms. This question will also serve to limit our investigation. The following study is not a systematic theology of Edwards's pneumatology. There will be points when we need to contextualize our analysis in the broader vistas of Edwards's thought, but we will primarily concern ourselves with what Edwards has to say about spiritual union, the Spirit's work as the bond of union, and the degree to which there is continuity between the Spirit's work *ad intra* and *ad extra*.

As a preliminary answer to this question, we may offer the following thesis: In the theology of Jonathan Edwards, the Holy Spirit's activity as the bond of the trinitarian union between the Father and the Son is paradigmatic for all other holy unions in his theology. In the personal union of Christ's two natures, the mystical union believers have with Christ, and the union of fellowship that believers have with each other, the Holy Spirit works *ad extra* in a manner that is patterned after his inner-trinitarian work. The following chapters will give us the opportunity for extended reflection on this thesis where we can address the questions that were raised above. Before we address these issues, however, we first turn our attention to the importance of this study.

I.2 Importance of Our Study

Edwards's theology of religious experience and his detailed accounts of the

---

Trustees of the College of New Jersey," October 19, 1757, in *The Works of Jonathan Edwards*, vol. 16, *Letters and Personal Writings*, ed. George S. Claghorn (New Haven: Yale University Press, 1998), 725-30, for details. For an excellent secondary study on the projected contents of the *History of Redemption* discourse, see John F. Wilson's introduction to volume nine (*Works*, 9:61-72). For two studies on *The Harmony of the Old and New Testament*, see Stephen J. Stein, "The Spirit and the Word: Jonathan Edwards and Scriptural Exegesis," in *Jonathan Edwards and the American Experience*, ed. Nathan O. Hatch and Harry S. Stout (New York: Oxford, 1988), 118-30; and Kenneth P. Minkema, "The Other Unfinished 'Great Work:' Jonathan Edwards, Messianic Prophecy, and 'The Harmony of the Old and New Testament,'" in *Jonathan Edwards's Writings*, 52-65.

marks of the Spirit of God in the life of a saint have long been the objects of study by both academics and church persons alike. What need is there, one may ask, for another study on Edwards's pneumatology? Three points may be identified which pinpoint the importance of this study for Edwards enthusiasts, Edwards academic specialists, and Christian theologians.

First, there does not yet exist a study that treats Edwards's pneumatology from the standpoint of its trinitarian foundations. While some studies have investigated portions of Edwards's pneumatology, such as Conrad Cherry's analysis of Edwards's theology of faith, and Amy Plantinga Pauw's study of Edwards's trinitarianism, these do not present thorough analyses of Edwards's views on the third person of the Trinity.[19] Other works have directly examined Edwards's pneumatology, such as Patricia Wilson-Kastner's *Coherence in a Fragmented World: Jonathan Edwards' Theology of the Holy Spirit*, and a chapter in Bruce M. Stephens's *The Holy Spirit in American Protestant Thought, 1750-1850*.[20] Yet these studies focus primarily on Edwards's understanding of the Spirit's economic work in redemption and limit their investigations to Edwards's well-known treatises and sermons such as the *Religious Affections* and "A Divine and Supernatural Light." Fred W. Youngs's dissertation, "The Place of Spiritual Union in the Thought of Jonathan Edwards," is an excellent study that attempts to understand the relationship between Edwards's theology and mysticism, and is not so much concerned with investigating the parallels between the immanent and economic activity of the Spirit in Edwards's thought.[21] The value then of our present study lies in the way it supplements these secondary studies by investigating a heretofore overlooked dimension of Edwards's pneumatology: the trinitarian foundations of the Spirit's economic work.

Second, this study features Edwards's eighteenth-century attempt to address a theological issue that theologians still recognize today as important: the apparent deficiency of pneumatological reflection found in the church's theological discourse. As we shall observe in chapter one, Edwards felt that in the traditional Reformed understanding of the Spirit's role in soteriology,[22] the

---

19 See chapters 2 and 3 of Cherry, *Theology of Jonathan Edwards*, 25-55, and Pauw's entire study, *Supreme Harmony of All*.
20 Patricia Wilson-Kastner, *Coherence in a Fragmented World: Jonathan Edwards' Theology of the Holy Spirit* (Washington D. C.: University Press of America, 1978) and Bruce M. Stephens, *The Holy Spirit in American Protestant Thought, 1750-1850*, Studies in American Religion, vol. 59 (Lewiston: Edwin Mellen Press, 1992).
21 Fred W. Youngs, "The Place of Spiritual Union in the Thought of Jonathan Edwards" (Ph.D. diss., Drew University, 1986).
22 Stephen Holmes nicely summarizes a workable definition of "Reformed theology" which I will be using in this study: "By 'Reformed theology' I am referring to the broadly coherent tradition of Christian thought and practice that, in its continental European manifestations, defined itself against the Lutheran and Roman Catholic

Spirit was not given equal honor and dignity in comparison with the Father and the Son.[23] Because of this, he became convinced of the fact that if Christian theology is to be fully trinitarian then it must work out a pneumatology that compares in sophistication and maturity with christology, trinitarianism and theology proper. He was passionate about this precisely because the Spirit is equally God as are the Father and the Son.[24] His particular strategy to remedy this pneumatological deficiency was to emphasize the fact that the Spirit is the bond of love of the Godhead.

> If it be said that more glory belongs to the Father and the Son because they manifested a more wonderful love, the Father in giving his Son infinitely dear to him, the Son in laying down his life; yet let it be considered, that the Holy Ghost *is* that wonderful love. Just so much as the two first persons glorify themselves, by showing the astonishing greatness of their love and grace, just so much they glorify that love and grace, who is the Holy Ghost.[25]

So important was this strategy to him that it appears in the blueprints he compiled for his "A Rational Account of the Main Doctrines of the Christian Religion," a projected treatise in philosophical theology for which he drew up plans around 1730.[26] While he never moved beyond the beginning stages of writing "A Rational Account," we find this pnuematological insight repeated in later writings such as his *Treatise on Grace* and his *Dissertation on the End for Which God Created the World*.[27] This study presents us with the opportunity to

---

traditions and in its Anglophone versions defined itself against Roman Catholicism and Anglicanism." See *God of Grace and God of Glory*, 253.

23 See below, pages 34-35. Also see Jonathan Edwards, *Discourse on the Trinity*, in *The Works of Jonathan Edwards*, vol. 21, *Writings on the Trinity, Grace, and Faith*, ed. Sang Hyun Lee (New Haven: Yale University Press, 2003), 137-38.

24 "As the persons of the Trinity are equal among themselves, so there seems to [be] an exact equality in each person's concern in the work of redemption, and in our concern with them in that great affair; and the glory of it equally belongs to each of them." Edwards, "Miscellanies" No. 402, in *Works*, 13:467.

25 Edwards, "Miscellanies" No. 402, in *Works*, 13:467.

26 In his "Outline of 'A Rational Account,'" he writes, "To explain the doctrine of the Trinity before I begin to treat the work of redemption; and of their equality, their equal honor in their manner of subsisting and acting, and virtue. But to speak of their equal honor in their concern in the affair of redemption afterwards, after I have done with all the doctrines relating to man's redemption." See Jonathan Edwards, "Outline of 'A Rational Account,'" in *The Works of Jonathan Edwards*, vol. 6, *Scientific and Philosophical Writings*, ed. Wallace E. Anderson (New Haven: Yale University Press, 1980), 396.

27 Jonathan Edwards, *Dissertation I. Concerning the End for Which God Created the World*, in *The Works of Jonathan Edwards*, vol. 8, *Ethical Writings*, ed. Paul Ramsey (New Haven: Yale University Press, 1989), 403-536. Hereafter I will refer to this work as *End of Creation*.

showcase "America's greatest theologian" addressing a currently live theological topic.

Third, this study also features Edwards addressing this pneumatological deficiency from the standpoint of a thoroughly Western and Augustinian trinitarianism.[28] Edwards's articulation of the Spirit as the bond of union of the Godhead, together with his formulation of the Son as the Father's image and understanding, and his embrace of the *filioque*, commit him to working out this deficiency from within the broader structures of a Western trinitarian theology. It is well-known that Augustine's articulation of the Trinity, most prominently featured in his *De Trinitate* (circa 420), set the tone for trinitarian theology in the Roman Catholic and Protestant West. One of his famous analogies of the Trinity emphasized the triad of memory, understanding, and charity which prominently features the Spirit as the charity or divine love of the Godhead.[29] As divine love the Spirit is the communion of the deity and the mutual love of the Father and the Son, a point he articulated with clarity earlier in his career: "Some have even dared to believe," Augustine wrote in *Faith and the Creed* (circa 393), referring to himself,

> that the Holy Spirit is the communion or deity, so to speak, of the Father and the Son, their θεότης as the Greeks call it. So, as the Father is God and the Son is God, the very deity which embraces both - the Father who begets the Son and the Son who cleaves to the Father - is equated with God by whom the Son is begotten. This "deity," by which they would have understood the mutual love and charity of

---

28 In this study I will use the term "Augustinian trinitarianism" in a very broad sense, namely to indicate that formulation of the Trinity which affirms an understanding the Holy Spirit as the bond of union between the Father and the Son, an affirmation of the *filioque*, and the recognition that the Trinity may be faintly imaged forth in creation through trinitarian analogies such as memory, understanding, and will. While this is admittedly a very basic definition, these points are distinctive characteristics of Augustine's formation of the Trinity, embraced by the majority of the Western Catholic and Protestant traditions, and are generally denied by Eastern Orthodoxy.

29 "So the love which is from God and is God is distinctively the Holy Spirit; through him the charity of God is poured out in our hearts, and through it the whole triad dwells in us. This is the reason why it is most apposite that the Holy Spirit, which being God, should also be called the gift of God. And this gift, surely, is distinctively to be understood as being the charity which brings us through to God, without which no other gift of God at all can bring us through to God." St. Augustine, *The Trinity*, in *The Works of Saint Augustine: A Translation for the 21st Century*, Part I, vol. 5, trans. Edmund Hill, O.P., ed. John E. Rotelle, O.S.A. (Brooklyn: New City Press, 1991), 421 (XV.v.32). See the entirety of Book fifteen for Augustine's extended argument.

both Father and Son, they say is called the Holy Spirit, and they adduce many proofs from Scripture for their opinion.[30]

It was this understanding of the Spirit that Edwards featured prominently in his theology, underscoring the Augustinian character of his trinitarianism.

There are two reasons why this observation about Edwards's trinitarianism is important. The first relates to contemporary trends in Edwards scholarship. A recent study argues that Edwards's trinitarianism evinces non-Western and non-Augustinian themes, approximating elements of a more Eastern Orthodox understanding of the Trinity in his writings.[31] Similarly, Amy Plantinga Pauw in her recent book on Edwards's trinitarianism, argues that Edwards embraced two contrasting models of the Trinity, a more Augustinian "psychological" model, and a "social" model which contains elements reminiscent of twentieth-century social trinitarianism. In the next chapter we shall examine her thesis in more detail. For now it is worth pointing out that Pauw discerns a significant degree of dissonance in Edwards's trinitarian reflections for he did not systematically connect these two trinitarian models in his thought. "The two sets of trinitarian images he employed required different theological vocabularies and different presuppositions about the Godhead, and his constant modulation between them was not always harmonious."[32] The resulting theology built upon such a foundation, she argues, reflects this unharmonious marriage between the contrasting social and psychological analogies found in his trinitarianism. Our study will not take issue with Pauw's thesis directly. Rather, due to Edwards's almost unanimous articulation of the Holy Spirit as the bond of union throughout the vast corpus of his writings, it calls into question the existence of a separate social trinitarian model in Edwards's theology. Whenever Edwards expands upon the nature of the Trinity in any significant manner, he always employs the same model of the Trinity, a model which shows a strong family resemblance to Augustine's trinitarianism.[33]

Second, the fact that Edwards seeks to address this perceived pneumatological neglect, mentioned above, from the standpoint of an Augustinian trinitarianism, is interesting precisely because it runs counter to the way many current theologians seek to restore a pneumatological balance to Christian theology. Augustine is generally identified as one of the main culprits funding this neglect and imbalance. Leading the list of reasons for the neglect of the Spirit, Bernd Jochen Hilberath writes, "With regard to the

---

30 St. Augustine, *Faith and the Creed*, in *Augustine: Earlier Writings*, trans. John H. S. Burleigh, The Library of Christian Classics, Ichthus Edition (Philadelphia: The Westminster Press, 1953), 364.
31 See Robert Jenson, *America's Theologian*, 91-98.
32 Pauw, *Supreme Harmony of All*, 50. William Danaher also generally agrees with this division of Edwards's trinitarianism into psychological and social analogies; see chapters 1-2 of his *Trinitarian Ethics of Jonathan Edwards*, 16-116.
33 See chapter one for more details.

doctrine of the Trinity, Augustine's 'de-personalized' approach to the Spirit (with his idea of the Spirit as the *vinculum amoris*, the bond of love between the Father and Son) laid not only the theological groundwork for *filioque*, the view that the Spirit proceeds both from the Father and Son, but also divests the Spirit of full personality."[34] Similarly, Roger E. Olson and Christopher A. Hall note that "Some critics of the Augustinian-Anselmian psychological model of the Trinity have averred that it necessarily implies a modalistic vision of the Trinity and reduces the Holy Spirit to a kind of 'glue' between Father and Son. That is, it may de-personalize the Holy Spirit, justifying reference to the third person of the Trinity as 'It.'"[35] For many the way forward lies in leaving the main contributions of Augustine behind.[36] Edwards, by contrast, did not share this sentiment, but worked creatively within the Augustinian trinitarian structures that predominated in his day. This study shall showcase Edwards's attempt to give equal honor to the Spirit from within the broad contours of an Augustinian trinitarianism.

I.3 Outline of Our Study

As we trace the pneumatological themes found in Edwards's writings, our path shall lead us through the major areas of his theology. Chapters one and two will give us a glimpse behind the scenes of the Spirit's work in redemption by analyzing the Holy Spirit and the immanent Trinity. In chapter one, after briefly addressing some of the philosophical principles that influenced his thinking, we shall address the structure of Edwards's trinitarianism by a study of his *Discourse on the Trinity*. There we shall consider the question of the unity of Edwards's trinitarian thought, and note his desire to bring equal honor to the Spirit in his theology.

Chapter two shall turn our attention to a section in Edwards's *Treatise on Grace* where he focuses specifically on the Spirit as the bond of union of the immanent Trinity. There we will consider Edwards's understanding of the

---

34 Bernd Jochen Hilberath, "Identity through Self-Transcendence: the Holy Spirit and the Communio of Free Persons," in *Advent of the Spirit: Orientations in Pneumatology*, Conference Papers from a Symposium at Marquette University, 17-19 April 1998 (unpublished), as quoted by Veli-Matti Karkkainen, *Pneumatology: The Holy Spirit in Ecumenical, International, and Contextual Perspective* (Grand Rapids: Baker Academic, 2002), 18.

35 Roger E. Olson and Christopher A. Hall, *The Trinity*, Guides to Theology, ed. Sally Bruyneel and others (Grand Rapids: Eerdmans, 2002), 56-7.

36 See for example Colin Gunton, *The Promise of Trinitarian Theology* (Edinburgh: T & T Clark, 1991), 48-55; Clark H. Pinnock, *Flame of Love: A Theology of the Holy Spirit* (Downers Grove, Ill.: InterVarsity Press, 1996), 32-33, 40. For a critical appropriation of Augustine's views of the Spirit, with particular reference to the *filioque*, see Gary D. Badcock, *Light of Truth and Fire of Love: A Theology of the Holy Spirit* (Grand Rapids: Eerdmans, 1997), 62-85.

Spirit as the affection of the Godhead, the object of divine love, the issue of the double procession of the Spirit from the Father "and the Son" (the *filioque*), and observe the Spirit's "hiddenness" at this foundational level of his theology. These issues deeply shape Edwards's economic pneumatology. From there we will address the sometimes confusing nature of Edwards's pneumatological concepts (i.e., his identification of the Spirit with holiness, fullness, divine goodness, and grace). Here we will also treat his own definitions of the concepts of "communion," "communication," and "participation."

In chapters three and four, we shall examine Edwards's understanding of the divine blueprints God drew up for creation and redemption. Chapter three will explore the theological bridges Edwards draws between the Creator and creation, including the issues of God's end in creation, his disposition to communicate his trinitarian fullness to the creation, the covenant of redemption, and an analysis of the *imago dei*. In chapter four we transition to an analysis of the mediator Jesus Christ, and the hypostatic union by investigating the Spirit's work as the bond of union between Christ's two natures. There we will investigate the relationship between pneumatology and christology in Edwards's thought by considering the effect that this pneumatological union has upon Edwards's christology.

Chapters five and six address the saints' union with Christ in this lifetime, and the Spirit's work in effecting this union. Chapter five treats the issues of regeneration and justification. Edwards often writes about the Spirit's union to the soul and its faculties, yet he rarely explains what he means by such a union. In this chapter we will analyze in detail Edwards's understanding of the Spirit's union with the saint, address the subjective signs that attend such a union (i.e., faith in Christ and love for Christ), and conclude by addressing how these views relate to his doctrine of justification by faith.

In chapter six we turn our attention to the saints' sanctification in both the personal and ecclesial dimensions. There it will become clear that Edwards's discussions on the nature of true religious experience are basically pneumatology in disguise due to the fact that the holy affections of which the saints partake are not to be too easily distinguished from the communications of the Holy Spirit himself. This point will be illustrated first by looking at Edwards's discussions on personal sanctification, where he prominently features the Spirit's work in the saint as the one who effects a spiritual vision of God in Christ. The saint "sees" God as God manifests himself in Christ, a glorious sight which inflames the heart with love and draws the individual to love Christ increasingly. Second, the Spirit draws the saint into his own bond of love by leading the individual to love others in the church. Here the Spirit's relationship to the saint's prayer, charity for the poor, and observance of the Lord's Supper will be treated. In each of these aspects of the Christian life, Edwards draws out the theme of the Spirit as the bond of union.

In chapter seven we will explore Edwards's fascinating meditations on heaven, noting the Spirit's work as the bond of union in his theology of glorification. There we will address such issues as the beatific vision, the difference between how the saints and angels are "in Christ," and the nature of the saints' ever increasing union with God throughout eternity. We shall conclude our study in chapter eight by drawing together all these streams, and summarizing our findings.

Even in his own day Edwards's pneumatological reflections were misunderstood by readers of his published works. Shortly after the publication of his *magnum opus* on religious experience, *A Treatise Concerning Religious Affections* (1746),[37] Edwards received a letter from an individual who was puzzled by some of its contents. From Edwards's response we gather that the issue had to do with the extent of the Spirit's communication to the soul. Does God communicate his essence to the soul? Edwards answers with an emphatic "no" by making a distinction between God's essence and his nature. Human beings can partake of God's nature, he says, not of his essence. After an examination of the meaning of the word "nature" (which we shall address in chapter five), he demonstrates his point with one of his favorite illustrations:

> Light and heat may in a special manner be said to be the proper nature of the sun: and yet none will say that everything to which the sun communicates a little of its light and heat has therefore communicated to it the essence of the sun, and is sunned with the sun, or becomes the same being with the sun, or becomes equal without that immense fountain of light and heat. A diamond or crystal that is held forth in the sun's beams may properly be said to have some of the sun's brightness communicated to it; for though it han't the same individual brightness with that which is inherent in the sun, and be immensely less in degree, yet it is something of the same nature.[38]

Did Edwards satisfactorily answer the question of his correspondent? In this study we shall address this question as well as the others mentioned earlier in this chapter. As we begin our way through Edwards's pneumatology, we turn our attention first to the "home" of the Holy Spirit by examining Edwards's doctrine of the Trinity.

---

37 Jonathan Edwards, *A Treatise Concerning Religious Affections*, in *The Works of Jonathan Edwards*, vol. 2, *Religious Affections*, ed. John E. Smith (New Haven: Yale University Press, 1959).

38 Edwards, Letter No. 66, "To an Unknown Correspondent," after March 13, 1745/6, in *Works*, 16:203.

Part I

Behind the Scenes

The Trinity and the Immanent Spirit

Chapter 1

Trinity: Jonathan Edwards's Trinitiarianism

> God has appeared glorious to me, on account of the Trinity. It has made me have exalting thoughts of God, that he subsists in three persons; Father, Son and Holy Ghost.[1]

So wrote Jonathan Edwards in the autobiographical account of his conversion, an event which took place in the spring of 1721, at age seventeen. For the remaining years of his life the doctrine of the Trinity would occupy many of his reflections on God's glorious nature, reflections which ultimately influenced the shape of his entire theology. His fascination with the Trinity stemmed not from an academic interest in remote theological topics, but from the great potential the Trinity had to enhance the spiritual life. "I used to think sometimes with my self," Edwards wrote in 1725, "if such doctrines as those of the Trinity and decrees are true, yet what need was there of revealing of them in the gospel? what good do they do towards the advancing of holiness?" Upon further pondering, Edwards realized that such questioning is indeed a sign of spiritual naivete, for without these truths one is refused the "glorious inlets into the knowledge and view of the spiritual world," necessary for communion with the only true God. "If such doctrines as these had not been revealed, the church would never have been let half so far into the view of the spiritual world, as God intends it shall be before the world is at an end." Far from being a remote theological truth, the Trinity was for Edwards a living truth with profound practical benefits: *"I know by experience,* how useful these doctrines be to lead to this knowledge [of the spiritual world]."[2]

Not everybody in his day exhibited such excitement for the Trinity. Under the influence of the recent Lockean and Newtonian philosophy, a new intellectual mood settled into the English speaking world that was inimical to mystery, metaphysical speculation, and theological subtlety. The "mystery" of the Trinity quite simply did not measure up to these new and improved

---

[1] Jonathan Edwards, "Personal Narrative," in *The Works of Jonathan Edwards*, vol. 16, *Letters and Personal Writings*, ed. George S. Claghorn (New Haven: Yale University Press, 1998), 800.
[2] Edwards, "Miscellanies" No. 182, in *Works*, 13:328, emphasis mine.

standards of rationality. As a result, several notable "scientific" theologians—men who both loved science and their Bibles, such as Isaac Newton, Samuel Clarke and William Whiston—resurrected the fourth-century Arian heresy, which taught that Christ is not divine but rather a highly exalted creature through whom God created the universe. This touched off a vigorous trinitarian controversy in the 1710s and 20s, evoking the concessions of some orthodox moderates such as Isaac Watts and Hubert Stogdon who admitted that the traditional doctrine of the Trinity, while true, is not plainly revealed in Scripture and thus ought not to be regarded as a fundamental doctrine of the Christian faith.[3]

As an interested observer of British and Continental intellectual life, Jonathan Edwards was well aware of these challenges to the Trinity. Yet he neither retreated from philosophy nor abandoned the orthodox position. Rather he perceived that the new philosophy could actually be turned to strengthen trinitarian orthodoxy and enable theologians to penetrate further into its glorious mysteries. In this chapter, as we lay the theological foundation of his pneumatology, I will argue that Edwards presents a generally unified and internally consistent trinitarianism which is basically Augustinian in character. This thesis will be defended first by briefly analyzing the philosophical trajectories he adhered to, trajectories which rendered the Trinity rationally possible to his mind. Second, we will examine the basic contents of his trinitarianism as portrayed in the unpublished *Discourse on the Trinity*, his most mature and detailed statement on the Trinity. Lastly, as we continue our look at the *Discourse*, we will highlight the broad affinities that Edwards's trinitarianism has with Augustine's, as well as note Edwards's strategy for dealing with the pneumatological deficiency he detects in traditional Reformed theology.

1.1 Explorations of Divinity: The Ontological Setting of Edwards's Trinitarianism

If the Trinity is indeed one of the deepest mysteries of the Christian faith, then how could Edwards privately declare "I think that it is within the reach of naked reason to perceive certainly that there are three distinct in God, each of

---

3 Gerald McDermott, *Jonathan Edwards Confronts the Gods*, 40. Also see Thomas Schafer's note in *Works*, 13:256n2. On eighteenth-century Arianism in Britain, see Maurice Wiles's chapter "The Rise and Fall of British Arianism," in his *Archetypal Heresy: Arianism through the Centuries* (Oxford: Clarendon Press, 1996), 62-164. For an excellent study documenting the trinitarian controversy see, Thomas C. Pfizenmaier, *The Trinitarian Theology of Dr. Samuel Clarke (1675-1729): Context, Sources, and Controversy*, Studies in the History of Christian Thought, vol. 75 (New York: Brill, 1997).

which is the same [God]"?[4] Edwards's profound confidence in "naked reason" to apprehend the Trinity apart from Scripture is stunning given the fact that virtually every Reformed and Puritan theologian denied this very possibility: "The common view of the Reformed," wrote Peter van Mastricht, one of Edwards's favorite theologians, "is that the Trinity can neither be investigated nor solidly proved by natural reason."[5] Such a caution from one he so highly esteemed probably drew Edwards back from an all-scale rationalistic invasion into the Godhead. Nonetheless, emboldened by his own version of the new philosophy, Edwards pressed forward, confident that his insights were only taking him further into Scripture where God has revealed his glorious nature. In this section we will briefly analyze three aspects of Edwards's philosophy which served as the ontological setting of his trinitarianism: his concept of God's being as "communicative," his idealism, and his theory of excellency. Edwards utilized these philosophical principles to explore the fabric of God's being, and they ultimately had an apologetic thrust. If true, they would recommend the Trinity to an age that was quickly dispensing with this central truth of the Christian faith.

The first philosophical principle important to Edwards's understanding of divine ontology is the concept that God's nature is inherently communicative.[6] This means, for Edwards, that God seeks to communicate the fullness of his infinite happiness to others. The origins of this idea are difficult to isolate in his early notebooks for they are tightly bound up in his reflections on God's purpose in creating the world.[7] Yet after years of reflection, the theme emerges clearly in "Miscellanies" No. 332: "The great and universal end of God's creating the world was to communicate himself. God is a communicative being."[8] Fundamental to God's essence is a dynamic inclination to diffuse, disseminate, or "communicate" his infinite, internal fullness. Like the sun, which cannot contain its inexhaustible light, God's happiness, love, and delight in his own glorious divine perfections are of such an infinite intensity that, as a principle of being, he seeks to diffuse this joy and radiance *ad extra,* or "outside" of himself. Creation is the result of this divine inclination. "Thus it appears reasonable to suppose that it was what God had respect to as an

---

4 Edwards, "Miscellanies" No. 94, in *Works*, 13:257.
5 Peter van Mastricht, *Theoretico-practica Theologia* (Utrecht and Amsterdam: 1714; new edition 1725), II, xxiv, 21, as quoted in Heinrich Heppe, *Reformed Dogmatics*, rev. and ed. Ernst Bizer, trans. G. T. Thomson (London: George Allen & Unwin, 1950), 109.
6 For an excellent study on God's communicative being, see Sang Hyun Lee's, *Philosophical Theology of Jonathan Edwards*, 170-210. For a less technical but still thorough summary, see Stephen R. Holmes's, *God of Grace and God of Glory*, 31-76.
7 See his early "Miscellanies" notes on God's end in creating the world; entry Nos. gg, ww, 3, 87, 92, and 104.
8 Edwards, "Miscellanies" No. 332, in *Works*, 13:410.

ultimate end of his creating the world, to communicate of his own infinite fullness of good; or rather it was his last end, that there might be a glorious and abundant emanation of his infinite fullness *ad extra*."[9] For most of his life Edwards argued that this vital impulse in God towards communication captures the traditional idea of divine goodness, a concept which he carefully defined. Goodness, in Edwardsean terms, is the inclination to seek the happiness of others through the communicating of one's own fullness, riches, or happiness to them.[10] As he meditated on this idea early in his theological development, he found that it had applicability to God's internal being as well as to his external work of creating. Not only does God create out of his goodness, but he has eternally and infinitely expressed this goodness within himself apart from creation. God's perfect and infinite expression of goodness, for Edwards, necessitates an infinite communication of his fullness, which in turn requires an infinite "other" to receive that infinite communication. "God must have a perfect exercise of his goodness, and therefore must have the fellowship of a person equal with himself." The conclusion from this is clear: if God is eternally good, then "there must be more than a unity in infinite and eternal essence."[11] Edwards's reflections on God's communicative disposition sows the seeds for the personal distinctions within the divine essence.

Edwards's idealism is the second philosophical principle that factors into his trinitarianism. As Wallace Anderson has observed, a central maxim that fills Edwards's early philosophical notebooks is the fact that "nothing can be without being known."[12] Existence and consciousness are necessarily connected. Statements to this effect abound in his early reflections: "nothing has any existence anywhere else but in consciousness. No, certainly nowhere

---

9 Edwards, *End of Creation*, in *Works*, 8:433. Later in this work (pages 445-50), Edwards carefully nuances his discussion to preserve God's immutability.

10 See "Miscellanies" No. 96, in *Works*, 13:263, where Edwards defines goodness as the "delight in communicating happiness." Later in his life he grew uncomfortable identifying this disposition toward communication as God's goodness as Paul Ramsay indicates in his helpful notes on *End of Creation* (see *Works*, 8:429n2, 433n7, and 438n4). Edwards rather remained content to describe this disposition merely as an unnamed disposition in God toward communication, terming it God's "fullness"; see Jonathan Edwards, "Miscellanies" No. 1218, in *The Works of Jonathan Edwards*, vol. 23, *The "Miscellanies," 1153-1360*, ed. Douglas A. Sweeney (New Haven: Yale University Press, 2004), 150-53.

11 Edwards, "Miscellanies" No. 96, in *Works*, 13:264 and 263 respectively.

12 Wallace E. Anderson, "Editor's Introduction," in *Works*, 6:75. Anderson, whose argument I am following in this section, provides an outstanding survey of Edwards's philosophical thought; see *Works*, 6:52-136. See also Danaher's excellent discussion of Edwards's idealism and its relation to his trinitarian thought in his *Trinitarian Ethics of Jonathan Edwards*, 18-35.

else, but either in created or uncreated consciousness."[13] He continues elsewhere: "We know there was being from eternity, and this being must be intelligent. For how doth one's mind refuse to believe, that there should be being from all eternity without its being conscious to itself that it was."[14] Edwards had good reasons for holding this philosophical position. Originally, it was part of a philosophical response to the atheistic materialism of Thomas Hobbes, whose dark shadow loomed over the Anglo-academic world. As Michael McClymond observes, "Idealism reflected a theocentric strategy of 'turning the tables' on materialism, making God in his immateriality into the central and defining reality, and rendering 'matter' a merely derivative phenomenon of consciousness."[15] Later, however, Edwards's idealism took on a logic of its own as he experimented with it in the context (again) of God's purpose in creation. Creation would be useless to God without intelligent creatures, Edwards argued in an early "Miscellanies" entry (No. gg).[16] Later he continues: "Intelligent beings are created to be the consciousness of the universe, they they [sic - read 'that they'] may perceive what God is and does."[17] Edwards applies this theory to God himself: because nothing, not even God, can be without being known, infinite divine being must be infinitely self-reflective. God supremely knows himself to an infinite degree. Furthermore, Edwards argues that there are ontological implications associated with God's infinite self-knowledge. The significance Edwards's idealism has for our discussion is that God's infinite self-reflection provides the ontological foundation for the eternal generation of the Son, a concept which we shall return to in the second section of this chapter.

Edwards's theory of excellency is the third basic philosophical principle that affected his theology in general and his trinitarianism specifically. Excellency concerns the aesthetic character of being and is foundational to Edwards's ethics. A being is excellent or beautiful when there is symmetry, harmony, and proportionality among its various components.

> That sort of beauty which is called 'natural,' as of vines, plants, trees, etc., consists of a very complicated harmony; and all the natural motions and tendencies and figures of bodies in the universe are done according to proportion,

---

13 Jonathan Edwards, "Of Being," in *The Works of Jonathan Edwards*, vol. 6, *Scientific and Philosophical Writings*, ed. Wallace E. Anderson (New Haven: Yale University Press, 1980), 204.

14 Edwards, "Miscellanies" No. pp, in *Works*, 13:188.

15 Michael McClymond, "God the Measure: Toward an Understanding of Jonathan Edwards' Theocentric Metaphysics," *Scottish Journal of Theology* 47 (1994): 53. See also Anderson's comments in *Works*, 6:53-68.

16 In "Miscellanies" No. gg, he writes that, "senseless matter . . . would be useless if there were no intelligent beings at all . . . for what would it be good for?" (see *Works*, 13:185).

17 Edwards, "Miscellanies" No. 87, in *Works*, 13:252.

and therein is their beauty. Particular disproportions sometimes greatly add to the general beauty, and must necessarily be, in order to a more universal proportion.[18]

Three points are crucial toward understanding Edwards's theory of excellency. First, these symmetries are real and objective, part of the fabric of being. Beauty is thus an objective characteristic of reality, logically independent of created minds. Second, excellency is the foundation of the soul's aesthetic sense. When the mind perceives an excellent object, there automatically arises in the soul pleasure, love, and a sense of happiness that draws the will toward that object in approval. This approval is defined as the "consent" of the soul, which is ultimately a willful act of love. When there is disharmony or lack of symmetry in an entity, such as a poorly performed concerto, or the feeling of pain due to an illness, the mind dissents and recoils from that object. Third, spiritual excellencies, or the loving consent and social harmony of sentient beings to each other and to God, are the highest excellencies of all. The symmetries we perceive in natural objects, such as a painting, a piece of music or a rose, are merely shadows of the spiritual world, whose excellencies far outweigh those of the natural.

Edwards's theory of excellency is significant to our discussion because God is infinitely excellent. As such it follows that God possesses an infinite array of glorious symmetries, which are infinitely beautiful and through which God infinitely consents to himself in love.[19] "'Tis peculiar to God that he has beauty within himself, consisting in being's consenting with his own being, or the love of himself in his own Holy Spirit."[20] Excellent divine being thus cannot be an undifferentiated unity, but necessitates a plurality within that unity: "One alone, without any reference to any more, cannot be excellent; for in such case there can be no manner of relation no way, and therefore, no such thing as consent."[21]

These three philosophical themes confirmed to Edwards that the doctrine of the Trinity had the potential to measure up to the standards of enlightened rationality. "Naked reason" indeed can perceive at least a plurality in the Godhead if it takes into account these philosophical principles. The question before us is whether or not Edwards fully developed his trinitarianism around one of these principles. In other words, is any one of these principles most foundational to his trinitarianism? This is an important question because major theses regarding Edwards's theology have been advanced based upon what is

---

18 Edwards, "The Mind," in *The Works of Jonathan Edwards*, vol. 6, *Scientific and Philosophical Writings*, ed. Wallace E. Anderson (New Haven: Yale University Press, 1980), 335 (§ 1).

19 For an extensive analysis of excellency and its relation to Edwards's aesthetics, see Roland Delattre's *Beauty and Sensibility in the Thought of Jonathan Edwards*, 58-67.

20 Edwards, "The Mind," § 45 ¶12, in *Works*, 6:365.

21 Edwards, "The Mind," § 1, in *Works*, 6:337.

perceived to be the most fundamental philosophical concept that pervades his theology.

For instance, in his fascinating studies on Edwardsian ontology, Sang Hyun Lee has argued that the fundamental dynamic in Edwards's doctrine of God is God's communicative disposition, the first philosophical theme we examined above.[22] Lee discerns in Edwards's doctrine of God a *dispositional* ontology (as opposed to a merely scholastic ontology of actuality) which affirms that the infinite actuality of God's being does not exhaust his disposition toward further communication. God, in Lee's reading of Edwards, is both infinitely actual, and at the same time disposed toward further "repetitions" of his prior actuality. "Edwards's intention is clear," writes Lee, "He wants to see God as essentially a disposition, but he does not want to compromise the prior actuality of God as the ultimate principle of all reality. The only way to state the matter may be to say quite paradoxically that the essence of God's being, for Edwards, is at once actuality and disposition."[23] In Lee's understanding of Edwards's doctrine of God, creation is the divine disposition exerting itself externally in time and space, repeating the prior actuality of the inner divine life. Furthermore, while the external exercise of the divine disposition accounts for creation, Lee argues that there is an internal exercise of this same divine disposition which results in the Trinity: "the internal exercises of the divine dispositional essence constitute the inner-trinitarian actuality of the Divine Being."[24] Thus the same divine disposition accounts for both the Trinity, as it is exercised infinitely *ad intra*, and creation, as it is exercised finitely *ad extra*. Lee continues, however, with a very key observation with regard to Edwards's trinitarian methodology: "Edwards articulates the inner-trinitarian exercise of the divine dispositional essence *with the help of the analogy of the human self as knowing and loving* as well as the Lockean notion of the self's reflexive knowledge of its internal acts."[25] With this acknowledgment, Lee recognizes that Edwards does not work out his trinitarianism completely from the philosophy of God's communicative disposition. Edwards's theology of the Trinity required something more, namely the "help of the analogy of the human self as knowing and loving." While it is true that his articulation of God's communicative being does sow the seeds for a personal plurality within the Godhead, Edwards

---

22 Lee offers a helpful summary of the main thesis of his magesterial *Philosophical Theology of Jonathan Edwards* in his essay, "Jonathan Edwards's Dispositional Conception of the Trinity: A Resource for Contemporary Reformed Theology," in *Toward the Future of Reformed Theology: Tasks, Topics, Traditions*, ed. David Willis and Michael Welker (Grand Rapids: Eerdmans, 1999), 444-55.

23 Lee, "Jonathan Edwards's Dispositional Conception of the Trinity," 448.

24 Sang Hyun Lee, "Edwards on God and Nature: Resources for Contemporary Theology," in *Edwards in Our Time: Jonathan Edwards and the Shaping of American Religion*, ed. Sang Hyun Lee and Allen C. Guelzo (Grand Rapids: Eerdmans, 1999), 18.

25 Lee, "Edwards on God and Nature," 18-19, emphasis added.

does not appear to develop his mature trinitarianism *solely* from the soil of this philosophical theme.

In contrast to Lee, Amy Plantinga Pauw identifies Edwards's theory of excellency as the most fundamental principle animating the deepest levels of divine ontology in his thought.[26] If divine being is primarily and fundamentally excellent, then there must exist a mutual consent among a plurality within that being, for, in Edwards's words, "in a being that is absolutely without any plurality there cannot be excellency, for there can be no such thing as consent or agreement."[27] Thus a Trinity of subject, object, and consent must obtain within God if he is truly excellent.[28] Divine excellency thus ensures not only that God must be triune, but that relationality is at the heart of divine ontology. "Relationality," Pauw writes of Edwards's metaphysics, "is at the heart of metaphysical excellence."[29] In her broader argument, Pauw contrasts Edwards's vision of divine excellency with that of the divine simplicity tradition which she argues characterized the theology of Edwards's Reformed heritage.[30] Drawing upon scholastic categories, Reformed theologians such as van Mastricht and Turretin began their reflections on divine ontology by asserting the priority of divine simplicity over that of any personal plurality within the Godhead. While trinitarian in profession, the gravity of this theological move she argues led them to articulate the Trinity in a way that minimized the personal distinctions within the Godhead. In short, divine simplicity affirms the unity, aseity, and independence of God while at the same time downplays the relational metaphysic of the trinitarian being. Divine excellency by contrast is more amenable to a truly trinitarian and therefore relational ontology. While Edwards affirms divine excellency at the deepest levels of divine ontology, Pauw argues that he does not make a complete break from the simplicity tradition. His doctrine of God, while conditioned by his theory of excellency, still shows signs of the influence of the simplicity tradition. As such Pauw argues that Edwards held not one but two different models of the Trinity, each reflecting the influence of these contrasting theories of God's being. This is the central thesis of her study. "Starting with his earliest reflections," she writes,

> Edwards employed two distinct models of the immanent Trinity, both with deep roots in the Christian tradition. One model portrayed the Son and Spirit as the Wisdom and Love of the one God, thus emphasizing divine unity. The other

---

26 See her extended argument in *Supreme Harmony of All*, 80-89.
27 Edwards, "The Mind," § 1, in *Works*, 6:337.
28 Pauw does not make this observation, but as we shall see below it appears to be what Edwards is saying in his discussions on the nature of divine excellency.
29 Pauw, *Supreme Harmony of All*, 80.
30 Pauw, *Supreme Harmony of All*, 59-69. For a more succinct statement of her thesis, see her essay "The Trinity" in *The Princeton Companion to Jonathan Edwards*, ed. Sang Hyun Lee (Princeton: Princeton University Press, 2005), 44-58.

model emphasized relationality within God by depicting the Godhead as a society or family of persons. Edwards alternated or modulated between them depending on the immediate theological and cultural context of his writing, but never repudiated either one.[31]

The differences between these two models in her mind are stark: one views the Trinity as a relational fellowship of persons in communion, the other views the Trinity from the perspective of a single human mind. In summary, Edwards's theory of excellency is strong evidence to Pauw that Edwards possesses a social model of the Trinity which he held in unharmonious tension with a more traditional, psychological model.

Edwards's remarks on divine excellency do support some of Pauw's assertions. Plurality does indeed seem to be woven deeply into the fabric of his first moves in divine ontology. Furthermore, Edwards does appear to develop his theory of excellency into the doctrine of the Trinity. Excellency as we have seen requires the "consent" of a plurality within a unity. "Indeed, what we call 'one' may be excellent, because of a consent of parts, or some consent of those in that being that are distinguished into a plurality some way or other."[32] The lowest common denominator for excellency is thus the triad of subject, object and consent.[33] Later in "The Mind" Edwards makes explicit the fact that metaphysical excellency serves as a foundation of the Trinity.

> As to God's excellency, it is evident it consists in the love of himself. For he was as excellent before he created the universe as he is now. But if the excellency of spirits consists in their disposition and action, God could be excellent no other way at that time, for all the exertions of himself were towards himself. But he exerts himself towards himself no other way than in infinitely loving and delighting in himself, in the mutual love of the Father and the Son. This makes the third, the personal Holy Spirit or the holiness of God, which is his infinite beauty, and this is God's infinite consent to being in general.[34]

Yet as we take a closer look at the shape of Edwards's understanding of excellency, and the way it funds his trinitarianism, we find that his writings do not support Pauw's contention that divine excellency undergirds a distinct social model of the Trinity over against a psychological one. In the quote above, Edwards quite clearly identifies the Spirit as the "infinite consent" of the Godhead, and as the one who is the mutual love of the Father and the Son. In other words, in Edwards's articulation of the "excellent" Trinity, the Spirit is not strictly a consenting person alongside of the Father and the Son, but the

---

31 Pauw, *Supreme Harmony of All*, 10-11.
32 Edwards, "The Mind," § 1, in *Works*, 6:337.
33 This observation in Edwards's thought was first suggested to me in conversation with Steven Studebaker. See reference to his studies below, page 37, note 73.
34 Edwards, "The Mind," § 45 ¶ 9, in *Works*, 6:364.

personal consent between them. This fundamentally is an Augustinian understanding of the Trinity, as we shall see below, not a distinct social model. Thus it appears that Edwards's articulation of divine excellency does not support the view that he held a distinct social model of the Trinity.

We shall later return to Pauw's other reasons why she discerns a social model of the Trinity in Edwards's writings. For now we may summarize this section by observing that Edwards's philosophical principles did shape his trinitarianism significantly, as both Lee and Pauw's analyses have revealed. As we shall see in the chapters to come his dispositional ontology, idealism, and emphasis on divine excellency exert a profound influence on his entire theology. Yet, as our examination of both Lee and Pauw's analyses have uncovered, the presence of other common themes in his trinitarianism emerge: first, the analogy of the human self as knowing and loving which aids his trinitarian formulation; and second, the Holy Spirit as the consent and mutual love of the Father and Son within the Godhead. These themes, which characterize the majority of Edwards's writings on the Trinity, locate his trinitarian reflections in the broad family of Augustinian trinitarianism as I will argue below. With this we turn our attention to Edwards's constructive statements on the Trinity.

1.2 Outlines of the Immanent Trinity: Edwards's "Discourse on the Trinity"

While a full treatment of Edwards's trinitarianism would require a complete survey of Edwards's writings, for our purposes an analysis of his *Discourse on the Trinity* is more than sufficient.[35] Indeed there are good reasons to believe that this document represents his mature statements on the Trinity. Written in the early 1730s, the *Discourse* is a systematic compilation of his trinitarian reflections as worked out in forty-four "Miscellanies" entries over the course of the previous decade.[36] Given the fact that he contributed only fifteen more "Miscellanies" entries on the Trinity in the remaining two and a half decades of his life, and that most of these merely extend arguments found in the *Discourse*, it is relatively safe to conclude that his mature trinitarianism can be found in its pages.[37] In this section we will cover half of the *Discourse*, highlighting the

---

35 Edwards, *Discourse on the Trinity*, in *Works*, 21:109-44.
36 Mark Valeri notes that Edwards began work on the *Discourse on the Trinity* about the same time he wrote his first published sermon, "God Glorified in Man's Dependence." See *The Works of Jonathan Edwards*, vol. 17, *Sermons and Discourses, 1730-1733*, ed. Mark Valeri (New Haven: Yale University Press, 1999), 197. Also see Edwards's "Table" to the "Miscellanies" for specific entries on the Trinity; (*Works*, 13:149).
37 "Miscellanies" No. 1062, entitled "ECONOMY OF THE TRINITY AND COVENANT OF REDEMPTION," is the exception to this general observation that he did not develop his trinitarianism further. In it Edwards carefully develops the connections between the

rational and scriptural reasons Edwards offers for why there are three persons in one God, and noting where he incorporates the philosophical themes surveyed above.

Edwards does not have much to say about God the Father in the *Discourse on the Trinity*, most likely because the critics had more problems with multiple persons within the Godhead than they did with the subject of God's Fatherhood. Nonetheless Edwards's brief comments are noteworthy. First, he "grounds" his trinitarian reflections in God the Father. "The Father," he writes, "is the fountain of the Godhead," and "the Deity subsisting in the prime, unoriginated and most absolute manner, or the Deity in its direct existence."[38] From this it follows secondly that whenever Scripture refers to "God" generally, without making intra-trinitarian distinctions, it is referring to the Father specifically, and not to the Trinity collectively, a point he brings out more clearly in "Miscellanies" No. 143: "Hence we see how and in what sense the Father is the fountain of the Godhead, and how naturally and properly God the Father is spoken of in Scripture as of the Deity without distinction, as being the only true God."[39] Third, it is the Father who possesses both knowledge and love, the only two "real attributes" and "faculties" in God.[40] It is this triad of God, his knowledge, and his love which ultimately provides the basis for the subsistent persons in the Godhead. The Trinity "grows" from the soil of this psychological triad.

Edwards's idealism clearly emerges in his discussion of the second person of the Trinity. God's understanding is infinitely comprehensive, according to Edwards, and therefore the object of God's knowledge is his own infinitely extensive and glorious being. Such divine self-reflection, however, does not result in a self-absorbed deity, but in the trinitarian community as the following reasoning will illustrate. The key to his argument lies in ontological nature of ideas of reflection (i.e., ideas of thought, choice, love, fear). "If we diligently attend to our minds," Edwards writes, "we shall find that [these ideas] are not properly representations, but are indeed repetitions of those very things."[41] To think about "thought" or "love" is actually to repeat the ontological reality of thought and love in the mind. When God, who knows with infinite perfection, thinks reflexively upon his own glorious being, he literally "repeats" his own

---

immanent Trinity and the economic plans for redemption in the covenant of redemption. The covenant is grounded in the ontological order which obtains among the three persons. See *The Works of Jonathan Edwards*, vol. 20, *The "Miscellanies" 833-1152*, ed. Amy Plantinga Pauw (New Haven: Yale University Press, 2002), pages 430-43. For my analysis on this topic, see the discussion in chapter three, pages 65-67.

38 Edwards, *Discourse on the Trinity*, in *Works*, 21:135 and 131 respectively.
39 Edwards "Miscellanies" No. 143, in *Works*, 13:298-99.
40 See his brief discussions on God's faculties and attributes in *Discourse on the Trinity*, (*Works*, 21:113 and 132).
41 Edwards, "Miscellanies" No. 238, in *Works*, 13:353.

divine essence.[42] "That [idea] which God hath of the divine nature and essence is really and fully the divine nature and essence again; so that by God thinking of himself the Deity must certainly be generated."[43] The conclusion is inescapable for Edwards, through self-reflection, God generates himself *again*, not outside of himself, but within his own being, so that there is a "duplicity" within himself: God and his divine self-knowledge. This substantial divine image, who is fully divine, Edwards concludes, "is the second person of the Trinity, the only begotten and dearly beloved Son of God. He is the eternal, necessary, perfect, substantial and personal idea which God hath of himself."[44]

Far from being vague speculation, Edwards believed that the word of God abundantly confirms this rationale for the generation of the Son. As we shall see, his Scriptural "proofs" are a conglomeration of mere textual references combined with complicated typological and metaphorical correspondences between biblical types and antitypes, and between biblical symbols and the Christocentric reality they mirror.[45] Their combined effect comprises a multi-faceted argument that the second person of the Trinity is truly God's infinite idea of himself. Furthermore, these proofs represent to us a classic example of what is today (unfortunately) called "pre-critical" exegesis.[46]

Edwards marshals many scriptural arguments to this end. First, he notes that

---

42 This repetition includes a repetition of substance because, "An absolutely perfect idea of a thing is the very thing, for it wants nothing that is in the thing, substance nor nothing else." ("Miscellanies""Miscellanies" No. 94, in *Works*, 13:258.)

43 Edwards, "Miscellanies" No. 353, in *Works*, 13:353-54.

44 Edwards, *Discourse on the Trinity*, in *Works*, 21:117.

45 For studies on Edwards's interpretation of the Bible, see Stephen J. Stein, "Jonathan Edwards and the Rainbow: Biblical Exegesis and Poetic Imagination," *New England Quarterly* 47 (1974): 440-56; "The Quest for the Spiritual Sense: The Biblical Hermeneutics of Jonathan Edwards," *Harvard Theological Review* 70 (1977): 99-113; "'Like Apples of Gold in Pictures of Silver': The Portrait of Wisdom in Jonathan Edwards's Commentary on the Book of Proverbs," *Church History* 54 (1985): 324-37; and "The Spirit and the Word: Jonathan Edwards and Scriptural Exegesis," in *Jonathan Edwards and the American Experience*, ed. Nathan O. Hatch and Harry S. Stout (New York: Oxford, 1988), 118-30. See also Conrad Cherry, "Symbols of Spiritual Truth: Jonathan Edwards as Biblical Interpreter," *Interpretation* 39 (1985): 263-71; Samuel T. Logan, Jr., "The Hermeneutics of Jonathan Edwards," *Westminster Theological Journal* 43 (1981): 79-96; and Douglas A. Sweeney's entry "Jonathan Edwards," in *Historical Handbook of Major Biblical Interpreters*, ed. Donald K. McKim (Downers Grove, Ill.: InterVarsity Press, 1998), 309-12; as well as his essay, "'Longing for More and More of It'? The Strange Career of Jonathan Edwards's Exegetical Exertions," in *Jonathan Edwards at 300: Essays on the Tercentenary of His Birth*, ed. Harry S. Stout, Kenneth P. Minkema, and Caleb J. D. Maskell (Lanham: University Press of America, 2005), 25-37.

46 "Unfortunate" because it might imply that his exegesis was "uncritical." Pre-critical exegesis generally refers to the exegetical methodology of the period before modern "critical" methods.

Christ is many times depicted as the "image" of God in the New Testament; he is "the image of the invisible God" as the apostle Paul writes (Col 1:15; see also 2 Cor 4:4; Phil 2:6; Heb 1:3). To Edwards spiritual images are none other than ideas: "An idea of a thing seems more properly to be called an image or representation of that thing than any distinct being can be."[47] Thus, by beholding the image one perceives the original, a fact to which Jesus attests: "whoever sees me sees him who sent me" (John 12:45). Second, God's loving his own idea of himself fittingly corresponds to the great love that God shows for Jesus Christ in the gospels. God's love for Jesus is particularly one of great delight, as seen in his baptism ("this is my beloved Son in whom I am well pleased," Matt 3:17) and as seen in their mutual rejoicing before the creation of the world ("I was daily his delight, rejoicing always before him," Prov 8:30). "It seems to be most probable that God has his infinite happiness but one way, and that the infinite joy he has in his own idea and that which he has in his Son is but one and the same."[48] Edwards's third argument comes interestingly from Exodus 33:14 where God promises to Moses that, "My presence will go with you, and I will give you rest." He first notes that the word for "presence" signifies "face, look, form or appearance." By identifying this presence with Christ, Edwards concludes that "Christ is called the face of God" in Scripture. He then reasons, "Now what can be so properly and fitly called so with respect to God as God's own perfect idea of himself, whereby he has every moment a view of his own essence? This idea is that face of God which God sees, as a man sees his own face in a looking glass."[49] Edwards's next argument derives meaning from the fact that Christ is portrayed as the "brightness, effulgence or shining forth of God's glory." Glory has a dual nature: it both shines forth and is beheld by an observer. God's own glory "antecedent to his idea of himself" would only be "latent" within himself, that is, he would not know of it though he infinitely shines forth. Yet through his infinite idea he beholds the fullness of his own glory, "'tis the idea by which [his glory] shines forth and appears to God's view, so that he can delight in it." This argument also applies to the fact that Scripture represents God as a luminary, and his idea as light.[50] Lastly, Edwards observes that Christ is often denoted in Scripture by concepts that are closely associated with ideas: Christ is called the "wisdom" of God (1 Cor 1:24; Proverbs 8; Edwards identifies wisdom with knowledge), and the *Logos* or Word of God (John 1). He is also the "Amen" or the truth of God (most likely John 14:6; "Now what is that which is the prime, original and universal truth but that which is in the divine mind, viz. his eternal or infinite knowledge or idea?").[51] Together these arguments reveal the systematizing gravity of

---

47 Edwards, *Discourse on the Trinity*, in *Works*, 21:117.
48 Edwards, *Discourse on the Trinity*, in *Works*, 21:118.
49 Edwards, *Discourse on the Trinity*, in *Works*, 21:118.
50 Edwards, *Discourse on the Trinity*, in *Works*, 21:119.
51 Edwards, *Discourse on the Trinity*, in *Works*, 21:119-20.

Edwards's mind: simple texts, typological concepts, metaphors and symbols are all drawn into orbit around the principle that God generates the Son through an eternal act of self-reflection.

As Edwards turns our attention to the third person of the Godhead, we find that his basic argument for the Holy Spirit is relatively simple once the plurality of Father and Son has been firmly established. God's willing and loving disposition, the second faculty of his nature, is drawn out as infinite divine love toward the glorious knowledge of himself in the Son: "there proceeds a most pure act, and an infinitely holy and sacred energy arises between the Father and Son: for their love and joy is mutual, in mutually loving and delighting in each other."[52] This "sacred energy" is of such an infinite intensity that the entire divine essence is again drawn out into another subsistence, whereby the "it" of the energy becomes the "he" of a third divine person. At the human level we do not normally think of our love for one another as being something that has personal attributes. But true human love is an intensely personal thing and often has the effect of "drawing us outside of ourselves." What Edwards is saying is that when we take this imperfect and vague notion that we experience in human love and infinitely multiply it in the context of divinity, we can catch a dim glimpse as to how infinite divine love can be "personified" in the Holy Spirit. "The Godhead therein stands forth in yet another manner of subsistence, and there proceeds the third person in the Trinity, the Holy Spirit."[53]

Again Edwards is confident that the Scriptural witness accords well with this theological portrayal of the Spirit. Later we shall investigate the immanent Spirit in more detail, so my comments here shall be brief. Edwards's primary argument is based on 1 John 4:8 and 16: "God is love." This is not merely a hyperbolic statement indicating the measureless degree to which God loves, it is an ontological statement describing the fundamental aspect of God's being. In the Spirit, "the entire Divine nature and essence subsists in love," and because the divine nature fully and personally subsists in this love, wherever this divine love is, there God is in his fullness. Thus "if we have love dwelling in [us], we have God dwelling in us."[54] Edwards next turns to a theological exegesis of the name Scripture gives to the third person of the Godhead: the "Holy Spirit." He observes that "spirit" generally refers to the dynamic orientation, "inclination or temper of the mind," when it is not put for the spiritual substance of the mind itself. Thus the Holy Spirit is the "disposition or temper or affection of the divine mind." "Holiness," whether creaturely or divine, consists in the loving orientation of a spirit's inclination. If that spirit perceives the glorious perfections of God and is motivated toward them in love, then Edwards would argue that a real holiness fills that spirit, and that this person actually "partakes" of God's nature, per 2 Peter 1:4. God's Spirit

---

52 Edwards, *Discourse on the Trinity*, in *Works*, 21:121.
53 Edwards, *Discourse on the Trinity*, in *Works*, 21:121.
54 Edwards, *Discourse on the Trinity*, in *Works*, 21:121.

infinitely delights in his own magnificence, as viewed in the glory of the Son. He is thus fittingly called by Scripture, the "Holy Spirit."[55] Edwards's last two arguments highlight how the Spirit is biblically portrayed as an active, dynamic agent in creation—a picture which concords with his immanent nature as the divine love, act and "sacred energy" of the Godhead. First, Edwards maintains that the Spirit's economic office reflects his immanent trinitarian activity: he *quickens* all things, moving over the face of the waters at creation and garnishing the heavens (Gen 1; Job 26:13); he *sanctifies* created spirits, "that is, he gives them divine love" (1 John 4:12-13); and he *comforts* and delights the souls of God's people, filling them with spiritual joy (Rom 14:17, "the Kingdom of God is righteousness and peace and joy in the Holy Ghost"). Lastly, Edwards observes that Scriptural metaphors that depict the Spirit, such as water, fire, breath, wind, oil, wine, a spring, a river, naturally coincide with the active divine affection, which, or better *who,* ever rejoices in God's inexhaustible glory.[56]

If we step back for a minute, the curvature of space in Edwards's trinitarian thought clearly emerges around three foci: God, his understanding, and his love. The divine idea of the Father, magnified to infinite heights, images forth the personal divine subsistence of the Son, and the divine love or act toward that idea, magnified to the same intensity, breathes forth a third divine personal subsistence in the Holy Spirit. As we conclude this outline of Edwards's trinitarianism, it should be mentioned that this triadic, personal unfolding is strictly a logical unfolding, not a temporal one. There was never a time when God did not think of himself, nor love himself; he has from eternity existed as Trinity. Edwards is merely describing the logical ordering of these triune relationships.

1.3 The Augustinian "Flavor" of Edwards's Trinitarianism

Any adequate trinitarian theology must not only biblically identify that there are three persons in one God, it must also address other difficult questions such as the definition of the word "person," the equality of the persons in relation to their ontological order, and the question of the procession of the Holy Spirit. Edwards treated these questions in the second half of his *Discourse on the Trinity*, and they are important for they reveal the particular "flavor" of his trinitarianism. In this section we will analyze two of these issues that emerge in the *Discourse*, and conclude with a discussion on the Augustinian shape of his trinitarianism.

First, we shall address the issue of the personhood of the Holy Spirit. Edwards recognizes that by identifying the Spirit with the divine love he runs the risk of depersonalizing the third person of the Trinity. If a person "is that

---

55 Edwards, *Discourse on the Trinity*, in *Works*, 21:122-23.
56 Edwards, *Discourse on the Trinity*, in *Works*, 21:123-29.

which hath understanding and will," as Edwards defines it, "how therefore can this love be said to have understanding," if the Son is the divine understanding and is a distinct person from the Spirit? He addresses this question through recourse to the traditional doctrine of circumincession or perichoresis, whereby the three coinhere or interpenetrate each other. "There is such a wonderful union between [the three]," Edwards writes, "that they are after an ineffable and inconceivable manner one in another; so that one hath another, and they have communion in one another, and are as it were predicable one of another." The divine Spirit knows because the Son is in an infinitely close union with him. The Spirit can thus be understood truly as a person. "So the Holy Ghost, or the divine essence subsisting in divine love, understands because the Son, the divine idea, is in him. . . . The understanding is so in the Spirit, that the Spirit may be said to know, as the Spirit of God is truly and properly said to know and to 'search all things, even the deep things of God' [1 Cor 2:10]."[57] Edwards's formulations here reveal his strong emphasis on articulating a plurality within the divine unity. Though there are three persons, there are not three wills, minds or deities. Rather through their interpenetration of one another, the one divine understanding and love subsist in their entirety in each of three persons.

Second, Edwards considers the equality of three persons of the Godhead, while at the same time recognizing that they each possess a "peculiar honor in the society." He explores these "peculiar" honors in three contexts: their immanent (*ad intra*) relationships, their united effort in redemption, and the distinctive dependence and allegiance that Christians owe to each of them. His concern throughout is not only to explore the equal yet peculiar dignities that each person has, but to emphasize the full equality and honor of the Holy Spirit, an emphasis he feels has not been adequately treated.

Within the immanent Trinity, the Father's peculiar glory and honor is that he is the "fountain of the deity," and the one from whom proceeds divine wisdom, joy, holiness, excellency, and happiness. The Son's honor is that he is the divine wisdom or image that the Father generates. The Son, however, shares with the Father the honor of being the person from whom the divine excellency and happiness proceed. The Holy Spirit's honor, equal with that of Father and Son, consists in the fact that he is the excellency, holiness, happiness and divine beauty of both the other persons.[58]

In the work of redemption, this same equality of honor is seen in his emphasis on the Holy Spirit's equal honor.

> Glory belongs to the Father and the Son, that they so greatly loved the world: to the Father, that he so loved that he gave his only begotten son; to the Son, that he so loved the world as to give up himself. But there is equal glory due to the Holy

---

57 Edwards, *Discourse on the Trinity*, in *Works*, 21:133-34.
58 Edwards, *Discourse on the Trinity*, in *Works*, 21:134-35.

Ghost, for he is that love of the Father and the Son to the world. Just so much as the two first persons glorify themselves by showing the astonishing greatness of their love and grace, just so much is that wonderful love and grace glorified who is the Holy Ghost.[59]

Likewise from the vantage point of the Christian's experience, Edwards argues that "our dependence is equally upon each in this affair [of redemption]." Whereas the Father provides the Redeemer and the Son is the Redeemer who offers himself, "the Holy Ghost immediately communicates to us the thing purchased by communicating himself, and he is the thing purchased."[60] Edwards then launches into a two-page discussion illustrating this very point. What Christ purchased for the elect was communion with God which is none other than partaking of the Holy Spirit. Far from being the agent who merely applies the work of Christ to the elect, the Spirit *is* the sum of all the good that believers commune in, all the grace that believers benefit from, and all the love that they enjoy in God. Edwards here is consciously trying to distinguish himself from what he views is a weakness in traditional Protestant theology. What used to be supposed about the Holy Ghost, he writes, "[m]erely to apply to us or immediately to give or hand to us the blessing purchased after it was purchased" is "but a little thing" compared to the work that God the Father and Son did toward securing the redemption of humankind. "But according to this [i.e., Edwards's understanding of Holy Spirit], there is an equality. To be the love of God to the world is as much as for the Father and the Son to do so much from love to the world; and to be [the] thing purchased was as much as to be the price."[61] As he sees it, in this paradigm the wonder at he who did not spare his own son, and the preciousness of Christ's death for sinners, is now matched by the glory of the one who fills the forgiven sinner with the personal, divine love of the Godhead. The vision he suggests here is bold and clear: the restoration of the full equality, honor, and dignity of the Holy Spirit among the economic Trinity. Because the Spirit is equal to the Father and Son in both his immanent and economic operations, pneumatology must be pursued with an equal thoroughness and intensity as both christology and the doctrine of God. This was Edwards's vision when he wrote these words in his late twenties, and it well summarizes his lifetime literary, sermonic, and ministerial accomplishments as we shall see in the chapters to come.

What can we conclude by these observations as a whole? If we step back and scan the broad outlines of his articulation of the Trinity, it is difficult to escape the conclusion of Stephen Holmes: Edwards's "approach [to the Trinity] is clearly that of a child of Augustine: the Trinity of the mind, the mind

---

59 Edwards, *Discourse on the Trinity*, in *Works*, 21:135-36.
60 Edwards, *Discourse on the Trinity*, in *Works*, 21:136.
61 Edwards, *Discourse on the Trinity*, in *Works*, 21:137.

knowing itself/God and the mind loving itself/God is straight from the master's work."[62] Whether writing in the context of excellency (subject, object, consent), Lockean psychology of selfhood (the self, its reflexive knowledge, and its internal acts), or his usual articulation of the Trinity (God, his understanding/image and his love for his understanding/image), it appears that he is following a similar strategy in each instance: that the Trinity consists of the divine mind, its understanding, and the mutual love of mind and understanding. This paradigm is strongly reminiscent of one of Augustine's famous psychological analogies of the Trinity: the analogy of mind, knowledge and love. "[W]hen mind knows and loves itself the trinity remains of mind, love, knowledge," writes Augustine,

> How they are all in all of them we have already shown above; it is when the mind loves all itself and knows all itself and knows all its love and loves all its knowledge, when these three are complete with reference to themselves. In a wonderful way therefore these three are inseparable from each other, and yet each one of them is substance, and all together they are one substance or being, while they are also posited with reference to one another.[63]

Furthermore, when we take into account that Edwards affirmed other well-known themes found in Augustine's trinitarianism, such as his affirmation of the *filioque* and his strong affirmation of the unity of divine operations *ad extra*, the affinities between Edwards's trinitarianism and Augustine's become even more apparent.[64]

Another factor illustrating this affinity is the observation that whenever Edwards discusses the Trinity in any significant detail, he consistently uses the general mind-knowledge-love triad to illustrate his trinitarianism. His earliest statement, "Miscellanies" No. 94 written in early 1724, is a lengthy seven page treatise based upon this triad.[65] In the early 1730s, as we have seen, Edwards uses this triad to frame the argument of his *Discourse on the Trinity*. A decade later (circa 1740) we find the same structure being used in his unpublished *Treatise on Grace*, where he writes that

> The Scripture therefore leads us to this conclusion—though it be infinitely above us to conceive how it should be—that yet as the Son of God is the personal word, idea or wisdom of God, begotten by God, being an infinitely perfect, substantial

---

62 Holmes, *God of Grace and God of Glory*, 69.
63 St. Augustine, *The Trinity*, 275 (IX.i.8).
64 For Edwards's treatment of the *filioque*, see pages 46-47; for Edwards's affirmation of the unity of the divine operations *ad extra* in the person of Christ, see page 83.
65 "'Tis often said that God is infinitely happy from all eternity in the view and enjoyment of himself, in the reflection and converse love of his own essence, that is, in the perfect idea he has of himself, infinitely perfect." See "Miscellanies" No. 94, in *Works*, 13:257. The entire entry spans pages 256-63.

image or idea of himself, . . . so the Holy Spirit does in some ineffable and inconceivable manner proceed and is breathed forth from the Father and Son, but the divine essence being wholly poured and flowing out in that infinitely intense, holy and pure love and delight that continually and unchangeably breathes forth from the Father and the Son.[66]

In the mid 1740s, Edwards observes in "Miscellanies" No. 1084 that God's dispositional overflow into creation is trinitarian in shape. Jesus' petition to the Father in John 17:26 ("And I have declared unto them thy name, and will declare it, that the love wherewith thou hast loved me may be in them, and I in them") serves as the basis of his argument. "In this last verse these two ways of God's flowing forth and being communicated, that are the end of all things, are expressed, viz. manifesting God's name and communicating his love or, in other words, Christ's being in the creature in *the name, idea or knowledge of God being in them*, and the Holy Spirit's being in them *in the love of God's being in them*."[67] This was not some passing observation, for it became one of the prominent themes coursing throughout his dissertation on the *End of Creation*, a decade later (mid 1750s).[68] Throughout the span of his career, Edwards consistently employs his own form of Augustine's mind-knowledge-love triad.[69] The question before us is this: does Edwards elsewhere regularly articulate a distinct social model of the Trinity?

As we observed earlier, the assertion that Edwards's theory of divine excellency provided a basis for his adoption of a non-Augustinian, social model of the Trinity does not hold weight precisely because his theory of excellency possesses Augustinian trinitarian themes.[70] Other hard evidences that are marshaled to support this thesis are the statements Edwards makes of the trinitarian members being an interpersonal "society" or "family" of three.[71] Danaher observes that because of the deficiencies inherent within the Augustinian psychological analogy of the Trinity, Edwards "therefore turns to

---

66 Edwards, *Treatise on Grace*, in *Works*, 21:185-86.
67 Edwards, "Miscellanies" No. 1084, in *Works*, 20:467, emphasis mine. Note here the example of Edwards articulating his trinitarianism in the context of his theology of God's divine dispositional ontology.
68 Edwards, *End of Creation*, in *Works*, 8:428-35.
69 I do not deny that there are some differences between Edwards's trinitarianism and Augustine's. Danaher has highlighted some of these differences, especially the way Edwards's commitment to his own version of philosophical idealism enables him to avoid the difficulties traditionally associated with Augustine's trinitarianism (see his *Trinitarian Ethics of Jonathan Edwards*, 26-35). Yet these differences do not obscure the fact that the basic, general shape of Edwards's trinitarianism fits broadly within the contours of an identifiably Augustinian trinitarianism.
70 Excellency, as the consent of a plurality within a unity (subject, object, and consent), shows a striking resemblance to the mind-knowledge-love triad.
71 See Pauw, *Supreme Harmony of All*, 14, 30-43, and Danaher, *Trinitarian Ethics of Jonathan Edwards*, 67-84.

explore the Trinity from the perspective of the 'love and society' of the Godhead." The psychological analogy cannot, Danaher argues, "account for the interpersonal relations of love among the three persons of the Trinity," nor can it "provide an account for of the order and manifestations of God's triune creation and redemption of the world through the missions of the Son and the Spirit."[72] By employing these social metaphors to represent the trinitarian persons, it is argued that Edwards conveys a very different portrait of the Trinity than when he when writes about the triune God from the perspective of the mind-knowledge-love triad.[73]

Edwards does use social language when speaking about the "society" of the Godhead (see the texts below). Upon examination of these wonderful passages, however, one issue leaps out which calls into question the conclusion that these

---

72 Danaher, *Trinitarian Ethics of Jonathan Edwards*, 67-8.
73 The conclusion that social and familial language about the Trinity must indicate the presence of an alternative model of the Trinity reflects the widely held belief that an Augustinian trinitarianism is conceptually incompatible with themes of interpersonal relation and communion. This attitude derives from two interrelated factors (a) an interpretation of Augustine's trinitarianism which envisions it as essentially derived from Neoplatonism and virtually modalistic, emphasizing the common divine substance to the detriment of the plurality of persons, and (b) a widely held narrative of the history of trinitiarianism, made popular in the late nineteenth century by Theodore de Regnon, which categorizes various "Trinities" into a Western, Augustinian trinitarian tradition that supposedly "begins" with the divine unity and then secondarily factors in the persons, and an Eastern, Cappadocian approach that places the emphasis on the personal plurality and interpersonal communion of the Godhead. When interpreting Edwards in light of this reading of historical theology, it is easy to see how social language in his trinitarian formulations could lead to the conclusion that he worked with two models of the Trinity. Recent studies however are seriously calling into question this reading of Augustine's trinitarianism and the de Regnon thesis. For an introduction to this revision, see Basil Studer, *The Grace of Christ and the Grace of God in Augustine of Hippo: Christocentrism or Theocentrism?* (Collegeville, MN: Liturgical Press, 1997); Michel Rene Barnes, "Rereading Augustine on the Trinity," in *The Trinity: An Interdisciplinary Symposium on the Trinty*, ed. Stephen T. Davis, Daniel Kendall, and Gerald O'Collins (New York: Oxford, 1999), 145-76; idem., "De Regnon Reconsidered," *Augustinian Studies* 26 (1995), 51-79; and Lewis Ayers, "The Fundamental Grammar of Augustine's Trinitarian Theology," in *Augustine and His Critics: Essays in Honour of Gerald Bonner*, ed. Robert Dodaro and George Lawless (London: Routledge, 2000), 51-76. If these recent studies are correct then it calls for a serious reinterpretation of Edwards's trinitarianism and how it fits into the history of the doctrine of the Trinity. For an excellent work that tackle's this task, see Steven Studebaker's "Jonathan Edwards' Social Augustinian Trinitarianism: A Criticism of and Alternative to Recent Interpretations" (Ph.D. diss., Marquette University, 2003), and his more succinct statement of in "Jonathan Edwards's Social Augustinian Trinitarianism: An Alternative to a Recent Trend," in *Scottish Journal of Theology* 56.3 (2003): 268-85.

statements reflect a separate social model of the Trinity in Edwards's writings, namely, that when he speaks about the immanent Trinity as a "family" or "society," he always has in mind the society of the Father and the Son who fellowship *in* the Spirit. We observed this earlier in his articulation of the "excellent" Trinity: the Spirit is not strictly a consenting person alongside of the Father and the Son, but the personal consent between them.[74] Likewise, in "Miscellanies" No. 571, Edwards writes of the marvelous communion that the elect have with the "household" of God in heaven. While he speaks of the "society of the three persons of the Godhead," he speaks only of the Father, Son and the elect as the communing persons. The Spirit, he explicitly notes, is he *in whom* they all have communion.

> Christ has brought it to pass, that those that the Father has given him should be brought into the household of God, that he and his Father and they should be as it were one society, one family; that his people should be in a sort admitted into that society of the three persons in the Godhead. In this family or household, God [is] the Father, Jesus Christ is his own natural and eternally begotten Son. The saints, they also are children in the family; the church is the daughter of God, being the spouse of his Son. They all have communion in the same spirit, the Holy Ghost.[75]

Similarly, in a pastoral letter he wrote to Lady Mary Pepperrell upon the death of her son, Edwards comforts her with words that magnify the glory of Christ:

> He is the image and exhibition of the infinite beauty of the [Deity], in the viewing of which God the Father had all his infinite happiness from eternity. The eternal and immutable happiness of the Deity himself is represented in Scripture as a kind of social happiness, in the society of the persons of the Trinity. Prov. 8:30, 'Then was I by him as one brought up with him: and I was daily his delight, rejoicing always before him.'[76]

The "society of the persons of the Trinity" here is clearly the Father and the Son. Christ is the "image and exhibition" of the Father, in whom the Father has infinite happiness. By quoting the Proverbs text, he indicates the mutual love between Father and Son ("I was daily *his delight, rejoicing* always before

---

74 See above, pages 27-28. For Edwards's reference, see "The Mind," § 45 ¶ 9, in *Works*, 6:364.

75 Edwards, "Miscellanies" No. 571, in *The Works of Jonathan Edwards*, vol. 18, *The "Miscellanies," 501-832*, ed. Ava Chamberlain (New Haven: Yale University Press, 2000), 110. Notice that although Edwards does mention the "society of the three persons" here, his expansion of his meaning in the latter half of the quote indicates that the third person of the Trinity is *He in whom* the others have their communion, for clearly those doing the communing are the Father, the Son, and the church communing *in* the Holy Ghost.

76 Edwards, Letter No. 136, "To Lady Mary Pepperrell," November 28, 1751, in *Works*, 16:415-16.

him"). There does not appear to be any evidence of Edwards "shifting gears" between two different models in these discussions. Rather, as Steven Studebaker has argued, Edwards employs the language of social themes *within the context* of a broadly Augustinian trinitarian framework.[77]

We may conclude therefore that Edwards does not operate with a distinct social model of the Trinity. Throughout his life he consistently formulates the Trinity in broadly Augustinian categories. The reason, I suggest, why Edwards employs social language in his discussions of the Trinity has more to do with his pneumatology than his trinitarianism. He does not modulate between two different models of the Trinity, but rather between two different ways of speaking about the Spirit. Throughout this study we shall see Edwards identifying the personal Holy Spirit with the divine love, communion, union, and fellowship of the Godhead. Thus, on the one hand, he had no problem speaking about the Spirit as the third person of the Deity and of the Trinity as a "family" or "society of the three." This language is merely his recognition that there are three persons in the Godhead, not evidence of another trinitarian model in his thought. On the other hand, he also had no problem speaking of the Spirit as the divine love, communion, and union of the Father and the Son. The important point is that these transitions in pneumatological language occur *within* a broadly Augustinian trinitarianism. Furthermore, as we observed earlier, Edwards's strong identification of the Spirit with the divine love of the Godhead was the way he sought to recover equal honor and glory for the Spirit in theology. Does he succeed at this? It is to these issues that we now turn.

---

77 See Chapter 4 of Studebaker's dissertation, "Jonathan Edwards's Social Augustinian Trinitarianism," 147-245.

CHAPTER 2

Pneumatology: The Holy Spirit as the Bond of Union of the Immanent Trinity

As [the Holy Spirit's] nature is the divine love that is between the Father and the Son, he is the bond of union between the two covenanting persons, whereby they with infinite sweetness agree, and are infinitely strongly united as parties joined into covenant.[1]

B. B. Warfield (1851-1921), the great Princeton theologian, is credited with first recommending John Calvin as *the* "theologian of the Holy Spirit."[2] In an age when the Spirit was receiving more attention by conservative American Protestants through the holiness movement, the doctrine of perfectionism, and the nascent Pentecostal movement, Warfield redirected attention away from these new and fantastic phenomena toward the tried and true wisdom of John Calvin, in whom he felt God had deposited a vast storehouse of pneumatological wisdom. Curiously, however, when we turn to Calvin's *Institutes of the Christian Religion* or to a list of his many other publications, we do not find any comprehensive chapter, treatise or monograph devoted to the Holy Spirit. How then does Calvin merit Warfield's praise? The answer lies in the fact that Calvin distributed his comments on the Spirit throughout his writings. The Holy Spirit hovers, as it were, over every facet of Calvin's theology – the inspiration of Scripture, the creation of the world, the justification and sanctification of the Christian, and the superintendence of the church – yet he is rarely the direct object of Calvin's theological eye. From cover to cover of the *Institutes* the Holy Spirit's presence is luminous yet hidden, and everywhere implicit.

The same can be said about Jonathan Edwards's pneumatology. To get a clear picture of his theology of the Spirit as the bond of union, we are obliged to piece together the numerous pnematological discussions that canvas his writings. Edwards's *economic* observations on the Holy Spirit, where he refers to the Spirit's work in creation, are far more numerous than his rare *immanent*

---

1 Edwards, "Miscellanies" No. 1062, in *Works*, 20:443.
2 B. B. Warfield, "John Calvin the Theologian," in *Calvin and Augustine*, ed. Samuel G. Craig (Philadelphia: Presbyterian and Reformed, 1956), 481-507, see particularly 484-87.

observations, which examine the Spirit's eternal, inner-trinitarian activity, irrespective of creation. Nevertheless, we are not left in the dark. In the early 1740s, as the Great Awakening was underway, Edwards pulled together dozens of "Miscellanies" entries on the nature of grace into a work entitled *Treatise on Grace*.[3] Given its contents it could have been titled *A Treatise on the Holy Spirit*, for his basic argument is that grace in the Christian soul summarily consists in the personal presence and influence of the Holy Spirit. While the majority of the treatise investigates the nature of grace and the Holy Spirit in the life of the saint, Edwards does come to a place where he treats the nature of the Holy Spirit himself as the Divine Love of the Godhead. This section represents his most extended discussion on the nature of the Holy Spirit *in himself*; i.e., as he is in his eternal essence and activity among the trinitarian community. As his essence summarily consists in divine love, so does he represent the union of the Father and the Son in the Trinity.

This chapter will showcase two issues related to Edwards's understanding of the Holy Spirit's immanent trinitarian life. First, we will investigate the rich vision that Edwards held of the Spirit as the divine love of the Godhead, exploring just how he envisioned the Spirit as the personal bond of union of the Trinity. Related issues such as the *filioque* and the "hiddenness" of the Spirit's presence in the Trinity will also be examined. Second, we will untangle the potentially confusing vocabulary that Edwards employs when he writes about divine love and the Spirit. He frequently equates terms such as holiness, excellency, happiness, fullness, and grace with divine love. Collectively these concepts are not merely related to the Holy Spirit as *Agape*, they actually *are* the Spirit and love viewed at from different angles. Together these two sections will enable us to grasp the contours of what Edwards held to be the shape of God's internal life.

2.1 The Immanent Spirit and the Shape of Union

In the last chapter, we observed that when Edwards writes about God's attributes from the vantage point of the Trinity, he localizes them around the tri-fold foci of God, his understanding, and his love. There are only "two real attributes" or "faculties" in the Godhead, Edwards maintains, *Logos* and *Agape*, divine understanding and divine will.[4] In the *Treatise on Grace*, written about a decade later, Edwards specifically focuses on the second of these pairs, identifying the Holy Spirit as the personalized, essential love of the Godhead:

> Scripture signifies that the Spirit of God is the Love of God, [and] therefore it follows that [the] Holy Spirit proceeds from, or is breathed forth from, the Father and the Son in some way or other infinitely above all our conceptions, as the

---

3 Edwards, *Treatise on Grace*, in *Works*, 21:153-97.
4 Edwards, *Discourse on the Trinity*, in *Works*, 21:113-14, 132.

divine essence entirely flows out and is breathed forth in infinitely pure love and sweet delight from the Father and the Son.[5]

Again, a survey of his exegesis is instructive for understanding the shape of his argument. He begins by an exegesis of 1 John 4:12-13. "No man has ever seen God," the apostle writes in verse twelve. "If we love one another, God abides in us and his love is perfected in us. By this we know that we abide in him and he in us, because he has given us of his own Spirit." Though the apostle speaks of two elements here (our love for one another as proof of God abiding in us, and the Spirit's presence among us as proof that we abide in God), Edwards maintains that only one reality is portrayed by the apostle: the love *by which* we love one another and *through which* we know of God's presence in our community (v.12), is the Spirit *in whom* we know of our abiding in God (v.13). Love and Spirit are one and the same reality.[6] He observes a similar argument in Galatians 5:13-16, where Paul exhorts the Galatian churches (1) to conduct their lives in love and (2) to walk in the Spirit. These exhortations, Edwards concludes, identify the Galatians' loving with the presence of the Spirit in their midst. Once again Edwards sees an identification of the Spirit with love in the Scriptures.[7]

In addition to these explicit biblical statements, Edwards argues that Scripture highlights the Spirit's nature as love in its extensive use of imagery. The dove, for instance, is "an emblem of love in the Holy Scriptures." This is seen in "the message of peace and love [she brought to Noah] after such terrible manifestations of God's wrath in the time of the deluge."[8] Similarly, the dove-like beauty that the beloved possesses in the Song of Solomon also reveals the deep connections that Scripture draws between the dove and love.[9] At the same time, the Spirit is also closely associated with the dove in Scripture, which can be clearly seen in Christ's baptism:

As God the Father then poured forth his Holy Spirit of love upon the Son without measure, so that which was then seen with the eye—viz. a dove descending and lighting upon Christ—signified the same thing to the eye as what was at the same time proclaimed to the ear—viz. 'This is my beloved Son, in whom I am well

---

5 Edwards, *Treatise on Grace*, in *Works*, 21:184.
6 Edwards, *Treatise on Grace*, in *Works*, 21:181-82.
7 Edwards, *Treatise on Grace*, in *Works*, 21:182.
8 Edwards, *Treatise on Grace*, in *Works*, 21:182.
9 Edwards, *Treatise on Grace*, in *Works*, 21:183 where Edwards notes Song of Solomon 1:15: "Behold, thou art fair, my love . . . thou hast doves' eyes"; 5:2: "'Open to me, my sister, my love, my dove, my undefiled'"; and 5:12: "His eyes are as the eyes of doves by the rivers of waters."

pleased.' This is the Son on whom I pour forth all my love, towards whom my essence entirely flows out in love.[10]

Edwards also discerns conceptual linkages between the "waters of life" portrayed in Revelation 22, Ezekiel 47 (which Christ identifies with the Holy Spirit in John 7), and the "rivers of [God's] pleasures" mentioned in Psalm 36.[11] God's "pleasures," which Edwards identifies as God's love of his own perfections, are associated with images of water (the "*river* of God's pleasures;" the "*waters* of life") which in turn are identified by Christ as the Holy Spirit (John 7). Thus, Edwards concludes, "This river of God's pleasures . . . is the same with God's love, or God's excellent loving-kindness."[12] Throughout his writings Edwards is fond of identifying the Spirit and love. Yet it is one thing to identify the Spirit and love, quite another thing to explore the nature of the Spirit *as* love. What, then, does Edwards consider to be the nature of the Spirit as divine love?

The answer to this question requires us to highlight the object of divine love. "God's love is primarily to himself," Edwards writes, "and his infinite delight is in himself, in the Father and the Son loving and delighting in each other."[13] At the inner-trinitarian level, "God's love" consists in the love enjoyed between the Father and the Son, and they serve as the dual objects of this love. Yet while their love is mutual, there is a logical ordering to this love, beginning first with the Father's love to the Son, a point he brings out in his well known sermon "Heaven is a World of Love." "[This Love] flows out in the first place [necessarily] and infinitely towards his only begotten Son, being poured forth without measure, as to an object which is infinite, and so fully adequate to God's love in its foundation. Infinite love is infinitely exercised towards him."[14] The Father's infinite love for the Son, who is the substantial image of himself, is the logical ground to Spirit's subsistence; the Spirit is "breathed forth" in the Father's infinitely intense love to the Son. Yet Edwards does not

---

10 Edwards, *Treatise on Grace*, in *Works*, 21:183-84.
11 Edwards, *Treatise on Grace*, in *Works*, 21:184-85. Rev 22:1: "And he showed me a *pure river of water of life*, clear as crystal, proceeding out of the throne of God and of the Lamb." Ezek 47:1: "Afterward he brought me again unto the door of the house; and, behold, *waters issued out from under the threshold of the house eastward.*" John 7:38: Jesus proclaimed, "'He that believeth on me, as the scripture hath said, *out of his belly shall flow rivers of living water.*' Now this he said about *the Spirit*, which those who believed in him were to receive." Psalm 36:8: "[The children of men] shall be abundantly satisfied with the fatness of thy house; and thou shalt make them drink of *the river of thy pleasures.*"
12 Edwards, *Treatise on Grace*, in *Works*, 21:185.
13 Edwards, *Treatise on Grace*, in *Works*, 21:184.
14 Jonathan Edwards, "Heaven is a World of Love," in *Charity and Its Fruits*, in *The Works of Jonathan Edwards*, vol. 8, *Ethical Writings*, ed. Paul Ramsey (New Haven: Yale University Press, 1989), 373.

consider this love to be unidirectional, for "Love is always mutual, and the returns are always in due proportion."[15] Therefore the Son returns that which he has received out of an infinite regard to the Father, and to the infinite degree that he has received it. The Son thus becomes both the subject and object of divine love.[16]

We are now in a position to pinpoint the nature of divine love and the Spirit of God in Edwards's theology. The picture we have painted so far is a very dynamic and intense view of God's inner reality. The Father and the Son are moved by valuing and sweetly rejoicing in each other to such a degree that their mutual activity, or the "meeting place" of their communion, stands forth as its own personal subsistence: the Holy Spirit. The Spirit is the dynamic, infinitely pure act of love which subsists between the Father and the Son, and is therefore the personal affection of the Godhead. "The Spirit of God is spiritual joy and delight,"[17] he writes in "Miscellanies" No. 364, a point which he explores further in a later entry:

> So the word "spirit," when it [is] used concerning God: when it is not used to signify the divine essence (as sometimes it is, as when we read that God is a Spirit) it signifies the holy temper, or disposition or affection of God, as when we read of the Spirit of God. If we read of the meek spirit, of the peaceable spirit, of the pure spirit or holy spirit of a man, we understand it of the meek, peaceable, pure or holy temper: so when we read of the good Spirit or holy Spirit of God, we should likewise understand it of the divine temper or affection.[18]

Four issues arise from this identification of the Spirit with divine love. First, it is the third person of the Trinity who is most properly responsible for the dynamic activity of the Godhead. While Edwards adheres to the traditional doctrine of the unity of the divine operations among all the trinitarian members, he feels at liberty to "locate" certain attributes around specific divine persons, while not denying their equal distribution among the Godhead. "Though all the divine perfections are to be attributed to each person of the Trinity, yet the Holy Ghost is in a peculiar manner called by the name of love, Ἀγαπη."[19] His general intent in this is merely to show that the Spirit is most essentially the divine love of the Godhead. While the Father and the Son love each other, they most originally consist in the "direct existence" and the "image, wisdom and idea" of God respectively. By contrast, Edwards is saying, from every possible angle, the Spirit is the divine love, affection, will and sacred energy which

---

15 Edwards, "Heaven is a World of Love," in *Charity and Its Fruits*, in *Works*, 8:377.
16 "The Son of God is not only the infinite object of love, but he is also an infinite subject of it." See "Heaven is a World of Love," in *Charity and Its Fruits*, in *Works*, 8:373.
17 Edwards, "Miscellanies" No. 364, in *Works*, 13:436.
18 Edwards, "Miscellanies" No. 396, in *Works*, 13:462.
19 Edwards, *Treatise on Grace*, in *Works*, 21:181.

courses through the Trinity. It is in this nuanced manner that the Spirit is responsible for the dynamic activity of the Godhead. As Bruce Stephens has correctly observed, "it is the Spirit and not Christ who lends an energetic and restless quality to Edwards's thought."[20]

The second point that unfolds from these observations is that Edwards adheres to the traditional Western trinitarian understanding of the Spirit's dual procession from both the Father "and the Son," the *filioque*. Centuries before the Reformation divided Western Christendom, the doctrinal flashpoint of the first great split in the Christian church centered upon the doctrine of the procession of the Spirit within the immanent Trinity.[21] The main question of this controversy runs as follows: does the Spirit proceed from the Father alone, as the Greek-speaking East asserts, or does he proceed from both the Father and the Son, as the Latin West maintains? The Eastern churches generally argue that Scripture explicitly mentions the single procession of the Spirit from the Father alone.[22] Consequently, they maintain a distinction between the Spirit's ontological procession and his economic "mission" in creation and redemption. *Ad intra*, the Spirit proceeds from the Father alone; *ad extra*, the Spirit is sent by both the Father (John 14:16) and the Son (John 15:26). Thus the Spirit is said to be the "Spirit of Christ" (Rom 8:9) with regard to his economic mission, while his procession in the immanent Trinity is *through the Son* from the Father, not conjointly *from the Son*. By contrast, the West counters that there is no distinction between the economic activity of the Spirit and the reality of his inner-trinitarian procession: the former is a window into the latter. Thus as the Father "spirates" or breathes forth the Spirit, the Son too possesses the same spirating ability with regard to the Spirit, as evidenced by his breathing the Spirit on to the disciples after his resurrection (John 20:22). Furthermore, the Spirit, as the "river of the water of life," is also said to flow from both "the throne of God *and of the Lamb*," (Rev 22:1, cf. John 7:38-39).[23] As these differing views took shape in the first millennium, Western clerics saw fit to insert the phrase "and the Son" (*filioque*) into the creedal formulae which were sung in the liturgy, a move that was considered by the East to be at worst a heterodox insertion into the very heart of the church's worship. This incredibly intricate controversy, involving many political, ecclesiastical, and theological elements, led to the Great Schism in 1054, accompanied by mutual anathematizations by both East and West.

---

20 Bruce M. Stephens, *The Holy Spirit in American Protestant Thought*, 2.
21 For an excellent historical summary of the *filioque* through the High Middle Ages, see Brian E. Daley S.J., "Revisiting the 'Filioque': Roots and Branches of an Old Debate," *Pro Ecclesia* 10.1 (2001): 31-62.
22 John 15:26: "But when the Comforter is come, whom I will send unto you from the Father, even the Spirit of truth, *which proceedeth from the Father*, he shall testify of me."
23 Daley, "Revisiting the 'Filioque,'" 34-35, 61.

With this admittedly brief summary of the two theological traditions, we can easily observe Edwards's Western pneumatological affinities. Edwards's conceptual development of the Spirit along the lines of divine love, a move advanced by both Augustine and Aquinas, naturally leans toward the Western position. Love as we have seen in Edwards's understanding requires at least the presence of two persons and an equal reciprocity between the parties. Citing Prov 8:30 ("and I [wisdom] was daily his [God's] delight, rejoicing always before him"), Edwards follows the standard scriptural witness used to support this mutual love model.[24] If the infinite act of love is the ontological rationale for the Spirit's subsistence in the Trinity, then the Spirit must proceed from both the Father and Son's mutual spiration.

> The Holy Spirit does in some ineffable and inconceivable manner proceed, and is breathed forth both from the Father and Son, by the divine essence being wholly poured and flowing out in that infinitely intense, holy, and pure love and delight that continually and unchangeably breathes forth from the Father and the Son, primarily towards each other, and secondarily towards the creature.[25]

Subsequently, because there is no distinction between the Spirit's immanent procession and economic mission, Edwards is able to affirm, along with the West, a high degree of continuity between the Spirit's inner-trinitarian life and economic work.[26]

Third, Edwards's presentation of the Holy Spirit as the immanent love of the Godhead underscores the "hiddenness" of the Spirit in the immanent Trinity. Love by nature highlights the object of its gaze, and does not call attention to itself. In the Trinity, the Spirit "highlights" God the Father's beloved, the divine Son, as well as the Son's beloved, the Father. He is the mediator of their communion, the bond of their love, and the sacred energy of their union. Consequently while he is equal in dignity with the other two, he remains hidden in the sense that he does not call attention to himself as divine love. Scripture, Edwards observes, leads us to these conclusions: "though we often read in Scripture of the Father loving the Son, and the Son loving the Father, yet we never once read either of the Father or the Son loving the Holy Spirit, and the

---

24 Edwards, *Discourse on the Trinity*, in *Works*, 21:121.

25 Edwards, *Treatise on Grace*, in *Works*, 21:185-86. For other statements on the *filioque*, see "Miscellanies" No. 143 (*Works*, 13:298-99); his *Discourse on the Trinity* (*Works*, 21:121, 135); and his sermon "Heaven is a World of Love," in *Charity and its Fruits* (*Works*, 8:373).

26 We see this in the last phrase of the above quote: "*primarily* towards each other, and *secondarily* towards the creature." The saint is caught up in this "love life" of the Godhead as she is in Christ: "The love of God flows out towards Christ the Head, and through him to all his members, in whom they were beloved before the foundation of the world." See "Heaven is a World of Love," in *Charity and its Fruits*, in *Works*, 8:373.

Spirit loving either of them."[27] This fact has puzzled Christians throughout the centuries: why does the New Testament shed so little light on the deity, nature, and personhood of the Spirit in comparison to the Son? "There is nothing in Scripture," Edwards notes, "that speaks of any acceptance of the Holy Ghost, or any reward, or any mutual friendship between the Holy Ghost and either of the other persons [of the Trinity], nor any command to love the Holy Ghost, or to delight in or have any complacence in [him], though such commands are so frequent with respect to the other persons."[28] The reason for this biblical reticence, he argues, stems from the fact that the Spirit is most often "present" in Scripture in the form of love, not as the third person of the Trinity. Subsequently, the Spirit, under the scriptural disguise of love, often rounds out the New Testament passages which appear to be "binitarian." Why do we find the Father and the Son loving each other, and never once see the Holy Spirit mentioned as either the subject or object of this divine love? "It is because the Holy Spirit is the divine love itself, the love of the Father and the Son."[29] Why does the apostle John appear to neglect the Spirit when he wrote that "our fellowship is with the Father and with his Son Jesus Christ" (1 John 1:3)? He does not neglect the Spirit, Edwards maintains, "because our communion [i.e., fellowship] with them *consists* in our communion of the Holy Ghost with them."[30] The Spirit's hidden presence radiates through the nature of "fellowship" in John's verse. How is it that "the apostle Paul so often wishes grace, mercy, and peace from God the Father, and from the Lord Jesus Christ, in the beginning of his epistles, without even mentioning the Holy Ghost"? It is because "the Holy Ghost is himself the love and grace of God the Father and the Lord Jesus Christ."[31] These texts, while "binitarian" in appearance, are ultimately trinitarian due to the Spirit's implicit presence.

Lastly, as the love of the Father and the Son, the Holy Spirit is the bond of union of the Godhead: "the holiness of God consist[s] in his love, especially in the perfect and intimate union and love there is between the Father and the Son. But the Spirit that proceeds from the Father and the Son is the bond of this union."[32] Love, Edwards held, is the only means of generating union between intelligent spirits,[33] a fact which renders the trinitarian community an infinitely unified society. While this bond of love unites the Father and the Son who are equal in deity, the union accentuates the divine understanding (i.e., the Son),

---

27 Edwards, *Treatise on Grace*, in *Works*, 21:186.
28 Edwards, *Discourse on the Trinity*, in *Works*, 21:140.
29 Edwards, *Treatise on Grace*, in *Works*, 21:186.
30 Edwards, "Miscellanies" No. 376, in *Works*, 13:448.
31 Edwards, *Treatise on Grace*, in *Works*, 21:186.
32 Edwards, *Treatise on Grace*, in *Works*, 21:186.
33 "Now there is no other way of different spirits' being thus united, but by love. . . . Such love as this makes a thorough union." Edwards, "Miscellanies" No. 398, in *Works*, 13:463.

for it is through him that the Father glorifies and loves himself. Divine love is not blind, but always presupposes knowledge in the order of nature:

> Even in creatures there is consciousness included in the very nature of the will or act of the soul; and though perhaps not so that it can so properly be said that it is a seeing or understanding will, yet it may truly and properly [be] said so in God by reason of God's infinitely more perfect manner of acting, so that the whole divine essence flows out and subsists in this act. The Son is in the Holy Spirit, though it don't proceed from him, by reason that the understanding must be considered as prior in the order of nature to the will or love or act, both in creature and in the Creator.[34]

Thus while the Father is both Lord and fountain of the Godhead and first in order, it is through the Son that the Father glorifies himself, and it is the Son as the divine understanding who is the direct object of the Spirit's love and unifying act. The shape of the inner-trinitarian union between the Father and the Son is thus "Son-centered."

So far we have probed the depths of Edwards's immanent pneumatology, noting various characteristics of the Spirit's inner-trinitarian life: he is the love and dynamic energy of the Godhead and is largely hidden in his paths. Many of these characteristics we will see later in our study when we turn our attention to the Spirit's economic work. For now we turn our gaze to the rich theological terms that Edwards employs to describe the Holy Spirit and divine love.

2.2 Facets of Divine Love: The Spirit as God's Holiness, Excellency, Happiness, Fullness, and Grace

Edwards's identification of the Spirit with divine love generates a magnetic field in his conceptual universe that powerfully attracts nearby theological concepts. Holiness, excellency, happiness, fullness, and grace are all facets of divine love, according to Edwards, and thus they all succumb to a gravity of identification where they are equated with the third person of the Trinity in various ways. While bringing a powerful unity to his theology, this characteristic of his work has the potential to confuse his readers. To avoid this confusion this section will conduct a vocabulary workshop in two phases. First we will explore the distinguishing features of the Spirit, divine love, and their conceptual cousins: holiness, excellency, happiness, fullness, and grace. Second, we will bring clarity to the dynamic, verbal language that he associates with these attributes, such as communication, communion, and partaking. By sharpening our focus on these terms, we will not only better understand the immanent Holy Spirit, but will later be better equipped to grasp the Spirit's economic activity.

---

34 Edwards, *Discourse on the Trinity*, in *Works*, 21:133-34.

2.2.1 Holiness

We begin with a look at the "objective" side of divine love: God's holiness. While holiness possesses overtones of "separateness" in Scripture, Edwards's theological interpretation of it leads him to associate it closely with divine love: "the holiness of God consist[s] in his love, especially in the perfect and intimate union and love there is between the Father and the Son."[35] When referring to it as a quality of God in general, he argues that the essence of holiness consists in God's infinite self-regard. "God's Holiness," he writes, "is his having a due, meet and proper regard to everything, and therefore consists mainly and summarily in his infinite regard or love to himself, he being infinitely the greatest and most excellent Being."[36] Holiness and love are thus two terms describing the same reality in God. We may distinguish them as follows: holiness seems to refer to God's love from the standpoint of the Godhead in general, whereas divine love indicates the holy activity of the inner-trinitarian members *within* the Godhead. Like divine love, holiness is not an *it* in God, or some*thing* God is. Rather, it is a *he*: the third person of the Trinity. The Holy Spirit, Edwards writes, "is not only infinitely holy as the Father and the Son are, but he is the holiness of God itself in the abstract. The holiness of the Father and the Son does consist in breathing forth this Spirit."[37]

2.2.2 Excellency

A nearby neighbor to both love and holiness is excellency, which we briefly explored in the last chapter. Like holiness, God's excellency "consists in the love of himself," a love which is played out through God's self-exertion and mutual consenting within the inner-trinitarian arena: "But he exerts himself towards himself no other way than in infinitely loving and delighting in himself, in the mutual love of the Father and the Son. This makes the third, the personal Holy Spirit or the holiness of God, which is his infinite beauty and this is God's infinite consent to being in general."[38] As God's excellency, the Holy Spirit represents the spiritual harmony and mutual consent that obtains among the Father and the Son. He is the meeting place of their communion, and is the spiritual beauty of the Godhead. Excellency is thus closely associated with holiness: both represent the objective side of love, and both are designations of the personal Holy Spirit. Perhaps the one difference between them lies in the

---

35 Edwards, *Treatise on Grace*, in *Works*, 21:186.
36 Edwards, "Miscellanies" No. 1077, in *Works*, 20:460. See a similar statement in *End of Creation* (*Works*, 8:422): "the moral rectitude and fitness of the disposition, inclination or affection of God's heart does chiefly consist in a respect or regard to himself infinitely above his regard to all other beings: or in other words, his holiness consists in this."
37 Edwards, *Treatise on Grace*, in *Works*, 21:187.
38 Edwards, "The Mind" §45 ¶ 9, in *Works*, 6:364.

separate contexts in which he employs each of them. Edwards uses excellency in ontological contexts when he speaks of the texture of being. Spiritual beauty, the consent of finite minds to being in general, and the harmony of being's various elements with the triune God, are all Edwardsean descriptions of ontology that conceptualize the outer surface of excellent being. By contrast, Edwards utilizes the language of holiness to refer to a personal agent's loving and radical God-centeredness (in both Creator and created). Holiness is more of the teleological aspect of divine love, whereas excellency has more to do with the ontology or shape of divine love. Both, as we have been arguing, are different ways in which Edwards refers to the Holy Spirit.

2.2.3 Happiness

In contrast to holiness and excellency, divine happiness is best understood as the subjective side of divine love, and is often described as the "delight" or "joy" experienced among the members of the Godhead. "The happiness of God doth also consist in this love: for doubtless the happiness of God consists in the infinite love he has to and delight he has in himself; or, in other words, in the infinite delight there is between the Father and the Son, spoken of in Prov. 8:30."[39] As the divine love, happiness is thus easily associated with the third person of the Trinity: "The Spirit of God is spiritual joy and delight," he writes in "Miscellanies" No. 364, and "that happiness spoken of that God will give his saints, is nothing but a fullness of his Spirit."[40] Happiness exults in God himself, yet Edwards often links it with the perception of excellency: "happiness is the perception and possession of excellency."[41] Thus merely to perceive spiritual harmonies is to be enveloped in this divine happiness. God's own perception of his glorious excellencies, which he "views" in the Son, is intimately linked with the act of divine love and the affection of infinite happiness. This again reminds us of the very close association between perception and affection, intellect and will, and ultimately Son and Spirit in Edwards's thought.

2.2.4 Fullness

The fullness of God, according to Edwards's use of the term, is a more difficult concept to grasp, primarily because its semantic range is broader than the terms that we have examined so far. While Edwards does not identify God's fullness explicitly with divine love, he does closely associate it with the Spirit, a fact which requires our attention. In several places he defines God's fullness as the totality of good which he possesses:

---

39 Edwards, *Treatise on Grace*, in *Works*, 21:186-87.
40 Edwards, "Miscellanies" No. 364, in *Works*, 13:436.
41 Edwards, "Miscellanies" No. 106, in *Works*, 13:276-77.

> Hence we learn that God's fullness does consist in the Holy Spirit. By 'fullness,' ... is intended the good that anyone possesses. Now the good that God possesses does most immediately consist in his joy and complacence that he has in himself. It does objectively, indeed, consist in the Father and the Son; but it doth most immediately consist in the complacence in these elements. Nevertheless the fullness of God consists in the holiness and happiness of the Deity.[42]

Fullness thus appears to be a "summary" concept that comprehends all of what Edwards means by divine love. It includes God's happiness, holiness and goodness and is another term which comprises the third person of the Trinity. In this sense it is similar to divine love in its scope. There are places, however, where fullness encompasses a wider reality than divine love. One noteworthy example occurs in *End of Creation*. There Edwards speaks of God's fullness as comprising all that God seeks to communicate to creation, including his knowledge, holiness and happiness.[43] He goes on to speak of fullness as that inclination in God's nature which seeks an *ad extra* communication of his internal glory: "as this fullness is capable of communication or emanation *ad extra*; so it seems a thing amiable and valuable in itself that it would be communicated or flow forth, that this infinite fountain of good should send forth abundant streams, . . . diffusing its excellent fullness."[44] Here fullness is not so much a summary term for God's goodness from a trinitarian perspective (where the Spirit is identified as God's goodness). Rather, it designates an undifferentiated inclination in God toward an external diffusion of all that God is. This more comprehensive meaning of fullness can be attributed to the fact that Edwards writes *End of Creation* not from the perspective of God as Trinity, but from that of God in general, where he was not prone in his language to locate specific attributes to certain members of the Trinity.

2.2.5 Grace

The last concept which Edwards identifies with the Spirit is grace. The distinguishing feature about grace with regard to the other terms we have examined is that it is properly an economic concept, relating to the redemption of sinners, rather than an immanent trinitarian reality. In spite of this difference, however, Edwards identifies grace with both divine love and the Spirit. Grace is divine love externalized, or the Holy Spirit's *ad extra* influence. His discussion begins with the varieties of grace: "'Tis common for us to speak of various graces of the Spirit of God as though they were so many

---

42 Edwards, *Treatise on Grace*, in *Works*, 21:187. See also *End of Creation* (*Works*, 8:433n7), where he writes that "I shall often use the phrase 'God's fullness,' as signifying and comprehending all the good which is in God natural and moral, either excellence or happiness."
43 See *End of Creation*, in *Works*, 8:438-43.
44 Edwards, *End of Creation*, in *Works*, 8:433.

different principles of holiness, and to call them by distinct names as such: repentance, humility, resignation, thankfulness, etc."[45] While we must distinguish this variety of graces in the soul, Edwards affirms that we err if we believe that they are all distinct realities. The truth is that while grace exists in many forms, it is ultimately "one common essence," and springs from one "original principle," which is essentially divine love: "[A]ll grace, and every Christian disposition and habit of mind and heart, especially as to that which is primarily holy and divine in it, does summarily consist in divine love, and may be resolved into it; however, with respect to its kinds and manner of exercise and its appendages, it may be diversified."[46]

As grace is none other than the divine love, so it is none other than the third person of the Trinity dwelling in the souls of the redeemed. He arrived at this conviction early in his life,[47] and it became the dominant theme throughout the *Treatise on Grace*. The New Testament, he observes, frequently contrasts spirit and the flesh as opposing principles within the life of the saint. That which is born of the Spirit is spirit, according to the apostle John (John 3:6). According to Paul, the flesh lusts against the spirit and the spirit against the flesh (Gal 5:17), and a law of sin and death opposes the law of the spirit of life (Romans 7). Edwards argues that Paul identifies this principle of the spirit with the Holy Spirit in Rom 8:9-16, thereby sealing the connections between grace as a divine principle, divine love and the third person of the Trinity. His conclusion masterfully summarizes the nature of grace, holiness and divine love as the Holy Spirit, and it reveals the conceptual "perichoresis" which characterizes Edwards's vocabulary as a whole:

> So that that holy, divine principle, which we have observed does radically and essentially consist in divine love, is no other than a communication and participation of that same infinite divine love, which is God, and in which the Godhead is eternally breathed forth and subsists in the third person in the blessed Trinity. So that true saving grace is no other than that very love of God; that is, God, in one of the persons of the Trinity, uniting himself to the soul of a creature as a vital principle, dwelling there and exerting himself by the faculties of the soul of man, in his own proper nature, after the manner of a principle of nature.[48]

With this we are getting ahead of ourselves and raising issues that will be

---

45 Edwards, *Treatise on Grace*, in *Works*, 21:166.
46 Edwards, *Treatise on Grace*, in *Works*, 21:168. For a very similar argument see "Love the Sum of All Virtue," the first sermon in the sermon series *Charity and Its Fruits*, in *Works*, 8:129-48.
47 See Jonathan Edwards, "Notes on Scripture," No. 14, in *The Works of Jonathan Edwards*, vol. 15, *Notes on Scripture*, ed. Stephen J. Stein (New Haven: Yale University Press, 1998), 52, where he writes (circa 1724) that "All grace is nothing but the Holy Spirit dwelling in us."
48 Edwards, *Treatise on Grace*, in *Works*, 21:194.

treated in subsequent chapters where we deal with the Spirit's economic activity. For now, however, we must note the interpenetration of these theological concepts under the banner of divine love and Spirit. We may summarize this interpenetration as follows: God's holiness constitutes divine love from the standpoint of the Deity in general, without reference to the inner-trinitarian community. From "outside" of the Trinity holiness consists in God's radical theocentricism, while the same reality viewed from "inside" the Trinity is more properly termed divine love. Excellency, like holiness, comprises divine love viewed from an objective stance. Yet unlike holiness, excellency pertains to God's love from more of an ontological angle, respecting the spiritual harmonies, mutual consent, and divine beauty that eternally obtains among the trinitarian persons, rather than from the teleological angle which the term holiness captures. By contrast God's happiness, joy, and delight, all synonymous concepts, denote the "subjective side" of divine love, illuminating the affectional experience of God's self-viewing and approving of his own perfections. We noted that God's fullness, in a narrow sense, is a "summary" term comprising all that divine love does, and as such is a term that is as extensive as love. Yet in a broader sense, God's fullness comprises all that God possesses, which includes his knowledge, and thus does not necessarily refer to the Holy Spirit in this more expansive sense. Lastly, we observed that grace is none other than divine love manifested *ad extra*. These concepts form much of the structural scaffolding of his thought. Because he identifies each of them with the third person of the Trinity at one point or another, his theology thus becomes charged with a hidden and luminous pnuematogical presence.

2.2.6 Communication, Communion and Participation

There is one other set of concepts which, while not identified with the Spirit, remains crucial to our understanding of him as he relates both within the trinitarian society and without. Edwards sometimes uses terms such as "communication," "communion," and "participation" when he describes the interrelations between the trinitarian persons. These words summarily refer to the dynamic intra-societal activity that obtains among the members of a community. In the trinitarian community we may define these verbal terms as follows. "Communication" and the verb "to communicate" refer to the active transfer of divine riches, fullness and glories from one person of the Trinity to another. God the Father communicates his infinite goodness to the Son by eternally generating him within the Godhead: "the Son is the adequate communication of the Father's goodness, [and] is an express and complete image of him."[49] Communication in the Godhead therefore is an extension of Father's own being, whereby the happiness of the Son is that of the Father.

Closely related are the concepts of "communion" and "participation."

---

49 Edwards, "Miscellanies" No. 104, in *Works*, 13:272.

Whereas communication has a unidirectional sense in Edwards's theology, focusing on one person's action toward another, communion is multidirectional, encompassing the total common activity of multiple persons. "Communion," Edwards writes, "is a common partaking of benefits, or of good, in union and society."[50] The communion of the Father and the Son is thus an activity whereby they enjoy the common goodness each possesses. This goodness is none other than the Holy Spirit, in which the Father and the Son are unified by divine love. By contrast, the terms "participation" and "partaking" are unidirectional concepts describing the act of communion from the standpoint of one of the parties. "[T]o have communion or fellowship with another," Edwards writes in *Treatise on Grace*, "is to partake with them of their good in their fullness, in union and society with them."[51] While Edwards is speaking in generalities here, the antecedent of "another" and "them" in the context is most likely "God the Father and God the Son," which illustrates that not only do the saints participate in the divine nature, but the members of the Godhead participate together in the divine communion as Trinity.[52]

Thus we have a triad of concepts that are used to describe the relationality of the immanent Trinity. The term "communion" (or fellowship, the terms are virtually synonymous in Edwards's writings) describes the common good that the Father and the Son partake of in their eternal love for each other. This common good we have seen is the third person of the Trinity. "Communication" references the active transfer of divine riches from one member to another. "Participation" by contrast is the reception of good that is communicated from another and the common enjoyment of good with another. We will see these terms used more frequently by Edwards in his discussion on the saints' salvation. For now we must note that it is this rich immanent trinitarian communion which serves as a basis for God's will to create the world. According to Edwards, God in his infinite trinitarian fullness is disposed toward seeking his glory *ad extra* or outside of himself. In the next two chapters we shall see how Edwards understood this divine disposition to magnify his glory *ad extra*, and the plans God made to begin this great work.

---

50 Edwards, "Miscellanies" No. 404, in *Works*, 13:468.
51 Edwards, *Treatise on Grace*, in *Works*, 21:188.
52 "Hence our communion with God the Father and God the Son consists in our partaking of the Holy Ghost, which is their Spirit: for to have communion or fellowship with another, is to partake with them of their good in their fullness, in union and society with them." (*Works*, 21:188)

Part II

Setting the Stage

Bridges to Creation and Redemption

CHAPTER 3

The Trinitarian Plan of Creation and Redemption

> The Father is as the substance, of the sun. . . . The Son is as the brightness and glory of the disk of the sun, or that bright and glorious form under which it appears to our eyes. The Holy Ghost is the action of the sun, which is within the sun, in its intense heat, and being diffusive, enlightens, warms, enlivens and comforts the world. The Spirit, as it is God's infinite love to himself and happiness in himself, is as the internal heat of the sun; but as it is that by which God communicates himself, is as the emanation of the sun's action, or the emitted beams of the sun.[1]

So far, our study has examined Edwards's explorations of the essential Trinity and the Holy Spirit's role as the bond of union among the "society of three." In this chapter we turn to our attention away from God's inner life toward that mysterious area of doctrine which has intrigued theologians for centuries, the boundary between Creator and creature. Move number one in any Christian theology has been to affirm without reservation that this boundary is firmly fixed, and that there is nor ever can be any ontological leakage between the two. Yet is this boundary likened more to a wall or to a window? In other words, to what degree can the creature discern the dimensions of God's inner life? Has God left vestiges of his trinitarian excellencies woven in creation? One of the striking features of Edwards's theology is the way he desires to demonstrate the continuity between God's inner trinitarian life with the new life experienced by the redeemed. While there is a sharp distinction between God and his people, Edwards seeks to emphasize at the same time that the redeemed know and love God much in the same way that God knows and loves himself.

The purpose of this chapter is twofold. First, we will trace the thematic lines Edwards uses to connect divine ontology and the divine intention in creation, noting specifically how for Edwards God's intention to create is pattered off and is in some sense an extension of his own trinitarian fullness. For Edwards God seeks to magnify himself in a trinitarian way through creation and redemption by a communication of his trinitarian excellencies to creatures who are suited to receive his communications and participate in his divine fullness. Second, we will examine Edwards's theological anthropology and note how

---

1 Edwards, *Discourse on the Trinity*, in *Works*, 21:138.

human beings are uniquely suited to partake of God's communications. Together these regions of his theology serve to show both the continuity between God *ad intra* and God's communication *ad extra*, as well as the pneumatological continuity between the immanent Spirit and his economic work. We will then conclude with a brief discussion of the fall, noting how it is essentially the loss of the Holy Spirit's gracious presence in the life of humankind, a circumstance which sets the stage for the work of a mediator-redeemer.

3.1 Outward Bound: God's Diffusive Disposition, the Covenant of Redemption, and the Holy Spirit

Readers of Edwards who are attuned to his trinitarianism find his work on the *End of Creation* to be deeply shaped by trinitarian themes. God is in the business of glorifying himself by an *ad extra* communication of his inner fullness primarily through a communication of the knowledge of himself (the Son) and a communication of the holiness and happiness of himself (the Holy Spirit) to the redeemed. For various reasons Edwards chose to mute these explicitly trinitarian references in the work.[2] By contrast, in "Miscellanies" No. 1062 we find Edwards explicitly connecting his doctrine of the end for which God created the world with his trinitarianism. In this entry, entitled "ECONOMY OF THE TRINITY AND THE COVENANT OF REDEMPTION," Edwards attempts to trace out the logical ordering of the pre-creation deliberations by the persons of the Trinity in order to demonstrate that the work of creation and redemption is ultimately shaped by his trinitarianism. The resulting structure of the way God determines to create and redeem reveals how the Spirit's operations *ad extra* are patterned from his inner trinitarian work.

In this entry Edwards envisions the logical unfolding of creation and redemption to take place in three logically sequential "moments:" (1) the eternal and necessary disposition of God to communicate himself, (2) God's decision to communicate his inner fullness *ad extra* in a way that reflects the immanent trinitarian order, and (3) the covenant of redemption. He writes that

> that particular constitution or covenant among the persons of the Trinity [i.e., the third "moment"] about this particular affair [of redemption] must be looked upon as, in the order of nature, after that disposition of the Godhead to glorify and communicate itself [i.e., the first "moment"], and so after the will of the persons

---

2 Among the many purposes of *End of Creation*, Edwards intended it as a work of apologetics to an enlightened community that was growing increasingly hostile to the Trinity as a rational doctrine. By accepting the argument in chapter one of the work ("Wherein Is Considered What Reason Teaches Concerning This Affair" of the divine purpose of creation), one basically becomes committed to a trinitarian view of reality without making an explicit reference to the Trinity.

of the Trinity to act, in so doing, in that order that is in itself fit and decent, and what the order of their subsisting requires [i.e., the second "moment"].[3]

Similar to a discussion of the order of the divine decrees, it must be noted that these three divisions or "moments" strictly portray a *logical* order in the divine decision to create. They do not involve temporality in any way, even though temporal indicators (i.e., before, after, first, next) may frequent these discussions. Together they illustrate the close parallels Edwards draws between God's immanent trinitarian life and his economic work.

3.1.1 God's Communicative Disposition

In formulating the purpose of God's creative act, Edwards's clear desire is to link this purposive act to God's being, and not merely to God's will. In other words, Edwards affirms that God does not merely decide to create, he creates because there is something about his nature that tends toward a communication "outside" of his own internal fullness. This view he develops most fully in *End of Creation*. God's "disposition to communicate himself or diffuse his own *fullness*," we may recall from our discussion earlier, "must [be conceived] of as being originally in God as a perfection of his nature."[4] Several paragraphs later he repeats the same point by writing that "*a disposition in God, as an original property of his nature, to an emanation of his own infinite fullness, was what excited him to create the world.*"[5] Creation is thus, in some sense, a communicative overflow of God's being.

At the same time, however, we must point out that this disposition in God toward a communicative emanation of himself *ad extra* is not an ontological *extension* of God's being. Nor does this opinion commit him to the position that creation is necessary to God. Edwards is neither a pantheist nor some eighteenth precursor to process theism.[6] He affirms divine independence,

---

3 Edwards, "Miscellanies" No. 1062, in *Works*, 20:432.
4 Edwards, *End of Creation*, in *Works*, 8:433-34.
5 Edwards, *End of Creation*, in *Works*, 8:435, emphasis in the original.
6 It is not the purpose of this section to address the intricacies of Edwards's doctrine of God but we might note that Edwards did leave to posterity a vision of God which, while breathtaking, did leave many questions unanswered regarding his relationship to classical Christian theism. Some have held that Edwards was really a closet pantheist or panentheist; see I. Woodbridge Riley, *American Philosophy: The Early Schools* (New York: Dodd, Mead & Company, 1907) and Douglas J. Elwood, *The Philosophical Theology of Jonathan Edwards* (New York: Columbia University Press, 1960). More recently the impressive studies by Sang Hyun Lee already noted have argued that at the heart of Edwards's doctrine of God lays a modern and new "dispositional ontology" which moved beyond the confines of scholastic, classical theism (see above page 25, notes 22 and 24). By contrast, a few scholars are just now beginning to call into question these readings of Edwards's doctrine of God

maintaining that God does not rely upon creation in any way to fulfill his being. He writes in *End of Creation* "That no notion of God's last end in creation of the world is agreeable to reason which would truly imply or infer any indigence, insufficiency and mutability in God; or any dependence of the Creator on the creature for any part of his perfection or happiness."[7] Thus, on the one hand, Edwards maintains that there is something about God's being that tends toward an *ad extra* communication of his internal trinitarian glory, while on the other hand, he affirms that creation is no way necessary to God's being. How does he hold together these two seemingly antithetical trajectories in his doctrine of God?

Edwards holds these two theological strands together by drawing a distinction between God's being and God's willing. To summarize his point, God's being is disposed toward a communicative emanation *ad extra*, but superadded to this divine inclination is God's choice to create. The former is both necessary to and a perfection of God's being; the latter comprises a divine volition which is not necessary to his being but which is consistent with the dispositional inclination of his being. Edwards calls this volition God's "wisdom intervening" or the "invention of wisdom" to highlight the fact that this decision by God to create is a volitional intervention consistent with and superadded to his dispositional nature, which results in the extension of God's glory *ad extra*. He speaks of this distinction between God's being and his choice to create in "Miscellanies" No. 1062:

> For God's determining to glorify and communicate himself must be conceived of as flowing from God's nature; or [i.e., "in other words"] we must look upon God, from the infinite fullness and goodness of his nature, as naturally disposed to cause the beams of his glory to shine forth, and his goodness to flow forth. Yet we must look on the particular method that shall be chosen by divine wisdom to do this as not so directly and immediately owing to the natural disposition of the divine nature, as the *determination of wisdom intervening*, choosing the means of gratifying that disposition of nature. We must conceive of God's natural inclination as being exercised before wisdom is set to work to find out a particular, excellent method to gratify that natural inclination. Therefore this *particular invention of wisdom*, of God's glorifying and communicating himself by the redemption of a certain number of fallen inhabitants of this globe of earth,

---

which appear to distance him from classical Christian theism. For instance, Stephen Holmes analyzes Lee's thesis and suggests that it simply does not stand on historical grounds: how could such a devoted Reformed thinker immersed in the Puritan tradition adopt a doctrine of God which would automatically place him outside of Reformed Orthodoxy? See Stephen Holmes, "Does Jonathan Edwards Use a Dispositional Ontology? A Response to Sang Hyun Lee," in *Jonathan Edwards: Philosophical Theologian*, ed. Paul Helm and Oliver D. Crisp (Burlington, VT: Ashgate, 2003), 99-114.

7 Edwards, *End of Creation*, in *Works*, 8:420.

is a thing diverse from God's natural inclination to glorify and communicate himself in general, and superadded to it or subservient to it.[8]

Edwards makes a similar observation in *End of Creation*. There he notes that "there is some impropriety in saying that a disposition in God to communicate himself *to the creature,* moved him to create the world." The reason for this is clear, it "presuppose[s] the existence of the object, at least in idea," which would commit him to the position that creation is necessary to God's being. By contrast, the divine disposition is a disposition "in general," a mere outward inclination in God's nature to communicate his fullness. "But the diffusive disposition that excited God to give creatures existence was rather a communicative disposition in general, or a disposition in the fullness of the divinity to flow out and diffuse itself."[9]

We might creatively enhance one of Edwards's own metaphors to elucidate this point. Let us imaging that the sun's internal light and glory does not require its beams to shine forth externally into the universe. Its internal energy is completely self-sufficient unto itself for eternity; shining forth into the universe rather is a product of a choice the sun makes. Yet there is a suitableness that this internal energy not only shine forth externally, but that it shines forth with beams of light that reflect the internal glory from which it originated. Edwards appears to be saying that apart from creation God is like the sun prior to its light shining forth (if we could imagine such a circumstance). Within his being there is infinite glory and sufficiency such that he does not need to "shine forth," though he is disposed to it. Thus it is fitting that he diffuse his internal glory *ad extra*. The act of creation thus becomes the particular way or the "wisdom intervening" whereby God chooses to "gratify" this eternal disposition of his nature.

3.1.2 The Continuity of God's Immanent and Economic Activity

What comprises this intervening wisdom whereby God creates the universe in a way that is consistent with his dispositional essence? How, in other words, does God "begin" the plans that eventuate in the work of creation and redemption? The second and third "moments" outlined earlier demonstrate Edwards's answers these questions. We find him addressing these issues respectively in the two major sections of "Miscellanies" No. 1062.[10]

In the first section of this entry, the "Economy of the Trinity," Edwards begins by observing that there appears to be a subordination of the members of the Trinity in their economic operations: "one acts from another, and under another, and with dependence on another . . . . So that the Father in that affair

---

8 Edwards, "Miscellanies" No. 1062, in *Works*, 20:432, emphasis added.
9 Edwards, *End of Creation*, in *Works*, 8:434-35.
10 Edwards, "Miscellanies" No. 1062, in *Works*, 20:430-43.

acts as Head of the Trinity, and Son under him, and the Holy Spirit under them both." Conversely, he notes that this economic subordination is not grounded in any ontological hierarchy between the three. Each is equally and fully divine: "'Tis very manifest that the persons of the Trinity are not inferior one to another in glory and excellency of nature." Yet this equality does not eradicate every distinction of priority and order within the Godhead. The Son for instance is eternally begotten from the Father; the Father possesses a "priority of subsistence" over the Son, and there is "a kind of dependence of the Son" upon the Father. "There is," he summarizes, "dependence without inferiority of Deity, because in the Son the Deity, the whole Deity and glory of the Father, is as it [were] repeated and duplicated."[11] In what way then are we to account for the subordination of the Son to the Father and of the Spirit to both in the economy of redemption? It is not because the Son and the Spirit are under a natural subjection to the Father, for in that case they would not be equal in dignity with the Father. Rather, they determined "by mutual free agreement" to act economically in a way that reflects the order that obtains in their immanent trinitarian relations. There is, Edwards writes,

> a subordination of the persons of the Trinity in their acting [*ad extra* which] be not from any proper natural subjection one to another, and so much be conceived of as in some respect established by mutual free agreement, whereby the persons of the Trinity of their own will have as it were form themselves into a society for carrying on the great design of glorifying the Deity and communicating its fullness [*ad extra*], in which is established a certain and order of acting.[12]

Several points are worthy of note at this point. First, this agreement is not the covenant of redemption. It is a distinct agreement from the covenant of redemption and logically prior to it.[13] Second, creation is not the object of this agreement. God at this stage merely determines that he will act externally in a way that reflects the internal trinitarian relations regardless of the manner of action: "The establishment of the economy is a determination that, *in whatever work is done*, the persons shall act in such a subordination; but the determining what works shall be done is not implied in that establishment."[14] Third, the Spirit's role in this agreement is equal with the other members of the Trinity; he along with the Father and the Son determine to act in creation in a way that reflects the immanent trinitarian relations. Hence the Spirit will reflect, in his external activity, the same hiddenness that we noted earlier in his immanent activity. He will not bring attention to himself, but will highlight the Son to the Father, and the Father to the Son. He will be the holy bond of union between the Father and the Son in his economic operations.

---

11 Edwards. "Miscellanies" No. 1062, in *Works*, 20:430.
12 Edwards, "Miscellanies" No. 1062, in *Works*, 20:431.
13 Edwards, "Miscellanies" No. 1062, in *Works*, 20:432.
14 Edwards, "Miscellanies" No. 1062, in *Works*, 20:438, emphasis mine.

3.1.3 The Covenant of Redemption

The "next" issue in the logical unfolding of God's decision to glorify himself *ad extra*, consists of the specific plan for glorifying the Godhead through the redemption of fallen sinners.[15] This plan, while it involves all the members of the Trinity, includes a special new arrangement between only the Father and the Son, an arrangement known as the covenant of redemption.[16] Introduced by the Father to the Son, it requires the Son to take on human likeness and become the substitutionary sacrifice for the sins of God's people, which shall draw forth a torrent of magnificent, God-glorifying praise from the redeemed. Because the Father's proposal requires the Son to accomplish a task that is far below his excellency and deity as the second person of the Trinity, the Father cannot merely prescribe this endeavor to the Son. A special covenant is required:

> The Father, merely by his economical prerogative, can direct and prescribe to the other persons of the Trinity in all things not below their economical character. But all those things that imply something below the infinite majesty and glory of divine persons, and which they can't do without as it were laying aside the divine glory, and stooping infinitely below the height of that glory, those things are below their oeconomical divine character, and therefore the Father can't prescribe to other persons anything of this nature, without a new establishment by free covenant empowering him so to do.[17]

The Son freely enters into this pact, thereby ensuring that the ensuing work of redemption is embraced and accomplished freely and gladly by the Son.

According to Edwards, "new" sets of mutual relations and obligations emerge as a result of this covenant.[18] Between the Father and the Son a "new kind of subordination and mutual obligation" obtains. The Father "acquires a new right of headship and authority over the Son" in this covenant, thereby having the authority to prescribe the Son what is needed to glorify himself

---

15 This theological foundation for this plan lies in the divine decrees. Edwards takes a unique approach to this issue, but ends up an infralapsarian: "both the decrees of election and rejection or reprobation, as so styled, must be considered as consequent on the decrees concerning creation and fall." "Miscellanies" No. 704, in *Works*, 18:317-18. See also "Miscellanies" No. 700, in *Works*, 18:282-83.

16 While most of his mature theology of the covenant of redemption is found in "Miscellanies" No. 1062, other aspects can be found in "Miscellanies" Nos. 617, 825 (*Works*, 18:148-51 and 536-38, respectively), and Nos. 919 and 1091 (*Works*, 20:167 and 475-79, respectively).

17 Edwards, "Miscellanies" No. 1062, in *Works*, 20:436.

18 "New" not in a temporal sense (as if this covenant was made in time, resulting in a new set of circumstances for God; Edwards held that God is eternal, not bound by time), nor in a sense that would imply any change in God (God is immutable, Edwards held, and had planned this covenant from eternity). Rather, this "newness" is merely the recognition that the covenant of redemption, as well as everything associated with creation, is not necessary to God's being.

through the difficult task of human redemption.[19] Yet the Father also is under a new obligation in the covenant: to enable and provide for the success of the Son's mission. Conversely, the Son, while eternally second in the order of the immanent Trinity, takes on an added dimension of being under the Father through undergoing the difficult, self-abasing work of securing redemption for his people. With regard to creation, the Son receives a new kind of rule and authority which is foreign to his position in the economy of the immanent Trinity: supreme ruler and head of the universe. "'Tis the Father that is economically the King of heaven and earth, Lawgiver and Judge of all; and therefore when the Son is made so, he is by the Father advanced into his throne, by having the Father's authority committed to him." With regard to redemption, the Son receives the Father's "own divine treasure," the Holy Spirit, "to dispense of it as he pleased to the redeemed. [The Father] made [the Son] Lord of his house, and Lord of his treasures."[20] As the Son is Lord of creation and redemption, he also, in the progress of redemption, is Lord over the third person of the Trinity having the authority to administer the Spirit to the elect as he pleases.

While not a covenanting partner in this pact, the Spirit is involved in it. Edwards identifies a "twofold subjecting of the Holy Spirit to the Son, as our Redeemer, [which is] in some respect new and diverse from what is merely by the economy of the Trinity."[21] First, in the course of redemption, the Spirit is to regard the Son as he regards the Father in the immanent Trinity because the Son is Lord and judge over creation. "Till the work of redemption shall be finished, [He] will continue to act under the Son, in some respects, with that subjection that is economically due to the Father." This relation shall terminate at the consummation of all things when Christ resigns his "vicarious dominion and authority."[22] Second, the Spirit is subject to the Son not only as the second person of the Trinity, but as the God-man who is the head of the church. Contrary to the first subjection, this relationship is eternal: "this subjection of the Spirit to Christ will continue to eternity and never will be resigned up, for Christ God-man will continue to all eternity to be the vital Head and Husband of the church, and the vital good that this vital Head will eternally communicate to his church will be the Holy Spirit."[23] While these new relations involve a subordination of the Spirit to the Son in a new way, this subjection "flows merely from the economical order of the persons," and does not involve any extraordinary self-abasement or emptying of dignity like the Son's humiliation.[24] Thus the Spirit's activity with regard to the Son in this plan does

---

19 Edwards, "Miscellanies" No. 1062, in *Works*, 20:437.
20 Edwards, "Miscellanies" No. 1062, in *Works*, 20:439.
21 Edwards, "Miscellanies" No. 1062, in *Works*, 20:439.
22 Edwards, "Miscellanies" No. 1062, in *Works*, 20:440.
23 Edwards, "Miscellanies" No. 1062, in *Works*, 20:440.
24 Edwards, "Miscellanies" No. 1062, in *Works*, 20:440.

not require a special covenant within the intra-trinitarian community. This was Edwards's reason why the covenant of redemption involves only the Father and the Son.

One might object that this scheme neglects the Spirit. How can the Spirit be equal to the Father and Son and yet be left out of the covenant of redemption, becoming the beneficiary of two new subjecting roles to the Son in the economy of redemption? Edwards was aware of this potential criticism, for we may recall in chapter one that his passion was championing the full and equal deity of the Spirit in the Trinity.[25] In the final analysis he did not feel that this criticism touched his formulation of the covenant of redemption. For one thing, the subordinate role of the Spirit is naturally part of the immanent ordering of the Trinity. Adding extra subordinating activities in a planned course of redemption is consistent with his immanent trinitarian position: the Spirit acts as third-in-order both *ad intra* and *ad extra*. More importantly, however, is Edwards's observation that the Spirit can be intimately involved in the covenant of redemption yet not be a covenanting partner. Edwards writes that "we may well suppose that the affair was as it were concerted among all the persons, and determined by the perfect consent of all, and that there was a consultation among the three persons about it." The Spirit's full involvement and "concern in this covenant is as great as theirs, and equally honorable with theirs."[26] He identifies three ways that the Spirit is intimately concerned in the agreement. First, he is the bond of union between the two covenanting persons and as such he is the ground of their mutual consent and agreement. Second, as he is the eternal love of God for himself, "so he is the internal spring of all that the other persons do in covenanting, and [the] moving cause of the whole transaction." Lastly, the Spirit, as the infinite richness of the Godhead, is the *telos* or end of the covenant, for he is that which is purchased for the redeemed in it.[27] The Spirit's full and equal dignity as deity is again discerned in Edwards's thought as hidden and behind the scenes as the divine love and the bond of union of God. This was Edwards's overall strategy in bringing a symmetrical equality to the Spirit in his theology.

These three theological "moments" were Edwards's way of establishing a very close relationship between God's immanent trinitarian life and his economic work. They ensure that the divine activity of redemption parallels the structure of the immanent divine life. In the following section we shall examine the way Edwards understands how God's divine glory is externalized in creation, namely through a communication of the knowledge and love of God to the redeemed.

---

25 See above, pages 34-35.
26 Edwards, "Miscellanies" No. 1062, in *Works*, 20:442.
27 Edwards, "Miscellanies" No. 1062, in *Works*, 20:443.

3.2 Anthropology: The Receivers of Communicated Divine Glory

As we read Edwards's statements on the psychological make up of a human being, it becomes clear that he is consciously patterning his understanding of the internal structure of man and the *imago dei* upon the Trinity. The "soul of a man" he writes is an "eminent and remarkable [image] of the Trinity among creatures.... There is the mind, and the understanding or idea, and the spirit of the mind, as it is called in Scripture, i.e. the disposition, the will or affection."[28] Repeatedly throughout his writings he emphasizes some version of this triad of mind-understanding-will when he discusses the "inner man" though his usual manner is to underscore the latter two. Hence in the opening paragraph of the *Discourse on the Trinity* he writes that "Though the divine nature be vastly different from that of created spirits, yet our souls are made in the image of God: we have understanding and will, idea and love, as God hath, and the difference is only in the perfection of degree and manner."[29] Likewise toward the conclusion of the *End of Creation*, Edwards speaks of the "creature . . . created in the image of God . . . as having these two faculties of understanding and will."[30] While Edwards's discussions of the *imago dei* appear to be binitarian on the surface, emphasizing humankind's rational and volitional capacities, the hidden variable in this trinitarian equation is the being of the created human mind which corresponds to God the Father. Thus as God (the Father) is gloriously triune through a perfect idea of his own perfections (the Son) and a perfect love of the same (the Spirit), so too does a human being mirror this triad, possessing the being of a human mind that has the twofold faculties of reason/understanding and will/affection.

What Edwards is doing in these discussions of the *imago dei* is that he is setting up a parallel between God's trinitarian communication of his inner fullness and the receivers of that communication. If God is to glorify himself *ad extra* in a trinitarian way that involves the eternal communication of his infinite fullness (as we explored in the last section), then the objects of this communication must be uniquely suited to receive these communications of the divine trinitarian fullness. The object of God's communication must be a creature that possesses a dual capacity to receive the two-fold communication of God's internal fullness: first to perceive the glory of God's infinite idea, the Son, and second to love that idea with God's infinite disposition of love, the Holy Spirit.

We might call this pattern in Edwards's thought the trinitarian blueprint for creation and redemption. This blueprint consists of an intimate connection between three major areas in his theology: (a) the trinitarian **fullness** *ad intra*, or his immanent trinitarianism, (b) the trinitarian **effulgence** *ad extra*, or his economic trinitarian theology of the end for which God created the world, and

---

28 Edwards, *Discourse on the Trinity*, in *Works*, 21:138.
29 Edwards, *Discourse on the Trinity*, in *Works*, 21:113.
30 Edwards, *End of Creation*, in *Works*, 8:529.

(c) the trinitarian **reception** in the redeemed human being created in the image of God. Throughout his "Miscellanies" notebooks we find Edwards consistently refining the connections between the trinitarian fullness, effulgence, and its reception in the redeemed. For instance, in "Miscellanies" No. 448 (circa 1730), Edwards explores the parallels between God's internal glory and his external glory.[31] God's internal glory is deeply informed by his trinitarianism:

> God is glorified within himself these two ways: (1) by appearing or being manifested to himself in his own perfect idea, or, in his Son, who is the brightness of his glory; (2) by enjoying and delighting in himself, by flowing forth in infinite love and delight towards himself, or, in his Holy Spirit.

Edwards goes on to connect this exposition of the divine fullness with its effulgence and reception *ad extra*:

> So God glorifies himself towards the creatures also in two ways: (1) by appearing to them, being manifested to their understandings; (2) in communicating himself to their hearts, and in the rejoicing and delighting in, and enjoying the manifestations which he makes of himself. . . . By one way it goes forth towards their understandings; by the other it goes forth towards their wills or hearts. God is glorified not only by his glory's being seen, but by its being rejoiced in.[32]

As God seeks his glory in creation through the redemption of his people it is necessary for them to possess understanding and heart, that is the image of God, for the circuit of God's glory to be complete.

Similarly, this blueprint appears later in a series of "Miscellanies" composed in the mid 1740s.[33] For example, in entry No. 1082 we see Edwards addressing the nature of the glory of God, where he proceeds first from the reception of divine glory before treating its origins in the trinitarian fullness and effulgence. God's glory is twofold consisting in the "manifestation of his perfection to [the saints'] understandings" and the communication of divine "blessedness" and "heavenly joy" to them.[34] From this base he then traces the origins of this twofold glory back its trinitarian foundations, the divine fullness *ad intra* and its effulgence:

---

31 For the dating of this entry, I rely upon Thomas A. Schafer's table in his brief essay "Note on the Text of the 'Miscellanies'" in *Works*, 13:153-60.
32 Edwards, "Miscellanies" No. 448, in *Works* 13: 495.
33 See "Miscellanies" Nos. 1066, 1082, 1084, and 1094. For the dating of these entries and entry No. 1142 (below) I rely upon Amy Plantinga Pauw's table in her "Editor's Introduction" to the volume (*Works*, 20:38). See her extended discussion of dating the entries in *Works*, 20:33-9.
34 Edwards, "Miscellanies" No. 1082, in *Works*, 20:466. "Therefore the diffusing the sweetness and blessedness of the divine nature is God's glorifying himself, in a Scripture sense, as well as his manifesting his perfection to their understandings."

> This twofold way of the Deity's flowing forth *ad extra* answers to the twofold way of the Deity's proceeding *ad intra*, in the proceeding and generation of the Son and the proceeding and breathing forth of the Holy Spirit; and indeed is only a kind of second proceeding of the same persons, their going forth *ad extra*, as before they proceeded *ad intra*.[35]

This "second proceeding" finds its termination in the understandings and hearts of the redeemed, a point he brings up two entries later (No. 1084) where he interprets John 17:26. There Jesus states "And I have declared unto them thy name, and will declare it: that the love wherewith thou hast loved me may be in them, and I in them." To Edwards, Jesus' high priestly prayer crescendos in this two-fold request (1) that Christ himself may be in them and (2) that God's love may be in them. These "two ways of God's flowing forth and being communicated," Edwards contends, "are the end of all things," the final purpose of creation and redemption, "viz. manifesting Christ's being in the creature in the name, idea or knowledge of God being in them, and the Holy Spirit's being in them in the love of God being in them."[36] These two entries demonstrate the logic of this trinitarian blueprint and the intimate connections he drew between his trinitarianism, his doctrine of the end for which God created the world and his articulation of the *imago dei*.

Edwards expands his thoughts on this blueprint thesis later in "Miscellanies" No. 1142 written around 1750. Here Edwards focuses on the connection between the trinitarian effulgence and its reception, or what he calls the "egress and reception of God's fullness."

> That glory of God that is spoken of in Scripture as the end of God's works is the egress and reception of God's fullness, the egress of it from God and the reception of it by the creature. The fullness of God is twofold: 'tis his excellency and his happiness, answerable hereto. There is a twofold faculty in the creatures that the egress has respect to and which is its recipient subject, viz. a faculty of perceiving and of approving; a twofold manner of egress or going forth, viz. manifestation and communication.[37]

This "twofold faculty in the creatures" Edwards elsewhere identifies as the image of God, a point which we saw earlier. The human faculties of "perceiving" (i.e. human understanding) and "approving" (i.e. human will) correspond to the twofold "egress or going forth" of God's glory, his "manifestation" of his glorious knowledge of himself in the Son to their perception, and the "communication" of the Holy Spirit to their "approving"

---

35 Edwards, "Miscellanies" No. 1082, in *Works*, 20:466.

36 Edwards, "Miscellanies" No. 1084, in *Works*, 20:467. See Paul Ramsey's perceptive remarks on the "ambiguous genitives" in this entry in his "Editor's Introduction" to volume 8 (*Works* 8:20ff).

37 Edwards, "Miscellanies" No. 1142, in *Works*, 20:517.

faculty, the heart.

Similar illustrations of the blueprint thesis may be observed throughout *End of Creation* (mid 1750s) where they find their fullest expression in numerous places.[38] The point to be made is that throughout much of his life, Edwards is clearly fashioning and reworking the thesis that the end for which God created the world is a trinitarian end which necessarily involves a trinitarian understanding of the *imago dei*. This "end" may be summarized as follows: in the divine master plan, God wills to create and redeem in order that he may be gloriously known to creatures through Christ, yet loved by them in the Spirit. Consequently, Christ will "objectify" God to the saints, manifesting the knowledge of God to their understandings, whereas the Spirit will "subjectify" God to them, communicating divine love to their hearts. That Edwards repeatedly refined and rearticulated this thesis throughout his life, and that he featured it prominently in *End of Creation* which was intended for publication, demonstrates that this was a central theme in his theology and one that we must take seriously if we are to understand his thought.

So far in this chapter we have seen Edwards trace the theological connections between God's immanent trinitarian life and the way he plans to glorify himself through creation and redemption. In conjunction with his eternal disposition to diffuse himself, God plans to glorify himself *ad extra* in a way that will be patterned off of his internal trinitarian glory. Subsequently, the covenant of redemption is planned between the Father and the Son, as well as the plan to create creatures made in the image of God who are uniquely suited to receive the divine glory. Edwards has nicely set up our stage. Yet dramas are meant to be played upon stages, and drama necessarily entails unexpected twists and turns in a plotline. The fall is one of the greatest twists in the drama of theology. Before we analyze the place of the redeemer in the plan of redemption and how the Spirit plays a vital role in the incarnation, we first need to examine briefly how humankind got into the situation that requires a redeemer.

3.3 Segue: The Fall and the Loss of the Supernatural Image

There was another way Edwards drew parallels between the *imago dei* in humanity and God, a way which corresponds to another great divide we perceive in his theology, the division between the natural and the supernatural or moral. In contrast to the psychological commonalities between God and humans, here Edwards stresses the distinction between natural capacities humankind is endowed with – such as the possession of moral agency, the ability to reason, the ability to act in accordance with what one perceives to be

---

38 See his discussion of how it is "fit and desirable" for God's glorious perfections to be both known and loved in section two of chapter one in *End of Creation* (*Works*, 8:430-32), as well as his summary in the concluding section (*Works*, 8:528-33).

the greatest apparent good, and rational speculation – and the supernatural capacity to know and love God truly, a capacity he sums up in one word, holiness. This distinction in humanity finds its origins in a fundamental distinction between God's own natural and moral attributes.

> As there are two kinds of attributes in God, according to our way of conceiving of him, his moral attributes, which are summed up in his holiness, and his natural attributes, of strength, knowledge, etc. that constitute the greatness of God; so there is a twofold image of God in man, his moral or spiritual image, which is his holiness, that is the image of God's moral excellency (which image was lost by the Fall); and God's natural image, consisting in men's reason and understanding, his natural ability, and dominion over the creatures, which is the image of God's natural attributes.[39]

Edwards prominently features this distinction in his discussion on the fall in his work *Original Sin*. "[W]hen God made man at first, he implanted in him two kinds of principles." First, there are inferior or natural principles, "being the principles of mere human nature." These principles consist of self-love, the "natural appetites and passions, which belong to the nature of man." Second, there are the superior principles, "that were spiritual, holy and divine, summarily comprehended in divine love; wherein consisted the spiritual image of God, and man's righteousness and true holiness."[40] These superior principles furthermore were meant to rule over the inferior, governing the entirety our existences and activities with a God glorifying disposition.

It was these superior principles which disappeared from the heart of humanity upon the first sin. "When man sinned," Edwards writes, "and broke God's Covenant, and fell under his curse, these superior principles left his heart: for indeed God then left him; that communion with God, on which these principles depended, entirely ceased."[41] Left by themselves, the inferior principles plunged Adam and Eve, along with the entirety of the human race after them, into a course governed by the self-oriented flesh and enmity against God. Having lost the supernatural image of God in them, which in essence is

---

39 Edwards, *Religious Affections*, in *Works*, 2:256. Edwards also calls the moral image of God in a human being the "spiritual" image his *A Careful and Strict Enquiry into the Modern Prevailing Notions of that Freedom of Will Which is Supposed to be Essential to Moral Agency, Vertue and Vice, Reward and Punishment, Praise and Blame* in *The Works of Jonathan Edwards*, vol. 1, *Freedom of the Will*, ed. Paul Ramsey (New Haven: Yale University Press, 1957), 166; hereafter referred to as *Freedom of the Will*. Similarly, he speaks of natural/inferior principles and superior/supernatural principles in *The Great Christian Doctrine of Original Sin Defended*, in *The Works of Jonathan Edwards*, vol. 3, *Original Sin*, ed. Clyde Holbrook (New Haven: Yale University Press, 1970), 381-83; hereafter referred to as *Original Sin*.
40 Edwards, *Original Sin*, in *Works*, 3:381.
41 Edwards, *Original Sin*, in *Works*, 3:382.

the departure of the Holy Spirit's gracious presence from the soul, the entire human race is doomed to act in ways that cross God's holy purposes, leading ultimately to their just and eternal damnation. Apart from divine intervention, apart from the Spirit's re-habitation in the human race, the original design of God glorifying himself through the gracious, trinitarian communication of his internal fullness *ad extra* cannot be realized. The problem is that this new situation requires not merely the creation of beings who can receive God's communications, but the recreation of the existing race of humans who have lost the supernatural image of God. Subsequently in Edwards's theology, the plan of redemption thus requires one who is both a redeemer from sin, and one who dispenses the Spirit to the redeemed without measure. In the next chapter we will examine how Edwards envisioned this close relationship between the incarnate one, Jesus Christ, and the Holy Spirit.

CHAPTER 4

Christology: The Holy Spirit as the Bond of Union of Christ's Two Natures

> What Christ says in the 3rd [chapter] of John, vv. 33-34, confirms that the Holy Spirit is the bond of union by which the human nature of Christ is united to the divine, so as to be one person.[1]

In a remarkable sermon entitled "The Excellency of Christ," Jonathan Edwards woos his listeners and readers to embrace Christ not only as an exalted Lord but also as a brotherly friend: "As there is such an admirable meeting of diverse excellencies in Christ, so there is everything in him to render him worthy of your love and choice, and to win and engage it. Whatsoever there is, or can be, that is desirable to be in a friend, is in Christ, and that to the highest degree that can be desired."[2] In Christ, as the doctrine of the sermon instructs, we find a unique conjunction of diverse excellencies which is not to be found in any other being. Consequently, he urges the unconverted to choose Christ precisely because he is not only God, but God-the-Word made flesh, accessible to humankind as a true human being:

> Though he be the great God, yet he has as it were brought himself down to be upon a level with you, so as to become man as you are, that he might not only be your lord, but your brother . . . . This is one end of Christ's taking upon him man's nature, that his people might be under advantages for a more familiar converse with him, than the infinite distance of the divine nature would allow of.[3]

These evangelistic appeals reflect Edwards's profound belief in the unity of the divine and human natures in Christ's person, a view which was rapidly falling out of favor by enlightened thinkers on both sides of the Atlantic. While he never wrote an extended treatise on christology comparable to his unpublished treaties on the Trinity and on grace, his "Miscellanies" reveal a fairly extensive

---

1 Edwards, "Miscellanies" No. 764b, in *Works* 18:411.
2 Edwards, "The Excellency of Christ," in *The Works of Jonathan Edwards*, vol. 19, *Sermons and Discourses, 1734-1738*, ed. M. X. Lesser (New Haven: Yale University Press, 2001), 588.
3 Edwards, "The Excellency of Christ," in *Works*, 19:589.

group of inquiries on the person of Christ, the unity of the two natures, the process of the incarnation, and the role the Holy Spirit played in the incarnation.[4] Following the theme we have been developing throughout our study, this chapter will explore how the Holy Spirit is the bond of union of Christ's two natures.

To meet this goal we must set this specific pneumatological union in the broader context of Edwards's own christology, an area which has not received much attention by scholars. The few substantial studies we have of Edwards's christology are divided in their estimations. Paul Ramsey, in a fascinating essay on Edwards's theology of heaven, observes strong parallels between standard Reformed christology, which emphasizes the communication of the human and divine attributes *to the person* of Jesus Christ, and Edwards's own christology. "Edwards' Christological affirmation," he writes, "is clear: the *communication* (and not only the union) of divine and human attributes in the person of Christ solved all such difficulties in the mind's endeavor to grasp and hold the truth of the incarnation."[5] Robert Jenson sees differently. To him Edwards's christology reveals strong associations with Alexandrian and Lutheran positions, and even pushes the traditional boundaries of their views: "Readers who come to Edwards' drafts from the traditional discussions must first be struck that this Calvinist teaches a 'real' communication of God's divine attributes to the human reality of Christ that might have seemed a bit unguarded even to Cyril of Alexandria or Martin Luther."[6] Jenson suggests that the crowning example of this unguardedness lies in Edwards's seeming affirmation of a mutual communication of the divine and human attributes *in abstracto*, where not only the divine attributes are communicated to the human (the Lutheran position), but where the human attributes are likewise communicated to the divine (Edwards's radical position).[7] In her dissertation, Amy Plantinga Pauw argues that both Ramsey and Jenson are correct to a degree by pointing out that Edwards's christological statements are fragmentary and do not cohere in a systematic whole. His "Christology is full of unresolved

---

4 Toward the end of his life, Edwards was planning to write a treatise on the divinity of Christ and was trying to get other orthodox divines to publish on it as well. See Douglas A. Sweeney's "Editor's Introduction," in *The Works of Jonathan Edwards*, vol. 23, *The "Miscellanies" 1153-1360*, ed. Douglas A. Sweeney (New Haven: Yale University Press, 2004), 29.

5 Paul Ramsey, "Heaven Is a Progressive State," in *The Works of Jonathan Edwards*, vol. 8, *Ethical Writings*, ed. Paul Ramsey (New Haven: Yale University Press, 1989), 734. Ramsey's benchmark for Reformed christology in his study is Francis Turretin, whom he engages extensively in lengthy footnotes. For his entire treatment of Edwards's christology, see pages 730-35.

6 Jenson, *America's Theologian*, 115. For his recent study on Edwards's christology, see Robert W. Jenson, "Christology," in *The Princeton Companion to Jonathan Edwards*, ed. Sang Hyun Lee (Princeton: Princeton University Press, 2005), 72-86.

7 See Jenson's discussion in, *America's Theologian*, 117-18.

tensions," she writes. "Often his writing reflected the traditional Antiochene bias of the Reformed tradition. However, in other places he adopted a vigorously Alexandrian Christology. Thus his success in deriving a coherent Christology from his practical trinitarianism must be judged at best partial."[8] The unsystematized duality in his christology is the byproduct, she argues, of a deeper duality in his thought: that two trinitarian models, a social and a psychological model, ground his theology and structurally affect its entire edifice.[9] Similarly, Stephen Holmes perceives the same theological incoherence in Edwards's christology that Pauw does, but argues that it is the result of other factors in his thought, not so much his trinitarianism: "There is an incoherence here, based on two different conceptions of what constitutes personal identity. From his own metaphysics, Edwards was led to Owenite Christology; from Locke's arguments he was led to a Lutheran form. He apparently never resolved this."[10] The lack of consensus on the nature of Edwards's christological views reveals that we are only in the beginning stages of understanding his complete christology.[11]

Two goals will be pursued in what follows. First and foremost, we will examine Edwards's affirmation that the Spirit is the bond of union of Christ's two natures by analyzing a series of "Miscellanies" entries, written over fifteen years, which develops this view both exegetically and theologically. Second, we will attempt to categorize Edwards's christology on the Antiochene-Alexandrian spectrum, where I will argue that we are limited from doing this because he never developed his christology to maturity. Edwards's christological concerns, in other words, paint only part of an entire picture, thereby keeping us from discerning the complete outlines of his christology. What we do have, I will argue, leads us to the conclusion that Edwards's christology was generally Reformed in its orientation, yet because of his fascination with the pneumatological basis for the union of Christ's two natures, his christology gives the appearance of possessing Alexandrian characteristics.[12] These two trajectories in his christology need not be deemed

---

8 Amy Plantinga Pauw, "The Supreme Harmony of All: Jonathan Edwards and the Trinity" (Ph.D. diss., Yale University, 1990), 205.
9 See our discussion of Plantinga-Pauw's argument above, pages 26-28, 37-40.
10 Holmes, *God of Grace and God of Glory*, 141.
11 For other fine treatments of Edwards's christology, see the brief section in Sang Hyun Lee's *Philosophical Theology*, 227-31; Bruce M. Stephens, *The Prism of Time and Eternity: Images of Christ in American Protestant Thought from Jonathan Edwards to Horace Bushnell*, ATLA Monograph Series, No. 42 (Lanham, Md.: American Theological Library Association and The Scarecrow Press, 1996), 1-16; and John H. Gerstner, *The Rational Biblical Theology of Jonathan Edwards* (Powhatan, Va.: Berea Publications, 1992), vol. 2, 368-423.
12 As demonstrated in the previous paragraph, Edwards scholars have employed the Antiochene-Alexandrian spectrum to compare and contrast Edwards's christology with others'. At the risk of over-simplification, Alexandrian christologies envision a

antithetical or contradictory. We will develop this argument in two stages. First, we will examine how Edwards understood the incarnation to fit into the overarching plan of redemption by examining his view of the necessity of the incarnation. From there, we will analyze the roles that each of the trinitarian members play in the incarnation, while focusing mainly, as Edwards himself does, upon the Spirit's role as the bond of union between Christ's human and divine natures.

4.1 The Redemptive Plan of the Incarnate Christ

The last chapter introduced us to Edwards's understanding of the covenant of redemption, and why it is fitting that the Son becomes the mediator of redemption. Here we are brought to consider the specifics of the Son's humiliation, and the pre-incarnate planning surrounding the type of being God the Son must assume in order to secure both the redemption of the elect and the glory of God *ad extra*. Two issues emerge in this context which Edwards found important: the necessity of the incarnation, and the necessity of that incarnation taking place *after* creation. The former issue illustrates his adherence to an Anselmian vision of the atonement. The latter issue reveals Edwards's poignant response to Arian capitulations by evangelical leaders such as Isaac Watts and Phillip Doddridge.

4.1.1 The Necessity of the Incarnation

According to Edwards, as the members of the Trinity "deliberated" ways to affect the redemption of sinful human beings, there were not many viable options open to them. There was only one way available: through the Son's assumption of human nature to himself, through which he would become the Lamb of God who takes away the sins of the world. Edwards explains his rationale in his celebrated sermon series, *A History of the Work of Redemption*, delivered to his Northampton congregation in the spring and summer of 1739: "For though Christ as God was infinitely sufficient for the work, yet viewed as to his being in an immediate capacity for it, it was needful that he should not only be God but man."[13] The works of redemption and atonement require two things from a divine being, obedience and suffering, both of which are improper and impossible acts of divinity. This impossibility, Edwards remarks, does not arise from any divine imperfection. By contrast, it is the result of his

---

"tighter" union between Christ's two natures than Antiochene christologies. While both affirm the unity of Christ's person and the completeness of his divine and human natures, Antiochene christologies have generally been more comfortable distinguishing both natures in the person of Christ. Edwards's Reformed heritage generally resembled an Antiochene strategy in relating Christ's two natures.

13 Edwards, *History of Redemption*, in *Works*, 9:295.

"absolute and infinite perfection." He explains:

> For Christ merely as God was not capable either of that obedience or suffering that was needful. The divine nature is not capable of suffering, for it is impassable and infinitely above all suffering; neither is it capable of obedience to that law that was given to man. 'Tis as impossible that one that is only God should obey the law that was given to man as 'tis that he should suffer man's punishment.[14]

Obedience and suffering are thus the central requirements of the divine person who acts as redeemer on behalf of humankind. Yet these requirements open up more than one option for the Son because, in addition to human beings, angels are also created beings capable of obedience and suffering. Could not God the Son, then, have assumed an angelic nature to secure redemption? No, replies Edwards, for "God saw need that the same world that was the stage of man's fall and ruin should also be the stage of his redemption."[15] Humanity's fall and ruin lies in the "world" of human nature, and it is this nature that needs redemption and restoration in order to affect salvation. Specifically, what is required is that God's divine Law, which was directed to humankind, be "answered" from one who is of that nature. "If he [Christ] had took on him the nature of an angel and had obeyed and suffered in that, it would not have been sufficient, for obeying the commands of God in an angelical nature would [not] have answered the law that was given to man."[16] Furthermore, this "answering" God's law must be two-fold. It must first answer to the law *in obedience* because no son of Adam has ever remained fully obedient to the law: "Man's law required the obedience of that nature, an obedience performed with the strength and under the circumstances [and] imperfections of that nature, and the temptations that it is liable to."[17] Second, the law must be answered *in punishment* to vindicate the honor of the one whose law it is that has been transgressed by representatives of humanity: "It was needful [that the Son become a man] to answer the law that the same nature that sinned should die."[18] Given these factors, the only way open to God in glorifying himself through human redemption is through an incarnation, or the assumption of human nature to the second person of the Trinity that would result in a unique individual, a God-man, who could "answer" the divine law as a man, effect forgiveness for humankind, and transform human nature. Such a view represents the objective side of Edwards's theology on the necessity of the incarnation. God could not have saved humankind apart from a divine invasion and transformation of that human nature which was stained with sin.

---

14 Edwards, *History of Redemption*, in *Works*, 9:295-96.
15 Edwards, *History of Redemption*, in *Works*, 9:296.
16 Edwards, "Miscellanies" No. 615, in *Works*, 18:147.
17 Edwards, "Miscellanies" No. 615, in *Works*, 18:147.
18 Edwards, *History of Redemption*, in *Works*, 9:296.

Yet Edwards is just as concerned about the subjective aspects of doctrine as he is with the objective. The incarnation was not only necessary to satisfy the objective requirement necessitating a divine union with human nature, but it was also necessary to catch our attention, and "engross our regard in every way." In "Miscellanies" No. 510, Edwards explains that God created us not only with vertical, spiritual inclinations to love and glorify God, but with horizontal, natural inclinations as well, "to friendship, to love and delight in a fellow creature, one that may be familiarly conversed with and enjoyed." In a move foreshadowing his arguments in *End of Creation*, Edwards maintains that while these two inclinations are distinguished, God is to be the ultimate object of both our vertical and horizontal inclinations. The only way for the exalted and infinite God of the universe to become the object of these horizontal inclinations for friendship and familiar conversing, is for him to be become one of us. "That God therefore might also be the object of the exercise of this natural inclination of ours, of our love and friendship to a companion, God is come down to us, has taken our nature, and is become one of us, that he might be our companion; so that there is now provision made, that we may have sufficient vent for all our inclination and love, in God and towards him."[19] Without this, our affections would be forever divided between a supreme regard for God and a subordinate regard for human companionship. Conversely, by the incarnation, God can become "all in all" to our every inclination.

We find a similar argument in an earlier "Miscellanies" entry (No. 460) with regard to sight. God directs the history of redemption, Edwards maintains, to this one end: that humankind might glorify God by seeing him intellectually and corporeally. The only way to achieve this is by way of incarnation.

> The saints in heaven will have two sorts of sight, intellectual and corporeal; it is the will of God that he himself, or a divine person, should be the principal entertainment of both those kinds of sight. Thus God saw it meet that it should be, and therefore assumed a body that appears with that transcendent visible majesty, glory and beauty, that is exceeding expressive of the divine greatness, holiness and grace.[20]

This subjective explanation of the necessity of the atonement is characteristic of Puritan piety with its emphasis on a close and familiar relationship with the infinite God of the universe through the incarnation and mediation of the Son. "One glorious end of the union of the human to the divine nature," Edwards writes in an early entry, "[is] to bring God near to us; that even our God, the infinite Being, might be made as one of us; that his terrible majesty might not make us afraid; that Jehovah, who is infinitely distant from us, might become

---

19 Edwards, "Miscellanies" No. 510, in *Works*, 18:54-55.
20 Edwards, "Miscellanies" No. 460, in *Works*, 13:501.

familiar to us"[21] The characteristically Edwardsean move, perhaps, lies in linking this Puritan spirituality with the traditional Reformed emphasis on the necessity of the atonement by way of aesthetics: one reason God *must* become man is so that we may be attracted to divine beauty and glory as it appears in and is united to human nature in the person of Jesus Christ.

4.1.2 The Necessity of the Incarnation Post Creation

Edwards not only affirms that the incarnation is necessary for the plan of redemption, he also affirms that the incarnation must take place *within* the time frame of creation, not *prior to it* in any way, which would result in a position that approximates Arianism. We have already seen in chapter one how a fashionable form of enlightened Arianism circulated in the early decades of eighteenth-century Britain. Several noteworthy evangelical leaders, while not desiring to abandon traditional trinitarianism, found the Arian criticisms of traditional christology compelling enough to modify their own christological views. Among these were Isaac Watts (1674-1748), the Puritan educator and celebrated hymn-writer, and Philip Doddridge (1702-1751), the erudite Calvinist minister who was widely known among evangelicals for his *Family Expositor*, a popular paraphrase and exposition of the New Testament. One christological modification they make is to advance the position that God the Son united himself to the human soul of Christ prior to the rest of creation. Furthermore, they teach that it was this God-"man" who created the universe.[22] These views were recognized as approximating Arianism due to the fact that they, like Arians, affirm the pre-existence of a human creature who created the universe. They differ in the fact that Watts and Doddridge affirm that this human creature is both God and man (i.e. the soul of the man who would later be clothed in flesh), whereas the Arians avoided attributing true divinity to this man. Nevertheless, Watts and Doddridge's position represents a significant departure from the orthodox position which affirms that it was God the Son, the eternal Logos, who created the universe and who then later assumed to himself an entire human nature in the incarnation.

In his work entitled *The Glory of Christ as God-Man Displayed* (1746), Watts argues that the only way to make sense of the scriptural passages that

---

21 Edwards, "Miscellanies" No. 81, in *Works*, 13:248.
22 For a summary of Watts's and Doddridge's theological aberrations, see Donald Macleod, "God or god?: Arianism, Ancient and Modern," *The Evangelical Quarterly* 46.2 (1996): 121-38. For a thorough study of the theology of Christ's pre-existent soul in early eighteenth century British controversies, see J. van den Berg, "The Idea of the Pre-Existence of the Soul of Christ: An Argument in the Controversy Between Arian and Orthodox in the Eighteenth Century," in *Tradition and Re-Interpretation in Jewish and Early Christian Literature: Essays in Honour of Jurgen C. H. Lebram*, ed. J.W. Van Henten, et. al., Studia Post-Biblia 36 (Leiden: Brill, 1986), 284-95.

speak of Christ as truly emptying himself and divesting himself of his glory (Phil 2:5-7; John 17:4-5) is to posit the pre-existence of Christ's human soul. "Now if nothing but his divine nature existed before this time [of his incarnation], this divine nature could not properly empty of divest itself of any glory; Therefore it must be his inferior nature, or his human soul, which did then exist and divest itself of its ancient glory for a season."[23] Divine nature alone cannot truly empty itself, according to Watts, for such an act would not be proper to God the Son, who is equal in dignity with the Father and Spirit and possesses no ontological subordination to either of them. By contrast, the pre-incarnate Logos, as united in a personal union to a human rational soul before the incarnation, can indeed properly empty himself of glory by appearing in the flesh and be spoken of in subordinationist language. Watts finds several advantages to this view. Scripturally, he believes it harmonizes well with the Johannine portrayal of Christ, where, for example, Jesus speaks about himself coming down from heaven not to do his own will but the Father's will (John 6:38). How, Watts reasons, can the Son truly have a will that is potentially at odds with the Father's will when traditional western trinitarianism teaches that the Father, Son, and Holy Spirit have one will via their perichoretic relations? If, by contrast, the Son is united to a created human will prior to the incarnation, then there is a genuine pre-incarnate capability of Christ to have a different will from the Father, a capability which Watts argues would not be genuine if there was just the Son's mere divinity prior to his incarnation.[24] Likewise, he argues that this position also offers a more understandable presentation of Christ's Old Testament appearances. "The appearances of Christ to the patriarchs are described like the appearances of an angel, or a man, a glorious man really distinct from God, and yet such a one in whom God or Jehovah had a peculiar indwelling, or with whom the divine nature had a personal union." These appearances of Christ, such as his visitation to Abraham at the oaks of Mamre (Genesis 18), or God's wrestling with Jacob (Genesis 32), "seem too low for the dignity of pure godhead" to undertake, but are more naturally understood as a God-"man" undertaking such things.[25]

Lurking underneath these arguments is Watts's desire to eliminate the Arians' greatest exegetical weapon against orthodox trinitarians. If a trinitarian, like Watts, can show how and why the divine Logos can be truly and fully God, and yet be truly subordinate to the Father at the same time (and not just subordinate in "economical order" as Edwards upheld), then trinitarianism could seemingly forever do away with its "archetypical heresy." To affirm that the Son was united to a human soul shortly "before" creation, and that only later he became incarnated bodily in Mary's womb, appeared to

---

23 Isaac Watts, *The Glory of Christ as God-Man Displayed*, in *Works of the Rev. Isaac Watts, D. D. In Seven Volumes* (Leeds, 1813), vol. 5, 387.
24 Watts, *Glory of Christ*, in *Works*, 5, 393-94.
25 Watts, *Glory of Christ*, in *Works*, 5, 385.

Watts to be the best strategy to undercut Arianism's greatest arguments against trinitarian orthodoxy.[26]

Edwards had little patience for Watts's views and kept a list of observations in "Miscellanies" No. 1174 that illustrate the potentially devastating effects such a view could have on theology. Of the thirteen observations he lists, two of them stand out. First, Edwards argues that Watts's view unsettles the trinitarian balance found in the covenant of redemption: "On this scheme it will follow that the covenant of redemption was made with a person that was not *sui juris*, and not at liberty to act his own mere good pleasure with respect to undertaking to die for sinners, but was obliged to comply on the first intimation that it would be well-pleasing to God and what he chose."[27] In sum, the covenant of redemption would not be a true covenant of equals, for Christ in his human nature would feel obliged to undertake the great work of redemption, and not feel free to accept or reject it.[28]

Second, Edwards believes that according to Watts's view, "the man Christ Jesus was not properly the son of the virgin and so the Son of Man." He explains:

> To be the son of a woman is to receive being in both soul and body in a consequence of a conception in her womb. The soul is the principle part of the man, and sonship implies derivation of the soul as well as the body by conception. Not that the soul is a part of the mother as the body is. Though the soul is not part of the mother and be immediately given by God, yet that hinders not its being derived by conception, it being consequent on it according to a law of nature.[29]

If Christ's human soul was pre-existent to creation, he would not have received the entirety of his humanity through the divinely appointed channel of his mother and would thus be significantly different from every other human being who ever lived. How then could he be the Son of Man and represent humanity

---

26 J. A. Dorner, the nineteenth-century commentator on the history of christology, wrote regarding Watts's strategy, "They [the Arians], namely, adduce passages which, even apart from the incarnation, – that is, therefore, in relation to the pre-existent element in Christ, – have a subordinatian [*sic*] tone, and by their means try to establish their Subordinatianism. If Christ's soul pre-existed, this objection falls to the ground. The Arian objection, further, that the orthodox doctrine is unable to acknowledge a true humiliation of Christ, seeing that God did not take part in suffering, and that consequently we must assume the existence in Christ of a higher being, subordinate to God, which truly humbled itself in the incarnation and truly suffered, also falls to the ground." *History of the Development of the Doctrine of the Person of Christ*, trans. D. W. Simon (Edinburgh: T. & T. Clark, 1880), II.2.331.

27 Edwards, "Miscellanies" No. 1174, in *Works*, 23:90.

28 Edwards does not address the possibility that the covenant of redemption could have taken place before the creation of Christ's human soul and its assumption to the Logos.

29 Edwards, "Miscellanies" No. 1174, in *Works*, 23:90.

before God in the work of redemption?

Edwards thus affirms the traditional christological view that God the Son assumed a complete human nature at the time of the incarnation, not part of a pre-existent human nature at the beginning of creation. While his positions are traditional on these subjects, when we turn our attention to the nature of the *unio personalis*, or the personal union of Christ's two natures, we find Edwards adopting a christological innovation advanced by Puritans like John Owen: namely, the fact that it is the person of the Holy Spirit, not the person of the Son, who is the immediate agent of union of Christ's two natures. We now turn our attention to this issue.

4.2 The Spirit as the Bond of the *Unio Personalis*

As we move forward in the logical unfolding of christology, we come to the tangled complex of issues surrounding the actual union of the divine and human natures, an area which has remained one of lively discussion in the church throughout the centuries. In exploring Edwards's views on these topics, we will notice his particular emphasis on the Spirit's work as the immediate agent of the *hypostatic* union. Before we consider this, it is necessary to note the trinitarian dimensions to the incarnational act in Edwards's thought. Edwards is quick to point out that while many of his discussions highlight the economic actions of one of the three divine persons, he affirms the unity of the divine operations *ad extra*:

> Though the creation of the human nature of Christ ben't by Christ economically, or don't especially belong to him as a work appointed him in the order constituted among the persons of the Trinity, with respect to their operations and actions *ad extra*, yet 'tis true the creation of the human nature of Christ is not without the Son, as all the persons of the Trinity do concur in all acts *ad extra*.[30]

Given this affirmation, however, the majority of his christological discussions center around one of the trinitarian-member's appropriated acts with regard to the incarnational act. Consequently, before we focus on the Spirit's specific work in the personal union, we will briefly observe what Edwards has to say about the Father's and the Son's activity in the incarnation.

The relationships between the distinctive works of the Father, the Son, and the Holy Spirit in the work of the incarnation are set out in "Miscellanies" No. 958, a rather lengthy entry where Edwards's design is to illustrate that the inner-trinitarian order of the persons is reflected in all the works of God *ad extra*, even in the work of the incarnation. Edwards's overall argument in the entry is that there are parallels between Christ's multi-faceted relationships with creation, and God the Father's relationship with the Son. For example,

---

30 Edwards, "Miscellanies" No. 958, in *Works*, 20:238.

while the Son is the source of knowledge and life of all creatures, it is the Father who is Christ's source of knowledge and life. Again, while all things are to conform to the image of Christ and show forth the glory of Christ, Christ himself derives his image from the Father and possesses his human glory from the Father. Hence the general theme that he traces throughout this entry is summed up as follows: "All the works of God *ad extra* are wrought by Christ, excepting those that are immediately wrought upon or about Christ, or in which Christ himself is the effect or object, and these are more immediately from God the Father."[31] Because of this, the inner-trinitarian order is reflected in God's external operations: the Father is the ground, source, and foundation of Christ's being and life, while the rest of creation finds its source in Christ. Christ is thus the mediator through whom God the Father rules over creation and through whom the redeemed find communion with God. By specifically applying this principle to the incarnation, Edwards affirms that while God created all things by the Son, "there is but one thing that is created that is more immediately the work of God the Father, and that is the human nature of Christ, and that both in its old and new creation."[32] Christ then, while he created all things, did not immediately create his human nature; that is the Father's work.

Several questions arise at this point, (1) what is the Son's role in the incarnation? and (2) how does the Father immediately create Christ's human nature? Edwards only addressed the former question, as we have already seen in "Miscellanies" No. 958: "Though the creation of the human nature of Christ ben't by Christ economically . . . yet 'tis true the creation of the human nature of Christ is not without the Son." The Son is part of the process, but Edwards does not exactly spell out this involvement. In a much earlier entry he suggests that the Logos's love to the human nature is the pre-requisite to the *unio personalis*: "Such was the love of the Son of God to the human nature, that he desired a most near and close union with it, something like the union in the persons of the Trinity, nearer than there can be between two distinct [beings]. This moved him to make the human become one with him."[33] This idea is not explicitly developed in later entries, but it foreshadows the Spirit's involvement in the union of Christ's two natures if we take the love here that the Son has for his human nature to be the "hidden" presence of the Spirit in Edwards's thought. While he does not explicitly make this connection, given the strong association Edwards makes between love and the Spirit in his thought, this connection is plausible.

With regard to the second question—"*how* does the Father immediately create Christ's human nature?"—we do have a sizable amount of material with which to work. In "Miscellanies" No. 958, he briefly mentions that while it is the Father who creates Christ's human nature, and while it is the Son who

---

31 Edwards, "Miscellanies" No. 958, in *Works*, 20:234.
32 Edwards, "Miscellanies" No. 958, in *Works*, 20:234.
33 Edwards, "Miscellanies" No. 183, in *Works* 13:329.

creates everything else, "All [these works] universally are *by the Spirit*." With this brief comment, we approach our central investigation: while it is the Father who immediately creates Christ's human nature, he only does so "by the Spirit." It is the Spirit who is the immediate agent whereby Christ's human nature is not only made, but sanctified and united to the divine Son in a personal union, a point which he summarizes in "Miscellanies" No. 764b: "There is such an union between this human nature that immediately speaks with God's words; which union is the consequence of God's communicating his Spirit without measure to [Christ's] human nature, so as to render it the same person with him that is God."[34] Edwards argues this point in eight separate "Miscellanies" entries across a considerable span of his life: from No. 487 (Oct. 1730) to No. 1043 (mid 1740s). Because we see him not only developing this view, but bringing theological and exegetical clarity to it throughout these entries, we can be fairly certain that it was his mature position.[35] In the following pages we will (1) explore Edwards's arguments for why the Spirit is the bond of union of Christ's two natures, (2) use this discussion as a platform to outline the broader distinctives of his entire christology, (3) suggest reasons as to why he held to this view, and (4) attempt to categorize his christological position *vis a vis* other schools of christological thought.

Edwards's opening thoughts in "Miscellanies" No. 487 (entitled "INCARNATION OF THE SON OF GOD AND UNION OF THE TWO NATURES OF CHRIST") consist of a lengthy reflection on the similarities he observes among the various unions that exist throughout theology. "There is a likeness between the union of the Logos with the man Christ Jesus and the union of Christ with the church," he writes, "though there be in the former great peculiarities."[36] For instance, as Christ dwells in believers as his temple (1 Cor 3:16-17; 2 Cor 6:16) so too does the Logos dwell in the human nature as his tabernacle; as Christ dwells in his church as his body (Eph 1:23), so too does he dwell in the human nature as his body (Heb 10:5). These are parallel sets of indwelling, and in each of them he observes Scripture's affirmation that the Spirit is the medium of this indwelling. The apostle Paul, for instance, comments in Col 2:9 that "in him [Christ] dwelleth all the fullness of the Godhead bodily." Given Edwards's strong association of God's "fullness" with the Spirit, it was

---

34 Edwards, "Miscellanies" No. 764b, in *Works*, 18:411.
35 The complete list is as follows: "Miscellanies" Nos. 487, 513, 624, 709, 738, 764b, 766, 1043. Like "Miscellanies" No. 94 is to his doctrine of the Trinity, No. 487 is in many ways the "charter" entry on this topic, where he explores the theological contours of this topic from as many different aspects as possible. For entries where he brings theological clarity to his position, see "Miscellanies" Nos. 624, 709, 738, 764b and 766. For entries where he brings exegetical clarity to his position, see "Miscellanies" Nos. 709, 764b, 766 and 1043.
36 Edwards, "Miscellanies" No. 487, in *Works*, 13:528.

quite natural for him to conclude from this verse that God's Spirit completely fills the God-man. The apostle John affirms a very similar thing in John 3:34, where he writes that the Spirit is given to Jesus Christ "not by measure" or "without measure" as Edwards often paraphrased it.[37]

Parallel to this indwelling of the Spirit in the God-man, Edwards discerns a similar movement of the Spirit with regard to the elect: "that fullness of the Godhead which the apostle Paul speaks of [in Col 2:9], I suppose to be the same with that fullness which John speaks of (John 1:16), as being that of which we receive." He notes that the saints too partake of God's nature (2 Pet 1:4) and may be filled with all the fullness of God (Eph 3:19) "though it don't dwell in them bodily."[38] While Edwards's scriptural observations are rough and a bit sketchy here, the overall drift is identifiable. While there are acknowledged differences between Christ's personal union and the union Christ has with the elect, the predominant emphasis of this entry lies in the *similarities* between these unions, and the centerpiece to these similarities is the Spirit of God who acts as the agent of union. "All divine communion, or communion of the creatures with God or with one another in God, seems to be by the Holy Ghost."[39] Hence the legitimacy of taking this insight and applying it in a christological direction to see whether or not the personal union of Christ is also by the Spirit: "As the union of believers with Christ be by the indwelling of the Spirit of Christ in them, so it may be worthy to be considered, whether or no the union of the divine with the human nature of Christ ben't by the Spirit of the Logos dwelling in him after a peculiar manner and without measure."[40]

Before we analyze the mechanics of this union in more detail, it must be noted that this strategy is distinguished from standard christological reflection which generally emphasized the *differences* between the hypostatic union and all other unions out of a desire to preserve the unsearchable mysteries of Christ's person. Francis Turretin, as a representative example, observes that the personal union of Christ's two natures is not a schetic or relative union "consisting in the union of souls and the consent of wills, such as the union of friends." Neither is it a "mystical union and grace of believers with Christ." Nor is it a substantial or "essential union of the person of the Trinity in one essence. Rather the question," he adds, "concerns the hypostatical union by the assumption of human nature into unity of the person of the Logos."[41] Each of these unions is formally distinguished in Turretin's theology, and must not be

---

37 Edwards, "Miscellanies" No. 487, in *Works*, 13:528-29.
38 Edwards, "Miscellanies" No. 487, in *Works*, 13:529.
39 Edwards, "Miscellanies" No. 487, in *Works*, 13:529.
40 Edwards, "Miscellanies" No. 487, in *Works*, 13:528.
41 Francis Turretin, *Institutes of Elenctic Theology*, in three volumes, trans. George Musgrave Giger, ed. James T. Dennison, Jr. (Phillipsburg, N.J.: Presbyterian and Reformed, 1992, 1994, 1997), vol. 2, 311 (13.6.3). See also Heppe's summaries from Reformed theologians, *Reformed Dogmatics*, 431-32 (17.17).

confused with one another. By contrast, Edwards's approach was to emphasize the commonalities between these unions. The relative union whereby human beings harmonize in community, the mystical union believers have with Christ, the essential union that is enjoyed by the members of the Trinity, and hypostatic union of Christ's two natures all share one common denominator: the Holy Spirit's immediate and personal activity acting as the bond of union among distinct persons.

How, according to Edwards, does the Spirit of God unite Christ's human and divine natures? The best way to understand his view is to watch his argument unfold in his "Miscellanies" entries. Edwards makes two basic moves in these "Miscellanies": first, he exegetically supports his argument that the Holy Spirit is the bond of union between Christ's two natures, and second, he explores the theological mechanics of this union. We shall consider each of these moves individually.

4.2.1 The Spirit as the Bond of the Unio Personalis: Exegetical Arguments

In "Miscellanies" Nos. 624 and 709, Edwards argues that John 10:36 "confirms that Christ's union with the Godhead is by the communication of the Holy Ghost not by measure to him."[42] In this text, the apostle records a heated interaction between Jesus and the Jewish leaders who attempt to stone him because of his startling statements that he is the Son of God, essentially equating himself with God. Jesus, in response to them, asks "Say ye of him, whom the Father hath sanctified, and sent into the world, thou blasphemest; because I said, I am the Son of God?" (John 10:36). Edwards comments on the scene: "The Jews [sic] objection was that he, *being a man*, made himself one with God [v.33]. Christ here answers directly to their objection, and shows how *he, a man*, is the Son of God, or how his manhood is united to the deity, and this is by his being sanctified," and being sent into the world.[43] Edwards's interest in verse 36 lies in its subordinate clause, where Jesus pairs the Father's sanctifying of the Son with his sending him into the world, acts which Edwards argues are ultimately one and the same. To say that the Father has sanctified the Son is to say "that it must be by his having the Holy Spirit given to him," for the Spirit throughout Scripture is the great Sanctifier, and the only way to be sanctified is to possess the Spirit. Subsequently, to say that the Son was sent into the world is to say that he was incarnated, or made flesh so as to dwell on earth as a man with human beings. The sanctification of the human nature, in uniting it with the eternal Son at the moment of its creation in Mary's womb, and his sending into the world are the same act:

---

42 Edwards, "Miscellanies" No. 624, in *Works*, 18:154.
43 Edwards, "Miscellanies" No. 709, in *Works*, 18:333.

> By sending the Spirit, assuming his flesh into being and into the person of the divine Logos, at the same time and by the same act, the Father sent him into the world, or incarnated him by an act of sanctification; for the incarnation was assuming flesh, or human nature, into the person of the Son, or giving communion of the divine personality to human nature, in giving that human nature being. And this was done by giving the Holy Spirit in such a manner and measure to that human nature in making it.[44]

The Father's work of sanctifying the Son and sending him into the world was immediately by the Holy Spirit, who worked *in* Mary's womb creating Christ's human nature, and at the same time worked *with regard to* the Son, miraculously uniting the person of the eternal Logos to that created human being, so as to make the two one God-man.

Edwards's other extended exegetical defense of the position that the Holy Spirit is the bond of union of Christ's two natures comes interestingly from Zechariah 3:8-9. There the angel of the Lord declares God's three-fold intentions to Zechariah: (1) God will send forth his servant, (2) a stone will appear before Joshua that has seven eyes engraved on it, and (3) God will then remove the land's iniquity in one day. To Edwards this stone is the Messiah. By virtue of its seven divinely engraved eyes, it has God's own perfect knowledge of all things, seven being the biblical number of perfection. Edwards argues that the only way that the Messiah, whom the Scriptures point to as being a human being, can have perfect divine knowledge is through a unique individual in whom exists a personal union between its divine and human natures.

> These eyes, in v. 10 of the next chapter, are said to be the eyes of the Lord, and yet they are represented as being, by the wonderful work of God, so united to the stone that they are the eyes of the stone, being graven by God in the very substance of the stone. So that here is God's sight, or perception, knowledge or consciousness united to the Messiah or Christ, which can't be less than a personal union.[45]

Through this stone God will remove iniquity from the land "in one day," a reference to Christ's work on the cross. Where does the Holy Spirit factor into this discussion? He is connected here through the seven eyes on the stone, which Scripture elsewhere identifies as the Holy Spirit himself (Rev 5:6).[46] The stone, as the typical Messiah, thus has perfect divine knowledge via the Spirit's indwelling. This entry reveals Edwards's long-term commitment to the

---

44 Edwards, "Miscellanies" No. 709, in *Works*, 18:334.
45 Edwards, "Miscellanies" No. 1043, in *Works*, 20:383.
46 Revelation 5:6: "And I beheld, and, lo, in the midst of the throne and of the four beasts, and in the midst of the elders, stood a Lamb as it had been slain, *having seven horns and seven eyes, which are the seven Spirits of God sent forth into all the earth.*"

fact that "the incarnation, or the union of the divine nature with the human, is by the Holy Spirit dwelling in the human nature,"[47] a commitment he first articulated some fifteen years earlier in "Miscellanies" No. 487. In summary, he felt this position exegetically cohered with the witness of Scripture.

4.2.2 The Spirit as the Bond of the Unio Personalis: Theological Arguments

How then does Edwards incorporate this exegetical conclusion into his christology? It is one thing to explain what Scripture says, quite another to explain how its exegetical contents fit with the broader currents of one's theology. Edwards's basic argument is that the Spirit, as the bond of this unique personal union, communicates the "personality" of the Logos to the human nature in such a peculiar manner that the two distinct natures, the divine and the human, become one person. In commenting again on the Father's "sanctifying and sending" of the Son into the world (John 10:36), Edwards writes, "By this sanctifying was given *communion in divine personality to human nature*. But the giving such *communion in the personality of the eternal Son to human* [nature], was the very same as sending Christ into the world."[48] Later, in paraphrasing John the Baptist's words in John 3:34 ("God hath giveth not the Spirit by measure unto him"), Edwards writes that this "union is the consequence of God's communicating his Spirit without measure to [Christ's] human nature, so as to render it the same person with him that is God."[49] How does this work?

Edwards experiments with the categories of Lockean psychology to explore further the mechanics of this union. We may recall that that which constitutes a person for Edwards is a being who possesses knowledge and will.[50] Thus the pneumatological communication of the Logos's hypostasis to the human nature is a communication of the Logos's understanding and will to that humanity, an issue that he explores in considerable detail in "Miscellanies" No. 766. There Edwards focuses on both Christ's teaching (i.e., his understanding) and his

---

47 Edwards, "Miscellanies" No. 1043, in *Works*, 20:383.
48 Edwards, "Miscellanies" No. 709, in *Works*, 18:334, emphasis mine.
49 Edwards, "Miscellanies" No. 764b, in *Works*, 18:411. This quotation illustrates Edwards's meaning when he writes that the Spirit is communicated to Christ's human nature "without measure." He does not mean that there is an infinite communication of the Logos's knowledge and love to the human nature (for reasons we shall discuss below). Rather, the Spirit's communication of the Logos to the human nature "without measure" is merely his shorthand way of saying that the result of this union of the two natures is one person.
50 Edwards, *Discourse on the Trinity*, in *Works*, 21:132-33. See also his comment in "Miscellanies" No. 766: "For those works of the divine power [in Christ's ministry] were his own no otherwise than as they were the works of the divine Logos, *united to the human nature, or to the human understanding and will*." (*Works*, 18:412, emphasis mine).

miraculous "works of power" (i.e., his will). He observes that both Jesus' teaching and his actions are portrayed in Scripture as being the joint work of Christ and the Spirit. For instance, it is Christ who heals ("I will; be thou clean"; Matt 8:3) and it is Christ who proclaims the good news to the captives (Mark 1:14-15). Yet by his own words he confesses that these words and works are by the Spirit (Luke 4:18-21).[51] Hence, to blaspheme Christ in his miraculous work of exorcism is to blaspheme the Spirit (Matthew 12), because there is such a close conjunction between the works of Christ and that of the Spirit. Thus what the Spirit directs Christ to do, Christ does of his own will and in his own name. When we ask of Edwards, who is the source of Christ's works of power and teachings, Christ or the Holy Spirit? his answer would be, both. "Though he was directed by the Spirit of God when and how to work these works, and was moved by the Spirit to work them, yet he wrought them as of his own wisdom and his own will."[52] This sort of conjunction between Christ's and the Spirit's willing and knowing obtains only among the perichoretic relations of the Trinity. Consequently, the only possible way for the existence of this unique conjunction between Christ's and the Spirit's willing, knowing, and working *in the God-man* whereby the personality of the Son is the personality of the human nature, is through the Spirit being the bond of union of Christ's two natures.

> Now this can't be, that he should [be] directed by the Spirit to work, and his will moved by the Spirit of God, and yet they be done as of his own will any otherwise than as the Spirit of God directed the human understanding, and moved the human will, as a bond of union of between the understanding and the will of the divine Logos, and the understanding and will of the human nature of Christ.[53]

As a man on earth, Christ can only have the personality of the heavenly Logos *through* a communication or "conveyance" of that rational, volitional consciousness *to* the human nature *by* him who is the agent of communion, the Holy Spirit. The Spirit therefore "comes between" Christ's two natures, yet because he is the agent of union *par excellence*, because he is the archetypical agent of union who infinitely unites the members of the eternal Trinity, his interposition between Christ's natures renders the unity of the God-man not less unified, but more unified.

What we have just examined in Edwards's thought is, I am arguing, his "basic" approach to the union of Christ's two natures. He does not appear to probe deeper into these mysteries, explaining the subtle mechanics of this

---

51 Luke 4:18: "The Spirit of the Lord is upon me, because he hath anointed me to preach the gospel to the poor; he hath sent me to heal the brokenhearted, to preach deliverance to the captives, and revering of sight to the blind, to set at liberty them that are bruised."
52 Edwards, "Miscellanies," No. 766, in *Works*, 18:412.
53 Edwards, "Miscellanies," No. 766, in *Works*, 18:412.

"conveyance" of the Logos's understanding and will to the human nature. This has generated considerable confusion in the secondary literature, a confusion that appears to be centered around what Edwards meant by an "identity of consciousness" between Christ's two natures.[54] Some have argued that Edwards employed this phrase to indicate a commitment to a strongly Alexandrian and Lutheran christology (which formally minimizes the distinctions between the two natures), over against the Antiochene and Reformed family of christology (which is more comfortable drawing sharper distinctions between the two natures).[55] For instance, in her dissertation Amy Plantinga Pauw observes an "unabashedly Alexandrian bias" in some of Edwards's christological reflections, where he held positions which were "eschewed by most Reformed thinkers. For example, he explicitly rejected the duality of Christ's knowledge and will. The 'communion of understanding' between the Logos and the human nature of Christ 'is such that there is the same consciousness' (Misc. 487)."[56] Similarly, both Robert Jenson and Stephen Holmes link his meaning of "identity of consciousness" with Edwards's idealism, and also end up seeing Alexandrian themes in Edwards's christology.[57] On the basis of these observations both Pauw and Holmes go on to argue that Edwards's christology is internally inconsistent, for he seems to affirm christological themes that show affinities with both Alexandrian and Antiochene christologies.[58] The problem with these arguments is that they invest too much in Edwards's phrases and language. In the few places where he uses the language of an "identity of consciousness" between Christ's two natures, Edwards's intent is not to incorporate Alexandrian themes into his christology; rather, his aim is much more modest: merely to affirm that the person of Jesus Christ is the same person that is God the Son. The two aims of these "Miscellanies" entries (Nos. 487, 624, 709, 738, 764b and 766) were (1) to show how it is that God the Son and the man Jesus Christ are the same person, and (2) to show how this *hypostatic* union is a result of the Spirit's immediate and continual work of communicating the understanding and will of God the Son to that human nature. Thus, when Edwards mentions that the two natures of Christ share the "same consciousness," he is merely highlighting this general point rather than addressing more complex christological issues.

One other question might serve to illustrate this point in more detail: if all

---

54 Edwards uses this phrase, along with "communication of consciousness," in "Miscellanies" No. 738. He also speaks of Christ's human and divine nature as possessing the "same consciousness" in "Miscellanies" No. 487.
55 It should be noted that both of these christological strategies fall within the allowable range of the orthodoxy codified in the Council of Chalcedon, though representatives from each side often are suspect of the other's christology.
56 Pauw, "Supreme Harmony of All," 208.
57 See Jenson, *America's Theologian*, 119-22; Holmes, *God of Grace*, 139-42.
58 See Pauw's dissertation, "Supreme Harmony of All," 205, and Holmes's *God of Grace and God of Glory*, 141.

Edwards is doing in these "Miscellanies" is merely showing the continuity of the personality of the Logos and of Jesus Christ, then *why* does he spill so much ink on this basic christological issue? Is not the position that the Son and the man Jesus Christ share the same divine subject a given in orthodox christological discussions? The reason for his special attention lies in the fact that he is arguing for a relatively new christological hypothesis: it is the Spirit who is the immediate agent who effects the union of God the Son and the man Jesus Christ.[59] Edwards recognized that this proposal was not held by the majority of the Christian tradition, who rather argued that the Son himself is the immediate agent who assumed the human nature into personal union with himself.[60] In addition, he was aware of the potential problems that such a position held: "The principle objection that I can think of against it, is that thus the union of the human nature with the Holy Ghost will be nearer than with the Son of God, because 'tis more immediate, and so he should rather be the same person with the Holy Ghost than with the Son."[61] This problem to his view reflects the assumption that it is the active incarnating agent who must be the one who is incarnated. Edwards denied that this had to be case. The immediate agent who unites these two diverse natures does not have to be the party which is incarnated, rather it can be an intermediary who mediates this unique union. Because this was a christological innovation, the burden of proof was on Edwards to show how this pneumatologically-mediated personal union resulted in one person. In other words, how can the Spirit "come between" two distinct natures and unite them into the *single* person of Jesus Christ? If it was difficult enough for traditional christology to argue that the Son and his complete humanity are one person, why confuse the situation even more by adding a third party? Such a move could only be seen as resulting in a christology that is *more* at risk of Nestorianism. Thus one of Edwards's greatest concerns in his christological reflections regarded the proper articulation of how there could be a unity to Christ's person as God-man when it is the Spirit who effects this union.

If the arguments in the preceding paragraphs are correct, then it seems we can avoid the "inconsistency" thesis that Pauw and Holmes advance. As we

---

59 John Owen in his *Pneumatologia or Discourse Concerning the Holy Spirit*, (reprint Carlisle, PA.: Banner of Truth, 1965), 159-87 argues for this very position. We know Edwards read this work from his reference to it in "Miscellanies" No. 1047. For a brief historical overview on Owen's christology see Alan Spence, "Christ's Humanity and Ours: John Owen," in *Persons Divine and Human*, ed. Christoph Schwoebel and Colin E. Gunton (Edinburgh: T & T Clark, 1991), 74-97.
60 His rhetorical question in "Miscellanies" No. 487 shows that he recognizes that his opinion differed from what is normally held: "If 'tis by the Spirit of God that the human nature of Christ was conceived, and had life and being, *why should we not suppose that 'tis also by the Spirit that he has union with the divine nature?*" (*Works*, 13:531, emphasis mine).
61 Edwards, "Miscellanies" No. 487, in *Works*, 13:531-32.

have seen, much of their argument is based on interpreting Edwards's language ("same consciousness" and "identity of consciousness") as possessing a technical sophistication which enables them to identify strong Alexandrian themes in his christology. Because they also observe strong Antiochene themes in his christology as well (which we shall examine below), their conclusion is unavoidable: Edwards cannot have an internally consistent christology because one cannot possess both Alexandrian and Antiochene themes in one's view on the person of Christ. If, however, Edwards's language is taken in a more general sense where he incorporates the language of "identity" merely to illuminate the unity of the person of Christ, then the basis for his "Alexandrian bias" and his christological inconsistency fall to the side.

4.2.3 Christ's Knowledge and Edwards's Reformed Christological Language

One illuminating aspect of this pneumatologically effected union between Christ's two natures concerns Jesus' human knowledge, an issue that Edwards treats in several "Miscellanies" entries. Edwards clearly teaches that Christ's post-incarnation knowledge is in continuity with the knowledge that the eternal Son had in his pre-incarnate state: "Christ taught the things of God as of his own knowledge, as being in the bosom of the Father, as he that had seen the Father and knew the Father."[62] What is the nature and extent of Christ's knowledge as God-man? Lurking behind this question stands broader issues concerning the kind of unity that exists between Christ's two natures. How can divine knowledge, which is infinite and of an order different from human knowledge, be communicated to and contained in a human understanding? If Christ's knowledge, as God-man, is not in complete continuity with the infinite knowledge he had in his pre-incarnate state, then is not his true deity threatened, rendering the union incomplete? If, on the other hand, Christ's knowledge is that of the Logos's infinite, eternal, and omnipotent knowledge, then in what way is his knowledge *human* knowledge—or in other words, how can he be truly human? These questions presuppose the classic Christian understanding of the relationship between God's knowledge and humanity's— namely that there exists a sharp distinction between infinite divine knowledge and finite human knowledge.

Edwards addressed some of these issues in "Miscellanies" No. 205, an early entry specifically devoted to the continuity and discontinuity that exists between the Son's pre- and post-incarnate knowledge. After affirming that Christ, "being the same person with the eternal Son of God, has a reminiscence and consciousness of what appertained to the eternal Logos," he comments on the distinction between Christ's human knowledge and that of the Son: "Now when he remembered those things, he could not remember [them] as they were in the infinite mind, for the idea of the Creator cannot be communicated to the

---

62 Edwards, "Miscellanies" No. 766, in *Works*, 18:413.

creature as it is in God; but the remembrance, as it was in his mind, was the same after a different manner, . . . as if they had been after the manner of a creature."⁶³ In this quote, Edwards demonstrates several christological characteristics. First, Edwards reveals his deference to the classic understanding that human knowledge is distinct from divine knowledge. Christ's knowledge, as the God-*man*, while it is continuous with the Son's pre-incarnate knowledge, is knowledge "after the manner of a creature."

Second and more revealing, Edwards appears to maintain the standard Reformed principle of the *finitum non capax infiniti*, "the finite is incapable of grasping, containing, or comprehending the infinite." Used as a principle of both epistemology and christology, Reformed theologians have emphasized that finite creatures, including the humanity of Christ, are unable to contain, grasp, and/or comprehend the entirety of the infinite and eternal attributes of deity. They have affirmed this out of a desire to preserve the glory of God by preventing any ontological "leakage" of divinity to the creation, and out of desire to do adequate justice to biblical texts which appear to limit Christ's human knowledge (as when he says that only the Father knows the time of the end; Matt 24:36). We see Edwards reflecting this principle a number of times in this relatively short entry:

> 'Twas impossible that the man Christ Jesus should remember this [i.e., the transactions of the covenant of redemption] as it was in the Deity, for then an idea of the eternal mind could be communicated to a finite mind even as it is in the infinite mind. . . . 'Tis very manifest that he speaks [in John 17:5] as remembering, but 'twas impossible that he should remember infinite glory and happiness but he remembered and was conscious [of it] to himself. His idea was finite.⁶⁴

If Jesus Christ's ideas are finite, then where is the "rest" of his knowledge? Are we to say that one of the persons of the Trinity has limited, finite attributes, and if so then can we still say that this person, this God-man, is still fully God? Edwards never explicitly addresses these issues. Yet he does say some things that echo the standard Reformed strategy in dealing with this difficult and subtle topic. Reformed theologians, in a logical extension of the principle *infinitum non capax finiti*, argued that while the Word is truly united to Christ's human nature, the Logos is not to be thought of as entirely contained in or by that human nature even in his incarnate state. In other words, the Logos's divinity is understood as being beyond or outside of (*extra*) the human nature even in the state of incarnation; the entirety of the second person of the Trinity, while fully united to the human nature, nonetheless is not infinitely communicated to that finite humanity. This distinction, known as the *extra calvinisticum*, enabled Reformed theologians to affirm simultaneously that the

---

63 Edwards, "Miscellanies" No. 205, in *Works*, 13:340.
64 Edwards, "Miscellanies" No. 205, in *Works*, 13:341.

infinite Word fills heaven and earth and is really omnipresent, and that he dwells among humankind as a finite man, with all the natural limitations of finite humanity including finite knowledge and the ability to grow in wisdom.[65] Thus Turretin's affirmation: "We acknowledge that Christ as God is indeed omniscient, but as man we hold that he was endowed with knowledge, great indeed beyond all other creatures, but yet finite and created, to which something could be added (and really was added)."[66] Edwards's echoes of the *extra calvinisticum* are faint, and are mostly comprised of tangential statements mentioning a distinction between the locale of Christ's divine nature in heaven and on earth: "the Holy Ghost that descended on Christ from heaven as a dove, was the bond of union that in descending from *the divine nature of Christ which was in heaven, on the human which was on earth*, united earth with heaven."[67] His statements on Christ's knowledge are also revealing. As we have seen, Edwards appears to have held that Christ's human knowledge is finite. This finite knowledge in no way diminishes the infinite omniscience of the second person of the Trinity because the infinite entirety of the Logos cannot be communicated to Christ's finite human nature. If the extended record of his "Miscellanies" tells us anything about his theological development, he does not appear to move away from this position later for he repeats his early arguments of "Miscellanies" No. 205 much later in his extended response to Watts's heterodox christology ("Miscellanies" No. 1174). Watts, we may recall, affirmed that the eternal Son was united to a created human soul shortly before his creation of the rest of the universe. One of Edwards's arguments against this was to point out that Watts's argument requires the Creator of the universe to possess an infinite understanding. If the Son was united to a finite human soul, Edwards argues, then he could not possibly carry out the task of creation. Though the universe is finite,

> things and circumstances, and dependencies and consequences of things in the world, are infinite in number; and therefore a finite understanding and power cannot extend to them: yea, it can extend to but an infinitely small part of the whole number of individuals, and their circumstances and consequences. Indeed, in order to the disposal of a few things, in their motions and successive changes,

---

[65] See Richard Muller, *Dictionary of Latin and Greek Theological Terms* (Grand Rapids: Baker, 1985), 111.

[66] Turretin, *Institutes of Elenctic Theology*, 2, 349 (13.13.3).

[67] Edwards, "Miscellanies" No. 487, in *Works*, 13:530 (emphasis mine). See also "Miscellanies" No. 709: "It was not merely giving being to the manhood of Christ, but the communicating the divine person *from heaven to earth* in giving being to Christ's manhood, that was sending Christ into the world." (*Works*, 18:334, emphasis mine).

to a certain precise issue, there is need of infinite exactness, and so need of infinite power and wisdom.[68]

Behind the logic of his critique stands the affirmation that Christ's knowledge is finite, and therefore it *must* be the case that it was the pre-incarnate Logos only who could have possibly created the universe. In his discussions of Christ's human knowledge, the evidence appears to support the fact that Edwards followed his Reformed christological heritage in affirming the *finitum non capax infiniti* and the *extra calvinisticum*.

4.3 Concluding Remarks

Is Edwards's christology "Reformed?" Such a question is both simplistic and reductionistic, and in answering it one runs the risk of missing the rich complexities and creativity of his christological views by submitting his statements to a mere checklist of issues. Edwards never felt constrained by his Reformed heritage, but creatively worked and reworked his views from within that tradition, and sometimes beyond it, because he plainly felt his views were scriptural, sanctioned by the Word of God. His christology is no exception. Furthermore, such a question is loaded for it implies that Edwards had a mature christology with all the details worked out. We have seen that this is not the case; Edwards never wrote a treatise on christology, or a systematic theology. What we have are merely christological themes running throughout his thought. Having said these things, the following points do seem to flow from our investigation in this chapter.

First, where Edwards is most explicit about his christological views, he reflects his Reformed tradition. We observed this especially in his discussion of Christ's human knowledge, where he appears to affirm the *finitum non capax infiniti* and the *extra calvinisticum*. Both of these positions are hallmarks of the Reformed view of the person of Christ. So while we might not be able to confirm that Edwards was a card-carrying Reformed theologian when it comes to christology, we can at least say that he approximates a Reformed view given the fact that he has no problem affirming these unique features of Reformed christology.

Second, Edwards's special concern in his reflections on the person of Christ has to do with the pneumatological origins of the union of Christ's two natures, not so much the exhaustive details of this union. In other words, Edwards wants to demonstrate *that* the Spirit unites Christ's two natures, not completely explain *how*. This concern of his coincides with his desire to recover equal honor and dignity for the Spirit in the theological enterprise, a concern which we observed in his trinitarianism.

Third, a contrary theological trajectory appears to result from Edwards's

---

68 Edwards, "Miscellanies" No. 1174, in *Works*, 23:91-92.

position that the Spirit is the bond of union between Christ's two natures. Because the Spirit unites Christ's human nature with the Logos, there is a "tightness" that exists between the two natures which does not appear to allow for the more loose union Reformed christologies allow. We have seen that the immediate and continuous presence and work of the Spirit effecting the personal union of Christ's two natures parallels the inner-trinitarian union, a union which cannot be closer. These two are really one person, Jesus Christ, and the two shall never be separate, even though the natures are not mixed or commingled. This fact about Edwards's christology most likely accounts for the reason why some have discerned Alexandrian themes in his theology. These signals were picked up in his writings, not because he formally developed Alexandrian concepts in his christology, for we have seen that he never developed his views to this level of sophistication. Rather the strong pneumatological presence in his christology "tightens up" his christology giving it an Alexandrian flavor. It is in this sense that we may say that there are Alexandrian *tendencies* in his christology.

Lastly, by way of segue into the next chapter, we may observe one of the soteriological benefits that result from this unique union of the divine and human natures in the person of Jesus Christ. While the man Jesus Christ has the Spirit in many ways that are unique to him, he also has the same Spirit in many ways that are common to all who partake of the divine nature. The pneumatological pattern established in assuming Christ's human nature to the divine, opens a way for the rest of humanity to find communion with the triune God.

> For Christ being united to the human nature, we have advantage for a more free and full enjoyment of him, than we could have had if he had remained only in the divine nature. So again, we being united to a divine person, as his members, can have a more intimate union and intercourse with God the Father, who is only in the divine nature, than otherwise could be.[69]

It is to this issue, to our being united to the person of Christ by faith, that we now turn.

---

69 Edwards, "The Excellency of Christ," in *Works*, 19:593.

Part III

Acts in the Drama of Redemption

The Spirit and the Stages of the Christian Life

CHAPTER 5

Regeneration and Justification: The Holy Spirit as the Bond of the Christian's Union with Christ

[T]he Trinity is exceeding analogous to the gospel scheme, and agreeable to the tenor of the whole New Testament, and abundantly illustrative of gospel doctrines.[1]

As we have already proved, all creature holiness consists essentially and summarily in love to God and love to other creatures; so does the holiness of God consist in his love, especially in the perfect and intimate union and love there is between the Father and the Son. But the Spirit that proceeds from the Father and the Son is the bond of this union, as it is of all holy union between the Father and the Son, and between God and the creature, and between the creatures among themselves.[2]

Edwards opens one of his earlier "Miscellanies" entries (No. dd) with a question asked by many young theologians who have anguished over the Bible's complexity: "Some may ask, why the Scripture expresses things so unintelligibly? It tells us of Christ's living in us, of our being united to him, of being the same spirit, and uses many other such like expressions. Why doth it not call directly by their intelligible names, those things that lie hid under these expressions?" Would it not have been easier if God had given us a systematic theology rather than the conglomeration of narratives, epistles, poetry, and apocalypse which make up the Bible as it now stands? As an astute theologian, Edwards realized the disadvantages to such wishful thinking. A "Scripture" in the form of a detailed systematic theology would not only be too massive to handle, but it would also be unintelligible to the average Christian. If God had given us such a revelation, "Then we should have a hundred pages to express what is implied in these words, 'ye are the temple of the Holy Ghost;' neither would it after all be understood by the one fourth part of mankind." The genius of the Scriptures as they now stand lies in the fact that in these diverse biblical

---

1 Edwards, *Discourse on the Trinity*, in *Works*, 21:134.
2 Edwards, *Treatise on Grace*, in *Works*, 21:186.

genres, the Holy Spirit has skillfully packed volumes of theological material into concise phrases, metaphors, stories, and "similitudes" which not only condense the richness of God's revelation into a manageable book, but also place their contents within the reach of all who inquire about God: "By such similitudes, a vast volume is represented to our minds in three words; and things that we are not able to behold directly, are presented before us in lively pictures."[3]

While Scripture may artfully pack volumes of theology into pregnant phrases and succinct stories, it is my task in this chapter to *un*pack Edwards's own understanding of what Scripture means when it says that believers are "indwelt by the Spirit" (e.g., Rom 8:9, 11), and when it indicates that believers are "united with Christ" (e.g., Rom 6:5). Edwards ties both of these scriptural concepts to the agency of Spirit; it is the Spirit who indwells the saints, uniting himself to the faculties of their souls, and it is the Spirit who awakens in them the faith and love which ultimately effects their union with Christ. This central role the Spirit plays in regeneration is not unlike his role within the Trinity. There the Spirit highlights the Son's glorious excellences to the Father and quite literally *is* the Father's infinite love to the Son. Likewise, the Spirit *ad extra* highlights the Son to the elect, and unites them to Christ in love. Conversely, within the Trinity the Spirit is the Son's own love to the Father, and it is *in the Spirit* where the Father and Son commune. Likewise, in redemption the Spirit is mysteriously the saint's love to the Father through the Son, and it is in the realm of the Spirit where they commune with their Redeemer and with God the Father. While these parallels are not perfectly symmetrical, it will become clear in the remainder of our study that Edwards conceived the entire scope of redemption to be, in one sense, an "externalization" of the Trinity, the Trinity turned "inside-out." In this chapter we will begin to explore this thesis in the initial stages of this "externalization," by examining how the Spirit acts as the bond of union in regeneration and in justification. Three issues will be analyzed. First, we will explore the nature of the Spirit's union to the saint, a union which serves as the logical foundation to the redemptive process. Second, we will investigate the logical unfolding of the regeneration process. Lastly, we will examine how these issues relate to the sinner's justification, and how it is by faith alone that one is justified.

5.1 "Grace After a Principle of Nature:" The Holy Spirit's Union with the Saint

Edwards's favorite way of expressing the Spirit's union to the saint was to speak of the Spirit indwelling the soul, uniting himself to the saint's faculties of understanding and willing, so that the regenerate person can know and love divine things. The Spirit "unites himself with the mind of a saint, takes him for

---

3 Edwards, "Miscellanies" No. dd, in *Works*, 13:181.

his temple, actuates and influences him as a new, supernatural principle of life and action. . . . The Holy Spirit operates in the minds of the godly, by uniting himself to them, and living in them, and exerting his own nature in the exercise of their faculties."[4] By virtue of this pneumatological union, the Spirit restores the supernatural powers of the soul that were destroyed by the fall. "[I]n the sanctifying work of the Holy Ghost, not only remaining principles are assisted to do their work to a greater degree, but those principles are restored that were utterly destroyed by the fall; [so that] the mind habitually exerts those acts that the dominion of sin had made the soul wholly destitute of."[5] Yet more is accomplished in the saint's union with the Spirit than just a partial restoration of the powers she would have had if the fall had never occurred. The saint's faculties of knowing and loving are actually enabled by the Spirit to know and love God in a way similar to the way that God eternally knows and loves himself. In short, she is caught up in the glorious currents of God's infinite self-regard, a self-regard that has eternally manifested itself as the mysterious reality of the Trinity.[6]

This is not merely regeneration, it is a participation in God's trinitarian life.

[T]he Spirit of God in the souls of his saints exerts its own proper nature; that is to say, it communicates and exerts itself in the soul in those acts which are its proper, natural and essential acts in itself *ad intra*, or within the Deity from all eternity. The proper nature of the Spirit of God, the act which is its nature and wherein its being consists, is (as we have shown) divine love. . . . The Spirit of God operates in the minds of the godly by only being in them, uniting itself to their souls, and living in 'em and acting itself.[7]

Edwards was as forthcoming about this in his public writings as he was in his private notes, as the closing sentence to "The Excellency of Christ" illustrates: "Christ has brought it to pass, that those that the Father has given him, should be brought into the household of God; that he, and his Father, and his people, should be as it were one society, one family; that the church should be as it were admitted into the society of the blessed Trinity."[8]

At a summary level, the main thrust of Edwards's agenda is clear: first, the regeneration of the soul's powers unto holy knowing and loving of God is the direct result of the Spirit's union with the soul; and second, this transformation

---

4 Edwards, "A Divine and Supernatural Light," in *Works*, 17:411. See also his extended discussion of this in *Religious Affections*, in *Works*, 2:201ff.
5 Edwards, "Miscellanies" No. 471, in *Works*, 13:513.
6 To avoid confusion throughout this chapter, when discussing the intricate work that the Holy Spirit performs on and in the soul of a saint in the work of regeneration, I shall use the feminine "she" and "her" to refer to the saint in whom the Spirit is working, and the masculine "he" and "him" to refer to the Holy Spirit.
7 Edwards, "Miscellanies" No. 471, in *Works*, 13:513.
8 Edwards, "The Excellency of Christ," in *Works*, 19:594.

of the individual is actually, from the widest possible angle, a participation in God's immanent trinitarian life. Yet as soon as we probe deeper into these issues, puzzling questions emerge: What does Edwards mean when he states that the Spirit acts as a "principle of life" in the saint? What is actually taking place when the Spirit "communicates" and "exerts" himself in the believer's soul? How does the concept of grace factor into this view? Who properly performs these acts of holiness, the Spirit or the saint? Each of these questions revolves around one central question that will govern the remainder of our discussion in this section: What is the nature of this union between the saint and the Spirit? Edwards does not explicitly respond to this question, but he does give us three important clues that enable us to discern the shape of his answer.

5.1.1 The Movement of the Spirit into the Soul: Illumination and Infusion

The first clue concerns the movement of the Spirit *into* the soul, a process which Edwards articulates by employing two alternative theological concepts: illumination and infusion.[9] When the Spirit regenerates the soul, coming into union with its faculties, he illuminates it with spiritual light enabling it to "see" and know the excellency of divine things.[10] Similarly, the Spirit also infuses divine grace into the soul, enabling her not only to know the excellency of divine things, but to love them as well through acts of divine love and holiness, resulting in a holy pattern of life. "Grace consists very much in a principle that causes vigorousness and activity in action. This is infusion, even in the sense of the opposite party. So that, if any operation of the Holy Spirit at all is allowed [in the soul], the dispute is only, how much is infused."[11] As Conrad Cherry rightly indicates, illumination and infusion basically describe the same reality in Edwards's theology; they are not to be distinguished from one another.[12]

---

9 Since these issues have been adequately addressed in the secondary literature, I will confine my comments to how Edwards's discussion of illumination and infusion further clarifies our understanding of the Spirit's union with Christians. For thorough treatments on Edwards's understanding of illumination and infusion, see Paul Ramsey's "Editor's Introduction" to Edwards's *Freedom of the Will* (*Works*, 1:42-43); and Conrad Cherry, *Theology of Jonathan Edwards*, 34-39. For other studies that set these issues in broader theological and historical contexts, see Paul Ramsey, "Infused Virtues in Edwardsean and Calvinistic Context," in *The Works of Jonathan Edwards*, vol. 8, *Ethical Writings*, ed. Paul Ramsey (New Haven: Yale University Press, 1989), 739-50; and Morimoto, *Jonathan Edwards and the Catholic Vision of Salvation*, 13-70.

10 See our extensive discussion on the nature of spiritual sight in chapter six, pages 142-55.

11 Edwards, "Miscellanies" No. p, in *Works*, 13:171.

12 Cherry, *Theology of Jonathan Edwards*, 27. See his entire discussion on pages 27-39.

By employing the concepts of illumination and infusion to describe the Spirit's regenerative indwelling, Edwards is taking a firm stand against the "Arminianism" of his day. As is widely recognized, this "Arminianism" that Edwards spent much of his life opposing was neither the continental Remonstrant tradition which stemmed from the writings of Jacob Arminius (1560-1609) nor the evangelical Arminianism associated with John Wesley (1703-1791).[13] Rather, it consisted of a very loose group of both churchmen and free-thinkers outside of the church who were attracted to newer, fashionable theologies circulating in the Anglo-American world, theologies which generally opposed the strict doctrines of the bondage of the will, justification by faith alone, the transmission of original sin, and eternal punishment.[14] Apart from a general adherence to the principles of liberty, these theologians possessed a wide diversity of opinions. As Norman Fiering observes, probably "no single individual held all the arguments for free will that Edwards opposed, nor was there a self-conscious 'Arminian' group based on the criterion of free will alone. Not only were there diverse arguments for free will, there were also a number of grounds on which one could turn against determinism, which itself was not a single, unified concept."[15] It is thus better to say that there was no identifiable Arminian "party" in Edwards's day, but rather a general theological mood that pervaded the intellectual climate of Great Britain and the New World, a mood which highly valued human ability in the process of salvation and viewed Calvinism as both theologically and devotionally bankrupt. In spite of this, New England Calvinist divines, Edwards included, viewed their ideas as a single unified threat to the integrity of their Puritan and Calvinist heritage, and consequently lumped them all under the general label of "Arminianism."[16]

It is not my intention to examine Edwards's understanding of Arminianism

---

13 See for instance Paul Ramsey's "Editor's Introduction" to Edwards's *Freedom of the Will*, (*Works*,1:2-3), where he observes that "In the eighteenth century there was probably more in common between Edwards' defense of orthodoxy and the restored Arminianism of Arminius, which emerged with new strength and warmth in the Wesleyan revival, than between the latter and some of the 'Arminians' whom Edwards opposed." (*Works*, 1:3)

14 Throughout his "Miscellanies" notebook Edwards identifies several of his "Arminian" interlocutors. They include Daniel Whitby (1638-1726), John Taylor (1694-1761), George Turnbull (1698-1748), and Henry Stebbing (1687-1763). For the impact of Whitby's work on Edwards's *Freedom of the Will*, see Ramsey's "Editor's Introduction," in *Works*, 1:81-9. For the impact of Taylor and Turnbull's work on Edwards's treatise on *Original Sin* see Clyde Holbrook's "Editor's Introduction" to that treatise in *Works*, 3:68-74.

15 Norman Fiering, *Jonathan Edwards's Moral Thought and its British Context* (Chapel Hill: University of North Carolina Press, 1981), 293.

16 As a result, I will designate Edwards's imagined interlocutors as his "Arminian opponents."

and the details of his response.[17] My goal is merely to illustrate how the overarching design of his response aids us in determining how he understood the Spirit's union with the saint. In one notebook Edwards summarizes the differences between his view and theirs in four succinct questions. This list helpfully illustrates what he took to be the central issues at stake between his own opinions on the nature of grace and the opinions of his Arminian opponents. It should be pointed out that Edwards is not responding specifically to certain individuals, but rather is responding to this general mood he discerns circulating in the theological world with broad brush strokes.

His first question relates to the nature of saving virtue: "Whether saving virtue differs from common virtue, or such virtue as they [have] that are not in a state of salvation, in nature and kind, or only in degree and circumstances?"[18] His opponents taught that saving virtue, or those uniquely Christian activities (such as divine love) which flow from a state of salvation, differs from "common virtue . . . only in degree and circumstances." In other words, there is a great deal of continuity between common and saving virtue, the only difference being that saving virtues are common virtues exercised to a greater degree. To illustrate, persons may have an "ordinary" or common amount of kindness, and goodwill toward others. Yet if they refine these virtues, working them out to higher degrees of goodness, kindness, and love, then they have passed over into a state of salvation. By contrast Edwards had a completely different understanding of the relationship between common and saving virtue. Like apples and oranges, saving virtue is different from common virtue "in nature and kind." Because fallen human beings by nature do not possess saving virtue, there is nothing they can do to work it into their lives; it must be worked into them by an external agent.

His second question concerns the origin of the heart's saving disposition: "Whether a holy disposition of heart, as an internal governing principle of life and practice, be immediately implanted or infused in the soul, or only be contracted by repeated acts and obtained by human culture and improvement?"[19] For his opponents, since saving virtue is merely the refinement of common virtue, they taught that holiness can be "contracted by repeated acts" which are then worked into virtuous habits that govern one's Christian practice. Thus the origin of a saving disposition of heart resides within the individual's nature; all that is needed is the willingness to work these habits into one's life. Edwards held to a completely different point of view. The heart's saving disposition originates not from inside one's life but from outside, from an external agent who "immediately implant[s] and infuse[s]" this

---

17 For a good summary of this, see Cherry, *Theology of Jonathan Edwards*, 186-215.

18 Edwards, "'Controversies' Notebook: Efficacious Grace," in *The Works of Jonathan Edwards*, vol. 21, *Writings on the Trinity, Grace, and Faith*, ed. Sang Hyun Lee (New Haven: Yale University Press, 2003), 301.

19 Edwards, "'Controversies' Notebook: Efficacious Grace," in Works, 21:301.

"internal governing principle of life" into the soul.

As a result of these previous two criteria, the timing of salvation thus takes place in two entirely different ways, an observation which Edwards makes in his third question: "Whether conversion, or the change of a person from being a vicious or wicked man to a truly virtuous character, be instantaneous or gradual?"[20] If salvation is the process of working out the virtues that naturally reside within one's nature, as Edwards's Arminian opponents taught, then the process of salvation is a gradual affair. If, however, it is wrought in the soul by an external agent, then it is reasonable to conclude that salvation is an instantaneous event, a position Edwards held from his earliest reflections:

> Now it is certain that [in] every man that becomes good, there is a last moment of his being bad and a first moment of his being good, a last moment of his being in a state of damnation and a first moment of his being in a state of salvation; or thus, there is a time before which if he had died but one moment, he would have gone to hell, and after which if he had died but one moment, he would have gone to heaven: this is self-evident.[21]

Edwards's last question contrasts two different models of the Spirit's assistance in salvation: "Whether the divine assistance or influence by which men may obtain true and saving virtue be sovereign and arbitrary, or whether God, in giving this assistance and its effects, limits himself to certain exact and stated rules revealed in his Word and established by his promises?"[22] From Edwards's perspective, his Arminian opponents taught that God had bound himself to the rules and promises revealed in Scripture concerning human salvation, so that upon an individual's performance of certain conditions, God would certainly respond with the rewards of grace and salvation. This made Edwards very uncomfortable because it ultimately obliges God to reward *unregenerate* human activity. If an individual seeks God, then God must respond by being found. If, through repeated acts of love and good deeds, that person cultivates habits of holiness in a state of nature, then God must reward her with salvation. Edwards, by contrast, understands God to be completely free from limiting himself to any external rules, when it comes to blessing individuals with salvation. His ways are "sovereign and arbitrary." An individual who has only common virtue, may indeed seek salvation, and cultivate habits of apparent holiness, but these sincere efforts place God under no obligation to bestow the eternal blessing of redemption in Christ. The decision is completely up to God.

Stepping back for a moment, we may observe that Edwards perceived two very different paradigms of salvation between his view and that of his Arminian opponents. His focused on the sovereign initiative of God who

---

20 Edwards, "'Controversies' Notebook: Efficacious Grace," in *Works*, 21:302.
21 Edwards, "Miscellanies" No. l, in *Works*, 13:168-69.
22 Edwards, "'Controversies' Notebook: Efficacious Grace," in *Works*, 21:302.

instantaneously works a saving disposition deep into the soul at regeneration. By contrast, his opponents envisioned redemption to be the result of a human enterprise whereby an individual concentrates her energies upon moral reformation, gradually attaining a degree of habitual virtue that merits God's reward of salvation. These contrasting visions of regeneration offer us a clue as to how Edwards understood the Spirit's union with the soul. For his opponents the Spirit's work is external to the soul, for Edwards it is internal. According to their principles, because human beings already have the natural means to attain salvation, the Spirit factors into the redemptive equation only as an external coach who presents moral motives to the mind. This, Edwards observes, is very similar to the way that the devil leads people astray by way of temptation:

> According to Dr. Whitby's notion of the assistance of the Spirit, the Spirit of God does nothing in the hearts or minds of men beyond the power of the devil, nothing but what the devil can [do] and nothing showing any greater power in any respect than the devil shows and exercises in his temptations. For he supposes that all that the Spirit of God does is to bring moral maxims and inducements to mind, and to set 'em before the understanding, etc.[23]

This external or "suasive" model of the Spirit's role in the soul's salvation was a common option for understanding the relationship between the Spirit and the soul in conversion. Reformed Protestants, Edwards included, generally found it to be a great assault on the gospel, justification by faith, and the sovereignty of God in humanity's salvation. They thus condemned these views, opting for a very internal work of the Spirit of God in the soul through the process of regeneration. Thus our first clue—Edwards's formulation of the Spirit's infusion in the soul and the Arminian theological background that it was meant to counter—aids us in determining what he meant by the Spirit's union with the soul by allowing us to rule out the "external" model of the Spirit's relationship with the soul. By contrast, Edwards held that the Spirit operates internally to the soul, transforming it from within, and enabling the saint to see, know, and love divine things in a way that is utterly impossible for anyone in a state of nature.

5.1.2 The Movement of the Spirit in the Soul: The Nature of Grace

The second clue Edwards presents that illuminates the nature of the Spirit's union to the soul concerns the nature of grace. From our discussion in chapter two we may recall that the indwelling Spirit is God's grace in the soul, a point Edwards never grows tired of making in his *Treatise on Grace*. "[T]rue saving grace is no other than that very love of God; that is, God, in one of the persons of the Trinity, uniting himself to the soul of a creature as a vital principle,

---

23 Edwards, "'Controversies' Notebook: Efficacious Grace," in *Works*, 21:294.

dwelling there and exerting himself by the faculties of the soul of man, in his own proper nature, after the manner of a principle of nature."[24] As such, grace is none other than the *ad extra* influence and presence of the Spirit. Like holiness, excellency, and happiness, grace is one of the "non-personal" labels that Edwards uses for the Holy Spirit. This, of course, does not mean that the third person of the Trinity is impersonal, it merely indicates that the personal Spirit is identified with these non-personal theological concepts, similar to identifying the Son with the "Word." In this Edwards was merely following the lead of Scripture.[25]

The point of this is that, for Edwards, grace is not some created spiritual substance distinguished from the Holy Spirit. In other words, the Spirit does not pour saving grace into the heart as if it is logically or ontologically distinguished from the Spirit himself. Rather, saving grace is merely the salvific presence of the Holy Spirit in the soul of the godly. This is important because it effectively rules out another model available for conceptualizing the Spirit's union with the soul: the "created grace" model. If, as we saw Edwards argue against the Arminians, the Spirit is not external to the soul but internal to it, transforming the individual through spiritual indwelling, then it might be plausible to posit an intermediary created principle of grace that subsists between the soul and the Spirit of God. This theological option was advanced by Thomas Aquinas in the thirteenth century in response to the position of Peter Lombard. Aquinas argued that if a saint's love were none other than the Holy Spirit causing the movement of love in the soul, as Lombard argued, then that person could not be the proper voluntary agent of love, but a mere instrument in the Spirit's hands. In order for the saint to be the proper actor of love, the Spirit must impart a created "habitual form" to her soul: "It is especially necessary for charity, therefore, that there should be in us some habitual form superadded to our natural power, inclining it to act with charity, and causing it to do so readily and joyfully."[26] Such a gracious created principle, infused by the Holy Spirit, properly becomes part of the individual and her natural disposition, making the soul suitable for both holy acts and the habitation of the Spirit. Two points render this model advantageous to the theologian. First, it prevents any ontological confusion between Creator and creature; if the Spirit is united to the

---

24 Edwards, *Treatise on Grace*, in *Works*, 21:194.
25 "Hence the Spirit of God seems in Scripture to be spoken of as to become *a quality* of the persons in whom it resided, so that they are called spiritual persons; as when we say 'a virtuous man,' we speak of virtue as the quality of the man. 'Tis the *Spirit itself that is the only principle of true virtue in the heart.* So that to be truly virtuous is the same as to be spiritual." Edwards, *Treatise on Grace*, in *Works*, 21:197, emphasis mine.
26 Thomas Aquinas, *Summa Theologica*, 2a2ae, q.23, a.2, in *Nature and Grace: Selections from the Summa Theologica of Thomas Aquinas*, trans. and ed. A. M. Fairweather, Library of Christian Classics, vol. 11 (Philadelphia: Westminster, 1954), 345.

soul via a created principle of grace, then there remains a clear distinction between the Spirit and the saint. Second, this model appears to affirm the integrity and free agency of the saint's actions. The saint, acting out the created principle of grace operating in her own nature, wills holy acts in harmony with the Spirit's indwelling presence, not as a result of any divine necessity that the indwelling Spirit may place upon the soul.

Edwards did not engage the created grace debate that scholastic theologians took up in the high and late medieval periods. Nevertheless, this position shares a few central features with the Arminian doctrine of grace we observed earlier. Both place theological intermediaries between the Spirit and the saint's soul: for Edwards's eighteenth-century opponents, the Spirit is an "external" coach; for the medieval advocate of created grace, the Spirit, while he indwells the soul, interacts with it through the medium of created grace. Furthermore, the Arminian concept of a "habit of grace" closely resembles the medieval understanding of "created grace" in the sense that both are created entities that properly belong to the individual. The saint owns her habit or grace; it is something that properly belongs to her. Thus Edwards's explicit rejection of the Arminian habit of grace can be taken as an indirect rejection of the concept of created grace:

> To speak of a habit of grace as a natural disposition to act grace, as begotten in the soul by the first communication of divine light, and as the natural and necessary consequence of the first light, it seems in some respects to carry a wrong idea with it. . . . The giving one gracious discovery or act of grace, or a thousand, has no proper natural tendency to cause an abiding habit of grace for the future.[27]

Furthermore, the entire drift of his theology was against submitting the Spirit to any created law, grace, or constraint which would limit divine sovereignty. Thus, regardless as to how Edwards would respond to Aquinas's concept of created grace, we can conclude that our second clue—Edwards's understanding of grace as the Holy Spirit's presence in the soul—enables us to rule out the "created grace" model as an option for determining how Edwards understood the Spirit's union with the soul. The Spirit, according to Edwards, does not unite to the soul by way of a created principle of grace which he infuses into the saint's being. For Edwards there is no created intermediary principle between the soul and the Spirit.[28] The Spirit's union with the saint, according

---

27 Edwards, *Treatise on Grace*, in *Works*, 21:196.
28 Thus Anri Morimoto is mistaken when he argues that "the Spirit forms in the regenerate an abiding and intrinsic reality, or an intermediary habit in Thomas [Aquinas]'s words, through which it operates." (*Jonathan Edwards and the Catholic Vision of Salvation*, 47; see his extended argument, 44-50). His argument is based on a metaphor Edwards used to describe the regenerate. The godly, Edwards says, are like jewels in whom the Sun of Righteousness shines, making them not only glow, but transforming them into "little suns" as well (see his *Religious Affections*, in

to Edwards, goes far deeper into the recesses of the saint's soul than the "created grace" model would lead us to believe. Having said this, we are still left with our question: what, according to Edwards, is the nature of the Spirit's union with the soul? Our third clue sheds even more light on the answer.

5.1.3 The Movement of the Spirit in the Soul: Grace "After a Principle of Nature"

While Edwards may not affirm the presence of created grace in the soul, this does not mean that there is no principle of grace in the soul of a saint, an observation which leads us to our third clue. There is indeed such a principle, yet it is not an "it" but a "he," namely the Holy Spirit himself, "acting in union with [the saint's] natural faculties, after the manner of a vital principle."[29] This is Edwards's standard way of describing the Spirit's activity in the soul of a saint: the Spirit of God "acts in the mind of a saint *as an indwelling vital principle.*"[30] He is "given to the true saints to dwell in them, as his proper lasting abode; and to influence their hearts, *as a principle of new nature*, or as a divine supernatural spring of life and action."[31] What does he mean by this? To answer this we must consider two points: first, what Edwards means by the terms "nature" and "principle of nature," and second, turn our attention to what is the essence of the Spirit's own nature.

First, when Edwards uses the term "nature" in these contexts, he has in mind the manner of an agent's activity, rather than the ontological concepts of being or essence. In a letter where he specifically addresses this issue, Edwards defines the term "nature" in the following manner: "That property which is natural to anyone and is eminently his character, I think, is, without abuse of language or going cross to the common use of it, called his proper nature, though [it] is not just the same with his essence. Thus we say concerning an

---

Works, 3:201 and 343). This luminosity is evidence to Morimoto that the saints possess a created gracious principle, distinguished from the Spirit's uncreated grace in the soul. Yet this is the only evidence that Morimoto marshals in support of his conclusion. Edwards makes no explicit statement that there is created grace in the heart of the saint. His metaphor is understood much better in light of the saint's union with the Spirit. The saints, in other words, shine with a light that is truly theirs, not because of a created principle of grace, but because they are completely and entirely united to the Spirit in such a way that his divine light becomes theirs. See below for further explanation. For a critique of Morimoto's thesis, see John J. Bombaro, "Jonathan Edwards's Vision of Salvation," *Westminster Theological Journal* 65(2003): 45-67.

29 Edwards, *Treatise on Grace*, in *Works*, 21:196.
30 Edwards, "Divine and Supernatural Light," in *Works*, 17:411, emphasis mine.
31 Edwards, *Religious Affections*, in *Works*, 2:200, emphasis mine.

exceeding good-natured man, that ingenuity is his very nature."[32] His point is to highlight the fact that the Holy Spirit can properly communicate his nature (i.e., holiness) to creatures, without imparting his essence to them. Thus an agent's nature, in Edwards's writings, most commonly refers to the abiding character of that agent's activity: the thing or things which that person does most naturally and most often. Similarly, Edwards uses the phrase "principle of nature" to emphasize the abiding and habit-like aspect that a nature exerts upon an entity. A principle of natural life in a plant, for instance, is a principle of nature governing that plant's biological growth from seedling to maturity. A principle of natural appetite in animals is a principle of nature which governs their hunger so that they may obtain food for survival. With reference to human volition, Edwards defines a principle of nature as that foundation which is laid in the soul governing a continued course of moral behavior. To put it in another way, it is that animating dynamic which acts as the basis off of which all choices are made.

> By principle of nature in this place, I mean that foundation which is laid in nature, either old or new, for any particular manner or kind of exercise of the faculties of the soul; or a nature manner or kind of exercise of the faculties of the soul; or a natural habit or foundation for action, giving a person ability and disposition to exert the faculties in exercises of such a certain kind; so that to exert the faculties in that kind of exercises, may be said to be his nature.[33]

A second element to consider is the Spirit's own proper nature. We may recall from chapter two that the Holy Spirit is the holy disposition and temper of the Godhead, being the love which the Father and the Son have for each other. Subsequently, there is no distinction between his essence and his principle of nature. The Spirit is not governed by a principle of nature, as if he were subjected to a principle or law above him; rather the Spirit is his own principle of nature; he *is* divine love substantialized and personalized.

We are now in a better position to understand Edwards's meaning when he states that the Spirit operates in the saint after a "principle of nature." While his basic meaning is difficult to pin down, it appears that for Edwards the Spirit mysteriously communicates his own principle of nature, that is his vital life and animating dynamic which summarily consists in divine love, to the saint in such a way that the new principle operating at the deepest levels of her being is the Spirit himself communicated. At the same time, however, this does not threaten the distinction between Creator and creature; the Spirit does not communicate his essence to the saint, merely his nature. *Ad intra*, God's essence and nature are identical and eternally indistinguishable. By contrast, Edwards appears to be saying that *ad extra* God's nature and essence *are*

---

[32] Edwards, Letter No. 66, "To an Unknown Correspondent," after March 13, 1745/6, in *Works*, 16:202.

[33] Edwards, *Religious Affections*, in *Works*, 2:206.

distinguishable: God can communicate his nature *ad extra* to the creature in a mysterious way that does not threaten the Creator-creature distinction.[34] The saints partake *ad extra* of the divine nature but do not partake of the divine essence. God thus "exists" *ad extra* only in his communicated nature, not in an enlargement or extension of his essence. In the rest of this section I will unpack this idea.

The Spirit who indwells the saint as a new principle of nature in her soul, has broken into the principle of her fallen nature, which was dominated by a self-oriented law of self-love, and has infused in her a new governing supernatural principle of divine love. This supernatural principle (which is the Holy Spirit) now exerts itself (himself!) at the deepest levels of saint's volition. What he infinitely desires (the glory of God), the saint now desires in finite, yet increasing, degrees. What he infinitely loves (the Father and the Son), the saint now loves in finite, yet increasing, degrees. She thus acts with acts that are the acts of the Spirit. She loves God with the divine love that is himself the Spirit. This does not result in divinization, as if the saint becomes an extension of God's own being, though Edwards's language at times seems to lean in this direction. This side of heaven, the old Adam remains, and for eternity the principles of created human nature remain. Yet Edwards wants to hold together these two realities in a mysterious tension: that the regenerate saint who loves God and performs acts of holiness is acting from a new nature in her soul that is the Holy Spirit himself communicated. "And indeed," Edwards writes in a 1737 sermon, "the new nature in a saint can *scarce itself* be distinguished from the communication or participation he has of the Spirit of God, or that Spirit dwelling in him united to him, acting as a vital principle in his soul."[35]

Three observations will bring more clarity to the Spirit's operation in the saint "after a principle of nature." The first is that this new supernatural principle of nature that operates in the soul operates in a manner that is patterned from the Spirit's own immanent trinitarian existence. The Spirit does not communicate himself *ad extra* in a way that is distinguished from his inner-trinitarian nature. In "Miscellanies" No. 471 Edwards writes that, "the Spirit of God in the souls of his saints exerts its own proper nature; that is to say, it communicates and exerts itself in the soul in those acts which are its proper, natural and essential acts in itself *ad intra*, or within the Deity from all eternity." In the saint there is a "communication of [the Spirit's] own nature, essential and eternal act."[36] What this ultimately means is that when the saint enjoys God, and has her religious affections stirred, she is actually participating in God's trinitarian life.

Second, this new principle of nature in the saint appears to operate as a non-

---

34 The failure to recognize this aspect of Edwards's theology is the probable source for the charge that Edwards was a panentheist or pantheist (see our discussion below).
35 Edwards, "Striving After Perfection," in *Works*, 19:693, emphasis mine.
36 Edwards, "Miscellanies" No. 471, in *Works*, 13:513-14.

personal natural habit much of the time. Because the Spirit's inner-trinitarian activity is constant, never deviating from being the divine love of the Godhead, his ways within the saint's soul often appear to mimic that of a non-personal habit which abides in the soul. Thus Edwards can say that "the Spirit of God seems in Scripture to be spoken of as to become a quality of the persons in whom it resided."[37] Edwards explores this idea further in "Miscellanies" No. 818, where he notes that the Spirit's activity in the soul reflects two alternative modes: sometimes he appears as a non-personal habit of grace, at other times he appears as a voluntary covenanting agent. "Rightly to understand the nature of the habit of grace, it must be observed that the Spirit of God in the heart of a saint acts both as a natural vital principle, and also as a voluntary agent manifesting care of that heart it is in, lest it should be overcome by temptations, and lest it should fall away."[38] On the one hand, the Spirit allows the saint to partake of God's own holiness, as we have already seen. Through his union to the soul, an abiding principle of divine love is habitually exerted within the life of the saint, giving the impression that a non-personal nature or habitual principle is at work in her faculties of holy knowing and holy loving. Yet at other times, most often in periods of great testing or danger in the Christian life, the Spirit reveals himself in the life of the saint as one who rewards diligence, answers prayer, and punishes spiritual "miscarriages" (or missed opportunities of growing in grace). In these times the Spirit reveals himself as a personal covenant partner in the great drama of redemption.

> The continuance of its actings [i.e., the Holy Spirit's actings] are in many respects like the continuance of the exercises of a nature; the exercises of that wherein nature consists will be continual because nature can't be destroyed. But in other respects 'tis owing to a covenant faithfulness. And more especially does the indwelling Spirit appear in its manner of acting as a voluntary agent – more than a natural necessary principle – in times of the greatest exigence, and in it [*sic* – read "its"] highest acts and fruits, as in those extraordinary exercises of grace that are often given under great trials, terrible persecutions and the like.[39]

What this means is that in those times when the saint is growing in grace, and enjoying close communion with God and Christ, there is some truth to the fact that the Spirit's ways in the soul are hidden, cloaked under an apparent habit of holiness in the individual's behavior. Edwards's Arminian opponents were right to a certain degree: grace is a habit of holy behavior. Yet Edwards would add that grace is so much more, it is really the personal presence of the third person of the Trinity abiding in the soul, united to her faculties and inspiring holy thoughts and actions in her behavior. Furthermore, he would also disagree with their assumption that this habit of holiness is really something that

---

37 Edwards, *Treatise on Grace*, in *Works*, 21:197.
38 Edwards, "Miscellanies" No. 818, in *Works*, 18:529.
39 Edwards, "Miscellanies" No. 818, in *Works*, 18:529.

originates from the individual. The divine love that the saints possess for God does not arise from their natures; rather, it is truly theirs by participation in the Spirit's own divine love, or by a participation in the Spirit's own supernatural principle of nature. The saints' love for God is in some mysterious way God's own love for himself.

This brings us to our third observation, which is best posed in the form of a question: What is the relationship between the Spirit's acts of holiness, and the saints' own holy acts? To be more succinct: Whose holiness is it? If the saint acts according to the supernatural principle of holiness in her soul, then it would appear that those acts are properly her own, for to act out of any principle which resides in one's soul is to own that act, and be the responsible agent for it. Yet as we have seen, this supernatural principle is the Holy Spirit himself who "operates in the minds of the godly by only being in them, uniting itself to their souls, and living in 'em and acting itself."[40] As *he* is this principle, so any activity that is generated from this principle would appear to be most properly the Spirit's own act. How can an act of holiness belong to two agents at the same time?

This is a very perplexing issue in Edwards writings, and it is no surprise that scholars have interpreted him in an number of different ways. On the one hand, we have already seen that one way around these difficulties is to opt for the "created grace" model. If the Spirit indwells the saint (uncreated grace) and infuses the saint with a created principle of grace (created grace), then the conceptual confusion appears to clear up. While the Holy Spirit personally indwells the saint, her holy acts are truly her own for they arise from a created principle of grace which the Spirit infused into her heart. Her acts thus harmonize with the Spirit's. Yet as we have seen, Edwards's writings do not support this model: "[T]he saints are said to be made 'partakers of God's holiness,' not only as they partake of holiness that God gives, but partake of that holiness by which he himself is holy."[41] This is more than a mere harmonization of two different holinesses; it is a real communication of God's own holiness to the saint. There is only one holiness.

On the other hand, some have found traces of pantheism and panentheism in Edwards's thought, positions which seriously compromise the ontological boundaries between Creator and creature. I. Woodbridge Riley, in an older study, wrote that in the mature phases of his career, Edwards lapsed into a "tentative pantheism . . . when a recrudescence of certain primary convictions led [him] to such a view of God's last end in creation as to constitute an almost monistic doctrine of immanence."[42] A more recent study by Douglas Elwood discerns hints of panentheism in Edwards's writings, which seeks to chart a

---

40 Edwards, "Miscellanies" No. 471, in *Works*, 13:513.
41 Edwards, *Treatise on Grace*, in *Works*, 21:195. This "holiness which God gives" is the Spirit, not created grace, for it is "the holiness by which he himself is holy."
42 Riley, *American Philosophy*, 127.

synthetic alternative to classical theism and classical pantheism.

> When he was not absorbed in some controversy or other, his reconstruction of Calvinism often took the form of an attempt at synthesis of the main lines of thought in traditional theism and classical pantheism. He was searching his mind always for an adequate 'third way' that would overcome the much-too-easy alternative between the two views.[43]

This way of understanding the mode of the Spirit's indwelling in the soul presents an alternative solution to the question that has been vexing us. By arguing that Edwards blurs the ontological boundaries between Creator and creature in any way, one can safely assert that the saint's acts of holiness *are* God's own acts of holiness. Yet again we run into problems when we measure this model with other statements Edwards makes where he explicitly denies that this was his position. In an often quoted passage from the *Religious Affections*, he wrote that the saints are not "made partakers of the essence of God, and so are 'Godded' with God, and 'Christed' with Christ, according to the abominable and blasphemous language and notions of some heretics."[44] He is even more clear in his personal correspondence, "the saints are made partakers of [the Holy Spirit's] holiness, as the Scripture expressly declares (Heb. 12:10), and that without imparting to them his essence."[45] Edwards quite clearly did not adhere to a divinization model of the relationship between the Spirit and the saint, where the saint somehow possesses God's essence. But, we may ask, does this get us any closer to answering the question before us? To know what he denies does not necessarily highlight what he affirms. Does Edwards say anything positive about the relationship between our holy acts and the Spirit's?

When Edwards speaks directly to this issue, he sticks close to scriptural terminology and emphasizes the conjunction of the Spirit's acting with the saint's, "So that when [the saints] act grace, 'tis, in the language of the Apostle, 'not they, but Christ living in them.'"[46] Everything pertaining to an individual's participation in redemption, even the saint's own holy knowledge and holy acts, find their ultimate basis in the triune God. The saints thus have spiritual life, not of themselves, but by virtue of a participation in Christ's life.

> The very principle of spiritual life in their souls is no other than the Spirit of Christ himself. So that they live by his life, as much as the members of the body live by the life of the head, and as much as the branches live by the life of the root and stock. 'Because I live, ye shall live also," (John 14:19). We are dead: but our

---

43 Elwood, *Philosophical Theology of Jonathan Edwards*, 6-7.
44 Edwards, *Religious Affections*, in *Works*, 2:203.
45 Edwards, Letter No. 66, "To an Unknown Correspondent," after March 13, 1745/6, in *Works*, 16:203.
46 Edwards, *Treatise on Grace*, in *Works*, 21:196.

'life is hid with Christ in God. When Christ, who is our life, shall appear' (Col. 3:3-4).[47]

He notes that Scripture leads the way in this peculiar conjunction of divine and human activity in many passages. There are many things which

> are represented [in Scripture] as from God and from us. So God is said to convert, and men are said to convert, or turn. God makes a new heart, and we are commanded to make us a new heart. God circumcises the heart, and we are commanded to circumcise [our hearts]. Not merely because we must use the means in order to the effect, but the effect itself is our act and our duty.[48]

For these reasons Edwards is not uncomfortable expressing the relationship between the saint's holy acts and the Spirit's in what we may call "compatiblist" terms, where there is a mysterious and even paradoxical conjunction of divine and human agency. In efficacious grace, Edwards writes, "We are not merely passive in it, nor yet does God do some, and we do the rest, but God does all and we do all. God produces all and we act all. For that is what he produces, our own acts. God is the only proper author and fountain; we only are the proper actors."[49] Thus while he explicitly denies the ontological implications of the divinization model, he affirms what this model affirms based on scriptural grounds: that our holiness *is* God's own holiness in some mysterious way.[50]

These trajectories in Edwards's thought appear to converge around the following idea: that the holy acts which the saint acts out are *truly* hers, yet are *most properly and originally* the Spirit's. On the one hand, the saint acts out a life of holiness and communion with God based upon a new supernatural principle which is infused in her soul and pervades her entire being. Because this principle actuates her behavior at the deepest levels of her soul, the acts that she performs in accordance with this principle are truly her acts. She is the responsible agent for them, and, as we shall see in the following chapter, she merits rewards due to them. Yet in distinction from other principles which animate her behavior (the principle of hunger, the principle of self-love), this supernatural principle does not ultimately arise from her being nor is it ontologically confused with it, but rather consists in the third person of the Trinity dwelling in her soul. Thus she does not "act holiness" in the same way

---

47 Edwards, *Treatise on Grace*, in *Works*, 21:195.
48 Edwards, "Efficacious Grace, Book III," in *The Works of Jonathan Edwards*, vol. 21, *Writings on the Trinity, Grace, and Faith*, ed. Sang Hyun Lee (New Haven: Yale University Press, 2003), 251.
49 Edwards, "Efficacious Grace, Book III," in *Works*, 21:251.
50 William Danaher calls this idea in Edwards's theology "theosis." See his extended discussion on what Edwards means by partaking in the divine nature in *The Trinitarian Ethics of Jonathan Edwards*, 39-49.

she does other human acts which arise from her natural being, such as non-moral acts (eating, sleeping) and "moral" acts which are not actuated by supernatural principles (i.e., sinful acts and good acts done in one's own strength). Acts of holiness are truly hers by way of "participation" in the Spirit's own acting, yet they are ultimately the Spirit's own acts of divine love. The Spirit "communicates" them to the saint not by infusing a created habit of grace in her, but merely by uniting himself to her soul and acting through her. As these acts are nothing but the *ad extra* repetitions of the Spirit's inner-trinitarian activity, the saint's participation in them can really be said to be God's own self-glorification *ad extra*. Thus to answer our question "Whose holiness?" we must keep the following distinction in mind: that a saint's holiness *truly* belongs to her, yet *most properly and originally* belongs to the Spirit.[51] Or, in other words, holiness belongs to both the Spirit and the saint, yet with this distinction: it primarily and fundamentally belongs to the Spirit, but secondarily belongs to the saint by way of participation.[52]

Our third clue—Edwards's understanding of the Spirit acting "as a principle of nature" in the soul—aids our investigation into the nature of Spirit's union with the soul in two ways. First it allows us to rule out yet another model available to us for understanding the nature of this union, the divinization model. However the soul and the Spirit are united through regeneration, Edwards affirmed in the strongest terms that there is no ontological blurring between Creator and the creature. Second, this clue underscores the compatiblist nature of the saint's holy activity and the Spirit's. The saint's holiness is the Spirit's holiness. With this observation we are in a position where we can discern what Edwards means by the Spirit's union with the elect.

5.1.4 The Nature of the Pneumatological Union: A Compatiblist Model

The following picture emerges from our analysis of the three clues we just examined. First, we know what model Edwards did *not* use when he spoke of the Spirit's union with the soul. In one way or another, Edwards explicitly

---

51 Similarly, Sang Hyun Lee observes: "In short, Christian deeds of regenerate persons are 'properly' the acts of the Holy Spirit himself and at the same time 'properly' the deeds of the regenerate human beings themselves." See Lee, "Editor's Introduction," in *The Works of Jonathan Edwards*, vol. 21, *Writings on the Trinity, Grace, and Faith*, ed. Sang Hyun Lee (New Haven: Yale University Press, 2003), 44.

52 Edwards distinguishes between "derived" and "underived" holiness: "Holiness in man, is but the image of God's holiness: there are not more virtues belonging to the image, than are in the original: derived holiness has not more in it, than is in that underived holiness, which is its fountain: there is no more than grace for grace, or grace in the image, answerable to grace in the original." See *Religious Affections*, in *Works*, 2:256.

denies the "external," "created grace," and "divinization" models.[53] Second, we observed that Edwards did not shy away from Scripture's intriguing yet mysterious portrayal of the conjunction of human and divine holy activity. The lives the saints live for Christ is Christ living in them; the holiness they perform is the Spirit's own performance. His strategy in describing the Spirit's union with the soul seems to be that of merely affirming the scriptural boundaries of such a theological concept, not putting forth another "model" which clears up all theological questions. For Edwards, while the Spirit remains ontologically distinct from the creature, he interpenetrates, suffuses, saturates and completely permeates every faculty of the soul when he unites himself to the saint at regeneration. The union is complete. When the saint acts in a holy manner, her acts are truly hers, yet they are hers by participation in the Spirit's holy activity. They become hers by the Spirit's communication of them to the soul, but they never originate with her soul. How can this be? Edwards quite simply does not say. The mechanics of this union lie beyond the reach of human reason, and thus beyond the ability of being placed into a "model." He knows how it works, not how it *is*. He thus does not try to answer the question, but merely articulates the correct dimensions of the biblical mystery.

We may employ a simple, though imperfect, analogy to illustrate Edwards's understanding of this union: the union of soul and body as it has been traditionally understood in the Christian tradition. In a human being we cannot point to where the soul ends and the body begins. Their union is so complete, so entire, that what one does the other does. Yet we know that the soul and the body are distinct. This is somewhat analogous to the union the Spirit makes with the soul of the saint; so complete is this union that the holy acts of divine loving which the saint participates in can truly be said to be her own loving acts of holiness, even though this holiness belongs to the Spirit, or to be more accurate, this holiness *is* the Spirit himself indwelling the soul and united to her faculties. Yet, as in the analogy of soul and body, the distinction between the Spirit and the soul remains. The two are completely united, but there is no ontological confusion between them.

If the preceding analysis is correct, then it would explain two important issues in Edwards studies: his characteristic vocabulary of "communication" and "participation," as well as the confusion in the secondary literature over Edwards's theology of this union. Edwards's vocabulary of the Spirit's "communication" of holiness to the saint, and the saint's "participation" in the divine nature, is not consistent with either of the alternative models others have thought they discerned in his thought. If the Spirit operates within the soul by way of a created principle of infused grace (the "created grace" model), then the saint does not really "participate" in the divine nature and holiness. She merely harmonizes with it through a created holiness that originates from her

---

53 He thus denies the Arminian, the Thomist and the pantheist or panthentheist models of the saint's relationship to God.

being. On the other hand, if the saint is deified, becoming a part of the divine essence, then there would be no need for a "communication" of God's nature to the saint, for the saint would already possess the divine nature by virtue of her virtual ontological identity with God. By contrast Edwards's view, which recognizes the mysterious nature of this union, maintains an inexplicable yet delicate balance: the saint, who is ontologically distinct from God, nonetheless can truly "participate" in the divine nature through a mysterious union with the Holy Spirit, whereby the latter "communicates" his own nature to the saint's mind and heart. How this works, Edwards did not know. That it does happen, Edwards was completely convinced.

Second, by not specifying the particulars of this union, Edwards may have remained biblical to his own satisfaction, but it opened him up to misinterpretation by scholars who later tried to make sense of his theology. Edwards's very "ontological" theological vision, especially in the *End of Creation* where he explores God's rationale for creation from the standpoint of divine ontology, leads him to express his theological opinions in language which at times appears to verge on pantheism. A divinization model of the Spirit's union with the soul would fit well with a pantheistic interpretation of Edwards's theism. This, of course, is not Edwards's view. Likewise, his portrayal of the Spirit as a "habit" of divine love and his consistent use of the neuter pronoun "it" to refer to the Spirit, make it easy to confuse his descriptions of grace in the soul of a saint with that of a created principle united to the soul. Without a detailed explanation given by Edwards himself as to the Spirit's union with the soul, it is not hard to see why scholars have been attracted to interpreting him in one of these other models, especially when the trajectories in his own thought seem to support several of these models. Edwards's own reluctance to speak definitively to the exact nature of this union, however, must caution us from concluding too much from the vectors in his thought. While there may be mild pantheistic tendencies in his language, and while there may be constructs that support a created grace model, Edwards affirms neither of these positions as we have seen. Instead he maintains that the pneumatological union is ultimately a mystery, a glorious and holy mystery, portrayed, yet not fully explained, in the pages of Scripture.[54]

5.2 Faith as a "Union of Soul to Christ as Savior:" The Saint's Union with Christ

Edwards's fascination with the ways of the Spirit in the soul of a saint began early in his life. On February 12, 1725, in one of his last "Diary" entries, he

---

54 For a comparison of Edwards and Gregory Palamas on this point, see "Salvation as Divinization: Jonathan Edwards, Gregory Palamas and the Theological Uses of Neoplatonism," in *Jonathan Edwards: Philosophical Theologian*, ed. Paul Helm and Oliver D. Crisp (Burlington, VT: Ashgate, 2003), 139-60.

writes, "The very thing I now want, to give me a clearer and more immediate view of the perfections and glory of God, is as clear a knowledge of the manner of God's exerting himself, with respect to spirits and minds, as I have, of his operations concerning matter and bodies."[55] In the last section, we examined in detail how he envisioned this union between the Spirit and the soul from the vantage point of its completion, where this union was treated as a given. As we turn our attention away from what this union *is*, and toward the *process* of its establishment, a new complex of issues emerges. What is the relationship between the Spirit's union with the soul and the saint's justification? How does faith in Christ relate to divine love? What is the first act of faith, and how does this virtue relate to that of divine love? What does the saint contribute, if anything, to her justification? In this section and the next we will address these issues, focusing on the saint's union with Christ in this section, and the fruit of this union, justification, in the next. It should be noted that the immediate product of the Spirit's union with the soul is bringing the individual into a union or a living communion with Christ. From this union derives all the benefits of salvation: justification, sanctification, and glorification. This Christ-centered orientation of the Spirit's work in the saint is merely an *ad extra* reflection of God's inner-trinitarian reality, because God, as we saw in chapter two, is "Son-centered" in the sense that he seeks to glorify and love himself through his own Son, who is the perfect substantial image of himself. The saint's movement toward God in the work of redemption, then, is merely God's own activity of seeking his own glory *ad extra*, in a way that mirrors his internal fullness.

Edwards does not explicitly detail the theological sequence that unfolds between the Spirit's union with the saint and the saint's union with Christ. For all intents and purposes, these two events in the soul's salvation are two sides of the same coin. They are the same reality and take place at that the same instant. Nevertheless, Edwards does distinguish them and more importantly affirms a logical order between them: the Spirit's union to the soul's faculties is logically prior to the saint's union to Christ. In this section of the chapter, we will explore the process of these two moments in the saint's regeneration, pausing in between them to examine the nature of faith and its relation to divine love.

5.2.1 The Spirit's Indwelling as the Logical Ground of the Salvation Process

"When the Spirit of God enters the soul" Edwards writes in *Charity in Its Fruits*, "love enters."[56] As mysteriously united to the soul, the Spirit operates there as a new principle of nature, engendering Christ-honoring acts of holy knowing and loving. Curiously, however, Edwards acknowledges that this

---

55 Edwards, "Diary," in *Works*, 16:787.
56 Edwards, *Charity and Its Fruits*, in *Works*, 8:132.

pneumatological union does not always immediately engender a divine love and knowledge *that has Christ as its explicit object.* An individual, in other words, can be united to the Spirit of God and thereby possess a holy regenerate disposition, yet not be aware that she is converted to Christ. Edwards thus distinguishes between the presence of a regenerate disposition in the soul (the Spirit's presence) from the subjective fruit of that disposition: conscious faith in Christ. The upshot of this is that while the Spirit's union to the soul is generally accompanied by a conscious faith in Christ, Edwards leaves the possibility open that an individual, in certain cases, may be saved and not consciously be aware of her faith in Christ: "'Tis the disposition and principle is the thing God looks at [with regard to salvation]. Supposing a man dies suddenly and not in the actual exercise of faith, 'tis his disposition that saves him."[57] Several factors influenced his thinking in this direction, which illustrate this idea in more detail.

The first was his quiet disagreement with his grandfather over the precise moment at which an individual crosses the line of salvation. Solomon Stoddard, along with other "old divines," argued that an individual is saved at the point of an explicit, active faith in Christ.[58] Edwards disagreed. To him, the manifold graces of the Spirit in the soul are so "nearly allied" and connected that, if the presence of one of them is discerned in the soul, one may safely conclude that the entire panoply of Christian graces resides there as well. Thus for an individual in the course of evangelical humiliation, an implicit principle of true faith in Christ may exist in the soul apart from the individual's conscious awareness of it. "So that humiliation that there is in repentance implies a principle of faith, and not only so, but something of the exercise too; so that a person according to the gospel may be in a state of salvation, before a

---

57 Edwards, "Miscellanies" No. 27b, in *Works*, 13:214. Edwards's reflections on this theme were generally developed in the theological context of preparation for salvation and with regard to the difficultly of discerning saving faith in the soul from false faith. Thus, while his ideas may have application to the current issues of religious pluralism and Christian inclusivism, Edwards most likely did not have the notion of an "anonymous Christian" in mind when he wrote on this topic. There is a big difference between not knowing the reality of one's own regeneration in the anxious environment of Puritan preparationism, and the theoretical possibility of the existence of "holy pagans" found in today's discussions of Christian inclusivism. For studies that explore this issue see McDermott, *Jonathan Edwards Confronts the Gods*; John J. Bombaro, "Dispositional Peculiarity, History, and Edwards's Evangelistic Appeal to Self-Love," *Westminster Theological Journal* 66 (2004): 121-57; and Steven M. Studebaker, "Jonathan Edwards' Pneumatological Concept of Grace and Dispositional Soteriology: Resources for an Evangelical Inclusivism," *Pro Ecclesia* 14.3 (2005): 324-39.

58 For the historical background to Edwards's disagreement with his grandfather, see the separate treatments by Thomas Schafer (*Works*, 13:22-24) and Kenneth Minkema (*Works*, 14:40-42) in their Yale edition introductions.

distinct and express act of faith in the sufficiency and suitableness of Christ as Savior."[59]

Second, Edwards's own experience confirmed to him that an individual may be truly converted to Christ without knowing it. In his own conversion experience in 1721, Edwards himself did not pass through the stages of spiritual angst generally acknowledged to be the sure road to conversion, a fact that caused him considerable unrest in the years following his "delightful conviction." "The chief thing," he wrote in his Diary in August 1723, "that now makes me in any measure to question my good estate, is my not having experienced conversion in those particular steps, wherein the people of New England, and anciently the Dissenters of Old England, used to experience it."[60] Later (circa 1740) when describing his own conversion experience in his "Personal Narrative," he likewise mentions that the legal humiliation he passed through before his conversion caused him great concern, "yet," he concedes, "it never seemed to be proper to express my concern that I had, by the name of terror."[61] This "unorthodox" humiliation was subsequently followed by an equally unorthodox conversion, an experience that took him quite by surprise. While he was meditating on 1 Timothy 1:17, "Now unto the King, eternal, immortal, invisible, the only wise God, be honor and glory forever and ever, Amen," a new sense of the glory of God dawned in his soul: "I thought to my self, how excellent a Begin that was; and how happy I should be, if I might enjoy that God, and be wrapt up to God in heaven, and be as it were swallowed up in him." This new sense and longing for God's glory enabled him to pray differently, to see new and glorious things in Scripture, and stirred new affections in his soul. Interestingly however, he did not think of these new experiences as being anything salvific: "it never came into my thought, that there was anything spiritual, or of a saving nature in this."[62] From the vantage point of his middle age, he concluded that at the time of his conversion he showed the signs of regeneration without fully knowing it and without consciously closing with Christ. Faith in Christ indeed was implicit in these early religious longings, for it manifested itself as an active wonder at God's glory, but at the time it did not appear to rise to the level of a conscious embracing of Christ. His theology later would reflect this religious experience. The Holy Spirit seems to have united to his soul, yet had not yet brought forth

---

59 Edwards, "Miscellanies" No. 393, in *Works*, 13:458. For places where he develops similar arguments, see "Miscellanies" Nos. 241, 284, 289, 302, and 317.
60 Edwards, "Diary," in *Works*, 16:779. This fear was not a single event in his early Christian life; see also the entries from December 18, 1722 (*Works*, 16:759) and July 4, 1723 (*Works*, 16:773) for similar confessions.
61 Edwards, "Personal Narrative," in *Works*, 16:791.
62 Edwards, "Personal Narrative," in *Works*, 16:793.

the full fruits of this disposition: a conscious consent to Christ.[63]

Similarly, in his pastoral experience, Edwards found exceptions to the rule that an individual is saved only at the point of active, conscious trust and faith in Christ. By navigating his Northampton congregation through two remarkable periods of revival (the Valley Awakening of 1734-35, and the Great Awakening of 1740-42), Edwards grew intimately acquainted with the religious experiences of dozens and perhaps hundreds of individuals. In his *Faithful Narrative of Surprising Conversions* (1737), he observed considerable latitude in the religious experiences of his parishioners undergoing conversion.[64] While many passed through the stages of preparation and legal humiliation in predictable fashion, some did not, which often resulted in true Christians who were unaware of their converted status: "It has more frequently been so amongst us, that when persons have first had the Gospel ground of relief for lost sinners discovered to them, and have been entertaining their minds with the sweet prospect, they have thought nothing at that time of their being converted."[65] In their experiences Edwards discerned a "secret disposition to fear and love [God through Christ], and to hope blessings from him in this way. And yet they have no imagination that they are now converted."[66] In effect, what Edwards has done here is that he has redefined the degree of saving faith required for salvation. When the Spirit regenerates the soul through union with it, he immediately effects a holy disposition or a "holy repose of soul in God" that may have Christ as its object only "implicitly." Whereas Stoddard demanded a conscious trusting of Christ as the *sine qua non* of salvation, Edwards allowed for the possibility of a nascent and virtually imperceptible faith to be the ground of an individual's salvation. Such a faith is indeed objectively related to Christ, but the individual is not yet conscious of this saving relation. Because of this, it appears that Edwards effectively distinguished between possessing a saving disposition of heart (i.e., a nascent faith, due to the Spirit's union with the soul), and a conscious embrace of Christ in an act of faith. "It must needs be confessed that Christ is not always distinctly and explicitly thought of in the first sensible act of grace (though most commonly he is); but sometimes he is the object of the mind only implicitly."[67]

Finally, when Edwards opened the pages of his Bible, he found other examples of this "implicit" saving faith. The salvation of Old Testament saints was based on Christ's sacrificial work on the cross, yet these individuals were not explicitly conscious of Christ and his work. "It need not be doubted but

---

63 This conscious consent to Christ naturally followed in the subsequent paragraphs of his "Personal Narrative"; see *Works*, 16:796-97.
64 See the second section of *A Faithful Narrative*, in *Works*, 4:159-91.
65 Edwards, *A Faithful Narrative*, in *Works*, 4:173.
66 Edwards, *A Faithful Narrative*, in *Works*, 4:173.
67 Edwards, *A Faithful Narrative*, in *Works*, 4:172.

that many of the ancient Jews before Christ were saved without the sensible exercises of those acts in that manner which is represented as necessary by some divines."[68] Their belief in God's promises and trust in God, according to Edwards, "had no distinct respect to Christ." Nevertheless, Christ was revealed to them apart from their conscious knowing so that "they closed with and cleaved to this their God, husband and Savior, in a way agreeable to the dispensation they were under, and [in] the manner in which Christ revealed himself to them."[69] Edwards argued that before Peter was sent to Caesarea to share the good news of Christ with Cornelius (Acts 10), the latter "did already in some respect believe in Christ, even in the manner that the Old Testament saints were wont to do."[70] Likewise, the paralytic whose sins Jesus forgave (Matt 9:2) and the disciples themselves before Christ's crucifixion, Edwards argued, were all saved prior to a complete understanding of the gospel.[71] What all these individuals share in common is a salvific disposition, which in essence *is* the Spirit united to their souls. As he seeks and loves the Son within the Trinity, so he will lead the individual to whom he is united, to grow more in the love and knowledge of Christ's excellencies, *even if that person is not yet aware of Christ and his work.* These examples demonstrate Edwards's openness to the possibility that the Spirit may indwell an individual, and yet due to various circumstances—such as bad theology, or living in a different dispensation in salvation history—that person may not possess a conscious faith in Christ and his salvific work.[72]

While the Spirit's union with the soul commonly accompanies a subjective faith in Christ, these exceptions to the general rule reveal that Edwards distinguishes between two "moments" in the process of salvation: the objective, pneumatological union with the saint's soul, and the soul's subjective faith in Christ. The Spirit's union to the soul, being the new holy disposition within it, is the bedrock of a person's salvation. For him, this principle is axiomatic to his soteriology: a principle of faith, grace and holiness must exist in the soul prior to any holy act of faith and grace. It "cannot be true," Edwards wrote with respect to theologians like Stoddard, "that none can be in a state of salvation before they have particularly acted a reception of the Lord Jesus Christ for a Savior." The reason? "There must be the principle before there can be the action, in all cases," later adding that "sanctification must be in the soul before one [act of grace] is in the mind."[73] Thus while there is an organic

---

68 Edwards, "Miscellanies" No. 27b, in *Works*, 13:214.
69 Edwards, "Miscellanies" No. 663, in *Works*, 18:201.
70 Edwards, "Miscellanies" No. 840a, in *Works*, 20:56.
71 Edwards, "Miscellanies" No. 1283 in *Works*, 23:230.
72 Edwards also argues that elect infants are truly saved apart from a conscious trust in Christ. See his various and somewhat scattered statements on infant salvation in "Miscellanies" Nos. 78, 289, 302, 492, 849, and the last section of 1129.
73 Edwards, "Miscellanies" No. 77, in *Works*, 13:244-45.

relation between the events that comprise an individual's salvation (the Spirit's indwelling, union with Christ, faith, and justification), Edwards conceived of the Spirit's union to the soul to be the most basic to the process. Like the Father in the Trinity, who cannot be separated from the Son and the Spirit, and who is fully equal with them yet first in order, the pneumatological union, while inseparable from union with Christ and justification in the progression of salvation, and equally necessary to the salvation of a sinner, is nonetheless "first" in the logical order of Edwards's soteriology. We are now in a position to analyze another union which is central in the reality of salvation, and in which the Holy Spirit plays a vital role: the saint's union with Christ. Yet before we treat this topic it is necessary to explore what Edwards considered to be the instrument of this union: faith.

5.2.2 Faith and Its Relation to Divine Love

The reason for treating faith at this juncture is not only because it is crucial to Edwards's discussion of union with Christ, but also because we here stand at the crossroads of what some have considered to be two very different "worlds" in Edwards's theology. On the one hand, it is said we have the "philosophical" Edwards: the one who was consumed with the intricacies of God's ontology, idealism, human psychology, and dispositional principles of activity. Here "divine love" takes center stage. On the other hand, we have the "Protestant" Edwards: the Edwards who is concerned with preserving Puritan theology and spiritual life, both of which are grounded in the forensic theology of justification by faith alone. Here "faith" takes center stage. The integration of these two sides in Edwards's thought has rarely been appreciated by scholars.[74] Edwards, however, addresses in detail the relationship between love and faith in his "Faith" notebook.[75] In this section, by exploring how he envisions the relationship between faith and divine love, I not only seek to prepare us for our discussion of union with Christ, but I also wish to suggest that a greater unity exists between these two supposed different sides of his thought than has been recognized.

The first point we encounter when trying to pinpoint Edwards's understanding of faith is the vast complexity of the subject. By his own

---

[74] Morimoto suggests the opposite is the case, namely, that Edwards failed to integrate his theology of justification with that of conversion and regeneration: "What is more surprising than the sparseness of its mention is that Edwards hardly shows any effort to relate the theme of justification to his thoughts on conversion. The pronouncements on justification stand, on their own, without being woven into a systematic whole." *Jonathan Edwards and the Catholic Vision of Salvation*, 72.

[75] Jonathan Edwards, "Faith," in *The Works of Jonathan Edwards*, vol. 21, *Writings on the Trinity, Grace, and Faith*, ed. Sang Hyun Lee (New Haven: Yale University Press, 2003), 417-68.

admission, faith is an extremely complex concept: "It may be more perfectly described than defined by a short definition. By reason of the penury of words, a great many words expresses better than one or two."[76] Throughout "Faith," Edwards wrestled with fine-tuning a definition of faith. "Upon the whole, the best, and clearest, and most perfect definition of justifying faith, and most according to the Scripture, that I can think of, is this, faith is the soul's entirely embracing the revelation of Jesus Christ as our Savior." Yet more definitions come later, even in this entry; "Faith is the whole soul's active agreeing, according and symphonizing with this truth, all opposition in judgment and inclination, so far as he believes, being taken away."[77] Key to his understanding of faith was a sense of personal need of Christ *as Savior* arising out of an awareness of one's own sinfulness.

> The whole act of reception suitable to the nature of the gospel and its relation to us, and our circumstances with respect to it, is best expressed (if it be expressed in one word) by the word [faith]. . . . [T]he Lord Jesus Christ in the gospel appears principally under the characteristic of a Savior, not so much of a person absolutely excellent; and therefore the proper act of reception of him consists principally in the exercise of a sense of our need of him and of his sufficiency, his ability, his mercy and love, . . . and an answerable application of the soul to him for salvation.[78]

Edwards's efforts to describe faith were attempts to encompass the multiple themes he found Scripture relating to faith rather than attempts at putting forth a definitive definition. Such was the complexity of what he found to be contained in the incredibly rich concept of biblical faith.

The primary reason for this complexity has to do with the fact that all Christian virtues and graces are ultimately one, or in his words, they are all "concatenated" or "implied" in one another. "The graces of the Spirit, especially those that more directly respect God and another world, are so nearly allied that they include one another; and where there is the exercise of one, there is something of the other exercised with it: like strings in consort, if one is struck, others sound with it; or like links in a chain, if one is drawn, others follow."[79] His interest in delineating Christian experience, and his desire to discern why it is that faith is singled out as that which justifies, led him further into the Scriptures in an attempt to discern the uniqueness of faith from the other Christian graces. As such, his notebooks are saturated with reflections on the connections and distinctions between the various graces, where he

---

76 Edwards, "Faith," No. 44, in *Works*, 21:424.
77 Edwards, "Faith," No. 46, in *Works*, 21:424.
78 Edwards, "Faith," No. 53, in *Works*, 21:427.
79 Edwards, "Miscellanies" No. 393, in *Works*, 13:458. Also see sermon 12, "Christian Graces Concatenated Together," in the Charity sermon series (*Works*, 8:326-38).

analyzes the relationships between faith and hope,[80] between faith and its Old Testament manifestations of trust, belief, and finding refuge in God,[81] and between faith and love.[82] While many of these entries remain unsystematized reflections on the various graces of the Spirit, two consistent themes run through them that relate to our discussion.

First, Edwards held that divine love in the soul is the foundation of saving faith. The two are organically related and cannot be separated. "[L]ove is the essence of faith," Edwards wrote in a "Miscellanies" entry on justification (No. 820); "yea, [it] is the very life and soul of it, and the most essential thing in it."[83] This is consistent with what we have observed throughout his theology: true virtue and the summation of grace in the heart is ultimately one reality, the presence of the Spirit united to the soul's faculties. As the Spirit is divine love, the individual to whom the Spirit is united will act all graces, including faith, out of a fundamental disposition of divine love. Thus in an earlier "Miscellanies" entry on justifying faith (No. 218), Edwards is able to categorize the Christian graces around a central hub of a loving disposition that is present in the heart:

> 'Tis the same agreeing or consenting disposition that according to the divers objects, different state or manner of exerting, is called different names. When 'tis exerted towards a Savior, [it is called] faith or trust; when towards one that governs us and orders our affairs for us, faith or trust; when towards one that tells and teaches us, faith or belief; when towards a Savior, a governor and instructor (or king, priest and prophet) in one, by no other name than faith; when towards doctrines, whither of things past, present or to come, faith or belief; when towards unseen good things promised, faith and also hope; when towards a gospel or good news, faith; when towards persons excellent, love; when towards commands, obedience; when towards God with respect to changes, 'tis properly called resignation; when with respect to calamities, submission.[84]

The second theme Edwards highlighted is the fact that while faith is organically related to divine love and springs from it, faith nonetheless is distinct from it in one significant aspect, an aspect which has nothing to do with the nature of divine love in itself, but rather has all to do with where it is expressed: divine love indwells a *sinful* soul in need of redemption. Because faith is essentially divine love in the soul, faith, in short, is the leading and primary act of divine love in a *fallen* human soul.

---

80 Edwards, "Faith," Nos. 49, 52.
81 Edwards, "Faith," Nos. 81, 92, 107, 110-20.
82 Edwards, "Faith," Nos. 20, 105, 108. See also "Miscellanies" Nos. 411 and 820; and sections from the Charity sermon series (*Works*, 8:137-41 and 330-31).
83 Edwards, "Miscellanies" No. 820, in *Works*, 18:531.
84 Edwards, "Miscellanies" No. 218, in *Works*, 13:344-45.

> Though true virtue be essentially the same in all – the same in mankind before and after the fall, the same in all intelligent creatures, both men and angels – yet the leading exercise of true virtue may differ according to the different nature, state and circumstances of the creature, the different relation it stands in to God, and its different concern with its Creator, and the diverse principal means and manner of God's manifesting himself to the creature, and the different intercourse he maintains with it. And if these things are considered, it will appear reasonable every way that FAITH should be the leading virtue of fallen man, a subject of the salvation of Jesus Christ, or candidate for it, to whom God principally makes himself known by the gospel of Jesus Christ.[85]

Edwards brings out this subtle distinction between faith and love in two private notebook entries. In "Miscellanies" No. 507 he wrote that faith is the "active, direct suiting and according of the soul to the Redeemer, and to his salvation and the nature of it—to salvation as salvation—and under the notion and quality of a free gift, a suiting with the way wherein it is procured and made ours." Faith respects Christ *as Savior*, and embraces him or "suits itself" to him as Savior. By contrast, Edwards argued that the other virtues, while intimately connected to faith, do not "directly" suit the soul to salvation and to Christ. For instance, he continues in the same entry, "love to God is rather a suiting or according of the soul to the nature of God" in general, not specifically to Christ as Savior.[86] Here divine love to God appears to be a broader, more general concept than faith; divine love "accords" itself to God's nature, which is Edwards's way of saying that there is a symphonizing of the soul's knowledge, affections, dispositions, and actions to God's glorious nature. Had human race not fallen into sin, their primary expression of divine love would not have been faith, but this more general according of the soul to God's nature. Yet because of the fallen condition of the human soul, Edwards appears to be saying that the way the Spirit communicates and expresses divine love in the soul is primarily through faith in Christ as one's Savior from sin. Faith is thus the leading expression of divine love in the soul of fallen humanity. "[Faith] is called 'believing,' because believing is the first act of the soul in embracing a narration or revelation; and embracing, when conversant about a revelation or thing declared, is more properly called by that name than loving or choosing."[87]

A similar distinction between faith and love can be observed in entry No.102 in his "Faith" notebook. There he describes faith as the "soul's active closing or uniting with Christ," and suggests that this act of uniting to Christ must be understood in a very specific way. "Such is the nature of it, that it is not merely like the various parts of a building that are cemented and cleave fast together,

---

85 Edwards, "Miscellanies" No. 1156, in *Works*, 23:70.
86 Edwards, "Miscellanies" No. 507, in *Works*, 18:53.
87 Edwards, "Faith," No. 39, in *Works*, 21:423.

or as two marbles and precious stones may be joined so as to become one."[88] Such a union of love as this one may be found among equals like among members of the church, or between "moral" equals like between God and the elect angels who both have no sin. Humanity, however, stained with sin, is not in this kind of relationship to God, and thus the kind of love or union that must exist between the soul and Christ must be understood in a different way using a different metaphor. He continues,

> [Faith] is such a kind of union as there [is] between a head and living members, between stock and branches, between which and the head, or stock, there is such a kind of union, that there is an entire, immediate, perpetual dependence for and derivation of nourishment, refreshment, beauty, fruitfulness and all supplies, yea, life and being. . . . Now such an union as this, when turned into act . . . is something else besides mere love: it is an act most properly expressed by the name of faith.[89]

The point of these entries suggests that Edwards understood the relationship between divine love and faith to be a complicated and subtle one. Divine love is the essence of all true virtues, including faith; yet faith is the "leading" expression of divine love in the soul of a *fallen* human being. "Mere love" is a glorious reality that exists infinitely as the Holy Spirit within the Trinity. It is enjoyed by the holy angels and would have been the norm among humanity had not they plunged themselves into sin. Yet as it now shines through the prism of a fallen human being, this love will show forth additional elements not originally included in "mere love:" a deep sense of dependence and trust in Christ as Savior, a personal closing with Christ, and a sense of humility before him. This disposition Edwards termed faith. Because of the presence of sin in God's image bearers, the whole affair of loving God by those image-bearers will center upon Christ through acts of faith. This leads us to our next topic of consideration, which is the essence of faith's act, an act of union with Christ.

5.2.3 Faith as an Act of Union with Christ

While Edwards believed that faith encompassed a complex, multidimensional reality that cannot be easily defined, he was sure about one of its essential features: faith is in essence an act of union with Christ. "Faith," he wrote, "is the proper active union of the soul with Christ as our Savior, as revealed to us in the gospel."[90] The efforts we saw Edwards making earlier at defining the essence of faith—faith as "embracing Christ," as "receiving a Savior," as "closing with Christ"—each reflect that a mysterious relation is established by faith between the believing individual and Christ, a relation which Scripture

---

88 Edwards, "Faith," No. 102, in *Works*, 21:444.
89 Edwards, "Faith," No. 102, in *Works*, 21:444-45.
90 Edwards, "Faith," No. 106, in *Works*, 21:446.

signifies by Christians being "members of Christ" and being "in Christ." In continuity with his Reformed theological tradition, Edwards called this relation the believer's union with Christ.[91] He distinguished himself from that heritage in two ways. First, rather than articulating faith as the instrument of justification, as his Reformed predecessors had done, Edwards articulated faith as the instrument of receiving Christ.[92] Since "receiving Christ" is not distinct from entering into a union with Christ, faith is not logically distinct from a believer's union with Christ: "God don't give those that believe, an union *with*, or an interest *in* the Savior, in reward for faith, but only because faith is the soul's active uniting with Christ, or is itself the very act of union, on their part."[93] Second, Edwards cast his theology of faith and the believer's union with Christ in the philosophical categories of his theory of excellency, which highlights once again the centrality of divine love. "[T]he proper active union of the soul with Christ as our Savior, as revealed to us in the gospel, is the soul's active *agreeing* and *suiting* or *adapting* itself in its act to the exhibition God gives us of Christ and his redemption."[94] The desperate soul, entombed in the prison of sin and sensible of her need for a Savior, in one act apprehends, embraces, loves, and "closes with" Christ as a glorious Savior, an act which "suits," "fits," or harmonizes its faculties with Him who is revealed and his message of salvation. Faith unites one to Christ, and this act of "unition" is at its core an act of love.[95]

Edwards's understanding of the believer's union with Christ comprises two important factors. First, as an individual's union to Christ is the act of love as we saw above, it is also a *mutual* act of love between Christ and the believer. "'Tis fit," Edwards wrote in "Miscellanies" No. 568, "that in order to an union between two living, acting beings, so as that they should be looked upon one, there should be the mutual act of each, the consent of both, that each should receive [the] other, and actively join themselves to each other."[96]

Second, the result of this union is a "oneness" between the individual and Christ. What is this oneness? Again, Edwards does not specify, but he does indicate that it is not something that is merely nominal, but rather has a real foundation in the objective order of being. To put it in another way, this union

---

91 See John Calvin, *Institutes of the Christian Religion*, trans. Ford Lewis Battles, ed. John T. McNeill (Philadelphia: Westminster, 1960), vol. 1, pages 569-71 (3.2.24); and Heppe, *Reformed Dogmatics*, 511-12. For an excellent study of the theme of union with Christ in Puritan literature, see R. Tudur Jones, "Union with Christ: the Existential Nerve of Puritan Piety," *Tyndale Bulletin*, 41.2 (1990):186-208.
92 Edwards, "Justification by Faith Alone," in *Works*, 19:153. See also Cherry, *Theology of Jonathan Edwards*, 92.
93 Edwards, "Justification by Faith Alone," in *Works*, 19:158.
94 Edwards. "Faith," No. 106, in *Works*, 21:446-47, emphasis mine.
95 Edwards writes in "Miscellanies" No. 398: "Now there is no other way of different spirits' being united, but by love." (*Works*, 13:463).
96 Edwards, "Miscellanies" No. 568, in *Works*, 18:105.

is not merely something in God's mind, as if God only looks upon the believer and Christ as being one; there is a mysterious, inexplicable bond between them, that unites them, and that enables believers to be treated under the new law of Christ, where he justly takes their punishment upon himself, and they mercifully receive his resurrection life. "This relation or union to Christ, whereby Christians are said to be *in* Christ (whatever it be), is the ground of their right to his benefits. . . . Our being *in* him is the ground of our being accepted."[97] Later he continues this reasoning: "What is real in the union between Christ and his people, is the foundation of what is legal; that is, *it is something really in them, and between them,* uniting them, that is the ground of the suitableness of their being accounted as one by the Judge."[98] This union, this "something really in them, and between them," entitles them to partake of the divine life in a way similar to the way the divine Son partakes of the inner-trinitarian life. "For, being members of God's own Son, they are in a sort partakers of his relation to the Father: they are not only sons of God by regeneration, but by a kind of communion in the sonship of the eternal Son."[99] Salvation ultimately brings the saint to partake of the eternal Son's relation to the Father, and to commune in his sonship. As the Son receives the Father's love in the Spirit, and returns to him the same love in the same Spirit, so the saints receive and return this love in the Spirit by virtue of their union to Christ. The shape of their redemption, from Edwards's point of view, is trinitarian; the internal dynamics of the inner-trinitarian community are thus *externalized* through the regeneration of a believer.

In summarizing the second section of this chapter, the unfolding logic of Edwards's theology of regeneration appears to run as follows. The Spirit first unites himself to the soul, whereby the gracious principles of divine love are infused into the soul's faculties. This divine love expresses itself primarily in the fallen soul as *faith* in Christ as Savior, which is essentially an act of union with Christ, a union which mysteriously makes Christ and the believer one. While both the pneumatological union and the believer's union with Christ are theologically distinct, they are essentially two aspects of one basic reality: the reality of regeneration. As we saw above, there are unusual exceptions to the temporal unfolding of regeneration. Explicit faith in Christ, where the individual consciously closes with him, may not be experienced due to various factors: a "silent" conversion (like Edwards's own), an infant conversion, or the conversion of an Old Testament saint. Nonetheless, Edwards held that in these exceptions, while there was not conscious faith in Christ, there was indeed an implicit or nascent faith in him, thus effecting a true union with Christ. What needs to be pointed out in all of these cases of conversion is the role the Holy Spirit plays at each step. It is clear that he is the active agent in the logical

---

97 Edwards, "Justification by Faith Alone," in *Works*, 19:156.
98 Edwards, "Justification by Faith Alone," in *Works*, 19:158; emphasis mine.
99 Edwards, "The Excellency of Christ," in *Works*, 19:593.

beginning of the process, at the point when he unites himself to the soul of an elect saint. He is most explicitly the bond of this union. Yet as he is united to the soul's faculties, and exerts himself there as a principle of nature, it is he who awakens divine love in the soul in the form of faith. The faith of the believer is most properly the saint's own act, yet by virtue of the mysterious union of the Spirit with the saint, and by virtue of the fact that faith is essentially divine love expressed in the soul, this faith is most originally the Spirit himself, acting in union with the soul's faculties. The union effected through faith, the believer's union with Christ, likewise is pneumatologically grounded in that the faith that one loves Christ with, and the love that Christ loves the saint with, are both the same reality: the Spirit himself. Thus in each of these stages at the beginning of the redemptive process, the Spirit's presence is sometimes explicit, sometimes hidden, yet "omnipresent" in the form of divine love, uniting disparate parties together in Christ, and ultimately in the trinitarian harmonies. We will explore these themes further in the believer's sanctification and glorification in the chapters to come. Before this we must deal with one other important issue which relates to the Christian's union with Christ: the believer's justification, and how it is by faith alone.

5.3 The "Real" and the "Legal:" Union with Christ and Justification

The theologically astute reader sensitive to Protestant issues may at this point be tempted to ask how it is that the doctrine of justification by faith fits into Edwards's soteriology. We have indicated that the real union between the believer and Christ is the objective basis for the forensic aspects of Edwards's soteriology, aspects which include the pardon of sin, the imputation of Christ's righteousness to the believer, and justification. A saint's union with Christ is in essence an act of faith, performed by the believer, a faith which we have seen is intimately connected with the divine love that the Spirit infuses in the soul at the moment of regeneration. Divine love in any form, including its expression in an individual's faith, is morally excellent and aesthetically beautiful in Edwards's theological world. If this is the case then does God bestow justification upon the believer *because* of his regard to the moral excellency inherent in the believer's faith in Christ? In other words, is faith a virtue that is meritorious of justification? If Edwards were to answer yes to these questions, then he would indeed be straying far from his Protestant Reformation heritage. Furthermore, the structure of his theology might seem to lean in this direction if we are to judge it solely on the data we have already reviewed. Edwards, however, does not come to these conclusions, and skillfully maneuvers through the corridors of theological subtlety to avoid the charge that an individual is justified by any moral excellency that is inherent in them. It is these issues that will briefly occupy our attention in this concluding section.

Edwards's understanding of the meaning of justification followed the standard definition that circulated in Puritan and evangelical circles.

Justification comprises two main elements: a "negative" righteousness, whereby the believer is "free[d] from any obligation to punishment," as well as a "positive" righteousness, whereby the same person possesses Christ's righteousness by imputation, a righteousness which entitles her to the reward of eternal life. "A person is said to be justified when he is approved of God as free from the guilt of sin, and its deserved punishment, and as having that righteousness belonging to him that entitles to the rewards of life."[100] Edwards, following Pauline language, was adamant to assert that the way a person comes to be justified is by faith, not by works.

> When it is said that we are not justified by works, nothing else can be intended but this, viz. that nothing that we do procures reconciliation with God for us and an admittance into his favor by virtue of the loveliness of it, or by reason of any influence the loveliness of it has to move God's love or favorable respect. . . . God don't justify us in this manner, upon the account of any act of ours, whether it be the act of faith or any other act whatsoever, but only upon the account of what the Savior did.[101]

Edwards's meaning cannot be clearer: Christ's work alone is that which merits justification for the elect; there is no act or disposition in the person which God regards as morally excellent in itself and meritorious of justification.

More important, perhaps, is what Edwards does *not* mean by these statements. He does not mean that we do nothing at all in the process of justification. Continuing the quote from "Miscellanies" No. 416 (quoted above), he states that

> But 'tis something that we do, that renders it in God's account (as the case now stands, there being a Savior) a meet thing, that God should let go his anger and admit us into his favor, as it may render it a meet thing in the sight of God that we in particular should be looked upon as united to the Savior, and [as] having the merit of what he did and suffered (upon the account of which we are so justified) belonging to us.[102]

This "something that we do" is of course trusting in Christ in an act of faith, an act that unites us to Christ. While Edwards affirms that this human act is *crucial to* justification, he is equally adamant that it does not *merit* justification. Furthermore, this act of faith is not void of spiritual goodness: "There is indeed something in man that is really spiritually good, that is prior in the order of nature to justification, viz. faith. But there is nothing that is accepted as goodness till after justification."[103] This is consistent with what we have seen

---

100 Edwards, "Justification by Faith Alone," in *Works*, 19:150.
101 Edwards, "Miscellanies" No. 416, in *Works*, 13:475.
102 Edwards, "Miscellanies" No. 416, in *Works*, 13:475-76.
103 Edwards, "Miscellanies" No. 712, in *Works*, 18:341.

so far: faith is divine love expressing itself in the heart of a sinner, and divine love in any form is spiritually good, excellent and worthy of God's regard. Yet the crucial point is that even though faith is something that we do towards justification, and even though this faith is morally excellent and virtuous, God does not regard it as worthy of reward "prior in the order of nature to justification."

What Edwards is attempting to juggle here are two realities which he envisions to be central to the biblical presentation of salvation. On the one hand, God does not justify the sinner based on the moral virtue and excellency inherent in the act of faith. To do so would not only contradict many biblical passages, it would also encourage spiritual pride and thus threaten the humility that is fundamental to the relationship between Christ and his people. On the other hand, there is a real, morally excellent principle of divine love infused and present in the soul "prior in the order of nature to justification," namely the Holy Spirit, united to the soul's faculties. These two biblical facts led Edwards to the following apparently awkward conclusion: that "prior in the order of nature to justification" God does not regard his own holiness present in the soul. If this is so, then what does God regard?

Edwards's answer is two-fold. The most obvious answer is that God regards Christ's righteousness. It is his moral virtue that he loves and regards as meritorious of salvation on behalf of the sinner. Yet how does this regard for Christ's righteousness include the saint? Edwards's intriguing answer is that God also has a *natural* regard to the unity of faith, union with Christ, and justification. God, in other words, out of a love to an external, natural order and not out of a love to the inherent worthiness of faith in the saint, has constituted the universe in such a way that these three realities—faith, union with Christ, and justification—go together.[104] If one is present, then by reason of divine constitution the others are present as well. An individual's faith in Christ is thus regarded by God as naturally "fit" to union with Christ and justification, not *morally* fit. Edwards explained this distinction in his sermon on "Justification by Faith:"

> There is a two-fold fitness to a state; I know not how to give them distinguishing names otherwise than by calling the one a *moral*, and the other a *natural* fitness: a person has a moral fitness for a state, when his moral excellency commends him to it, or when his being put into such a good state, is but a fit or suitable testimony of regard or love to the moral excellency, or value, or amiableness of any of his qualifications or acts. A person has a natural fitness for a state when it appears meet and condecent that he should be in such a state or circumstances, only from the natural concord or agreeableness there is between such qualifications and such circumstances; not because the qualifications are lovely or unlovely, but only because the qualification, and the circumstances are like one another, or do in

---

104 Samuel Logan, "The Doctrine of Justification in the Theology of Jonathan Edwards," *Westminster Theological Journal* 46 (1984): 37.

their nature suit and agree or unite one to another. And 'tis on this latter account only that God looks on it fit by a natural fitness, that he whose heart sincerely unites itself to Christ as his Savior, should be looked upon as united to the Savior, and so having an interest in him; and not from any moral fitness there is between the excellency of such a qualification as faith, and such a glorious blessedness as the having an interest in Christ.[105]

Edwards does not artificially concoct this distinction to protect the Protestant concerns in his soteriology. It is rather a derivative of a fundamental distinction he makes in his theology, a distinction which runs through his thought like a continental divide. Throughout his theology, we find Edwards distinguishing between supernatural and natural dimensions in his thinking. For instance in aesthetics he distinguishes primary beauty from secondary beauty;[106] in ethics, moral and natural ability/inability;[107] in epistemology, the "sense of the heart" from natural knowledge;[108] and in theology proper, God's "moral" attributes from his "natural" attributes.[109] By employing this distinction to the kind of fitness faith has to the state of justification, Edwards was merely extending this fundamental characteristic of his thought to his soteriology.[110]

---

105 Edwards, "Justification by Faith Alone," in *Works*, 19:159. See also "Miscellanies" No. 1260a, in *Works*, 23:196, as well as his comments on this distinction in the justification passages found in his "Controversy" notebook; Jonathan Edwards, "'Controversy' Notebook: Justification," in *The Works of Jonathan Edwards*, vol. 21, *Writings on the Trinity, Grace, and Faith*, ed. Sang Hyun Lee (New Haven: Yale University Press, 2003), 339-40, 354, and 366.

106 See the first three chapters of Jonathan Edwards, *Dissertation II. The Nature of True Virtue*, in *The Works of Jonathan Edwards*, vol. 8, *Ethical Writings*, ed. Paul Ramsey (New Haven: Yale University Press, 1989), 539-74, for a detailed analysis of the differences between primary and secondary beauty. For helpful secondary sources, see Paul Ramsey's comments in his editor's introduction to volume eight of the Yale edition (*Works*, 8:35-7), and Roland Delattre's "Beauty and Theology: A Reappraisal of Jonathan Edwards," in *Critical Essays of Jonathan Edwards* ed. William J. Scheick (Boston: G. K. Hall & Co., 1980), 136-50; Delattre's article is a succinct summary of his monograph-study, *Beauty and Sensibility in the Thought of Jonathan Edwards* (New Haven: Yale, 1968).

107 See Part I, section 4, "Of the Distinction of Natural and Moral Necessity and Inability," in *Freedom of the Will* (*Works*, 1:156-62). For historical context and helpful critique of Edwards's views, see chapters 1-2 in Allen Guelzo's *Edwards on the Will: A Century of American Theological Debate* (Middletown, Conn.: Wesleyan University Press, 1989), 17-86.

108 See Edwards's well-known "Sense of the Heart" entry in his "Miscellanies" No. 782, in *Works*, 18:452-66; as well as his sermon, "A Divine and Supernatural Light," in *Works*, 17:408-26.

109 See *Religious Affections* (*Works*, 2:253-59).

110 George Hunsinger analyzes this and other aspects of Edwards's doctrine of justification in his article, "Dispositional Soteriology: Jonathan Edwards on

In summary, God's natural regard for the unity of faith, union with Christ, and justification, and not his love for the moral excellency of faith in the believer, leads him to justify the sinner who in faith has joined herself to Christ. Because the believer's own act of faith is the product of the Spirit's union to the soul's faculties, the entire affair, from the widest possible angle, is ultimately and entirely of God: God reaches down in his Spirit, uniting himself to the soul, awakening in her faculties divine love in the form of faith in Christ, which effects the believer's union with Christ. God then, in the same act, looks down upon Christ, his beloved Son, in whom resides the image of his own excellent holiness, and automatically grants all those united to him by a real, mysterious bond of union, the pardon purchased by Christ, and the eternal blessings that are due to him. The individual truly acts, uniting herself to Christ. But behind the believer's acts is the Holy Spirit, catching up the believer in the external loop of God's self-regard by uniting her to Christ, and causing her to love, cherish, and humbly devote herself to the Redeemer who saved her from the wrath to come. What we have here in effect is the same pattern of the inner-trinitarian dynamic externalized: God the Father's self regard (the Spirit), manifesting itself in love to his own glorious, infinite and eternal image (the Son). The only additions to this formula are those elect ones who are mysteriously caught up in this current by the Spirit of God. The Holy Spirit works as the bond of union, uniting the sinner to God, in very much the same way he unites the members of the eternal Trinity. With these acts, the Spirit introduces the saint into the glorious society of the Trinity. In the following chapters we shall see how the Spirit continues this work in the ongoing sanctification of the believer at both the individual and corporate levels, and in the final glorification of the church.

Justification by Faith Alone," *Westminster Theological Journal* 66 (2004): 107-20. There he argues that Edwards's soteriology significantly stretches the limits of the normative Reformed understanding of justification. For an analysis of Edwards's doctrine of justification which sees more continuity between Edwards and his Reformed heritage, see Jeffrey C. Waddington, "Jonathan Edwards's 'Ambiguous and Somewhat Precarious' Doctrine of Justification," *Westminster Theological Journal* 66 (2004): 357-72.

CHAPTER 6

Sanctification: The Holy Spirit as the Bond of Union in the Christian Life

[The saints] partake of the same Spirit, of the same holiness and the same happiness; they are branches in him and partake of the same sap and nourishment with the vine. Christ and believers are partakers of the same Spirit. Christ has the Spirit not by measure, and they have of the same Spirit by measure [John 3:34]. Christ has all fullness of grace in him, and believers have grace for grace [John 1:16]. . . . Believers also in the gospel feast have communion one with another. They partake of that one bread. They have one Lord, [one] faith, one baptism. All drink into one Spirit, are all united together by partaking of the same influence of the same head. 'Tis one Spirit that unites them all, so that they make but one body.[1]

As the above quotation illustrates, Edwards's pneumatology profoundly shaped his entire theology. The Spirit reaches into and transforms the far corners of his thought. The last chapter detailed Edwards's understanding of the Spirit's regenerative work in believers and how this work relates to their justification. With the exception of the section on faith, that discussion centered on issues which are one-time occurrences in the Christian life. Neither the Spirit's union with the soul nor justification are repeatable events in the progress of individual redemption. By contrast, in this chapter we shift our attention to the ongoing pneumatological realities of the Christian life, realities which are tangible everyday Christian experiences in the Spirit, able to be discerned through sanctified self-reflection and measured against the straightedge of Scripture.

The entire complex of issues Edwards addressed on the Christian life—the nature of spiritual "sight," the testimony of the Spirit, assurance, true love to neighbor and to God, the true signs of Christian spirituality, and the communion the saint has with Christ in the Lord's Supper—together comprise his theology of sanctification. Thus, while Edwards never wrote a treatise systematically linking these diverse topics together under the *locus* of "sanctification," and while we surprisingly find only one reference to

---

1 Jonathan Edwards, "The Spiritual Blessings of the Gospel Represented by a Feast," in *The Works of Jonathan Edwards*, vol. 14, *Sermons and Discourses, 1723-1729*, ed. Kenneth P. Minkema (New Haven: Yale University Press, 1997), 287.

sanctification in his "Table" to the "Miscellanies,"[2] the degree to which he treated each of these other issues can only lead us to the conclusion that sanctification, broadly considered, was one of the theological topics he was most passionate about.[3]

For Edwards, sanctification is a thoroughly pneumatological affair. At every turn in his thought on the subject we find the Spirit's presence influencing, communicating, loving, affecting, etcetera. Yet not only is the Spirit merely present throughout his theology of sanctification, he is present and active in a *trinitarian* way, a way that mirrors his being and activity within the Godhead. If the Spirit repeats his inner-trinitarian activity *ad extra* through the church, being the bond of union in the multiplicity of their relationships, then we would expect to find Edwards shaping the pieces of his doctrine of sanctification into this master narrative. This is indeed what we find him doing in several statements he makes which summarize the continuities between the Spirit's internal and external work. "The Spirit that proceeds from the Father and the Son," Edwards writes, "is the bond of this union [between the Father and the Son], as it is of all holy union between the Father and the Son, *and between God and the creature, and between the creatures among themselves.*"[4] The Spirit "exerts itself in the soul in those acts which are its proper, natural and essential acts in itself *ad intra*, or within the Deity from all eternity."[5] In this chapter we will consider whether he remained faithful to this proposal in the specific details of his thoughts on sanctification.

One of the difficulties we confront in tracking down the theme of union found in Edwards's doctrine of sanctification, lies in the fact that he did not articulate the Spirit's work of union from a single vantage point. As his doctrine of the Christian life is complex and varied, so too is his discussion of the Spirit's work. We can identify at least three perspectives from which he detailed the Spirit's work as the bond of union in the Christian's sanctification, each of which corresponds with a well-known feature of his theology. First, when Edwards speaks from the perspective of the Christian's personal experience of God in the Spirit, he generally employs the categories of spiritual light and spiritual sight, a theme associated with his well-know sermon, "A Divine and Supernatural Light." Here the metaphors of "sight" and "light" predominate, underscoring the subjectivity of this perspective. The saint,

---

2   Edwards, "Table to the 'Miscellanies,'" in *Works*, 13:145.
3   This is especially true of his sermons. John Gerstner has observed that "Of the twelve hundred plus sermons which Edwards wrote, I estimate that sanctification was the central and most emphasized theme." *Rational Biblical Theology of Jonathan Edwards*, 3:224.
4   Edwards, *Treatise on Grace*, in *Works*, 186, emphasis mine.
5   Edwards, "Miscellanies" No. 471, in *Works*, 13:513. See also "Miscellanies" No. 183 (*Works*, 13:330) and the end of "Miscellanies" No. 1082 (*Works*, 20:466), for similar statements.

indwelt by the Spirit, possesses a spiritual vision whose object is not the Spirit himself, but the objects of the Spirit's loving gaze, namely the Father and the Son. From this perspective, the Spirit's work as the bond of union is discerned implicitly *within* true Christian experience. Having glimpsed the overwhelming glories of God and the excellencies of the gospel, the saints cannot help but be drawn outside of themselves to love, adore, and worship God's divine Majesty. Such spiritual vision, effected by the Spirit, draws the saint into loving union with the Godhead.[6]

Second, when Edwards shifts the perspective and writes *objectively* about the Christian's personal love to others and to God, and the nature of that love, he often modulates into the discourse of "overflowing dispositions," which is simply his way of articulating the fact that love is other-centered. Love, considered objectively as the divine disposition who is the Holy Spirit, is dynamically charged toward overflowing the boundaries of one's being, seeking union and communion with the other. Here, terms such as "principles" and "dispositions" predominate the discussion, as well as the analogies of a "fountain" and the "sun," each of which cannot contain within themselves their own inner fullness. As we have seen, Edwards applies this logic to God's being as the rationale for the creation of the world in *End of Creation*. In this chapter, we shall see that he also applies it to humanity as the rationale for their loving others. It is the Spirit, united mysteriously to the saint's faculties as the ultimate foundation of their activity, who leads the believer to love God with all her heart, soul, mind, and strength, and to love others as herself. Thus from this perspective, the Spirit's work as the bond of union is seen in the dynamic that draws the saints outside of themselves and lovingly into communion with God and others. In contrast to the first perspective above, which views the Spirit's role as mainly illuminatory and centering on spiritual apprehension, Edwards articulates the Holy Spirit's role in this perspective as foundational to the soul's faculties, motivational to the saint's willing, outward-seeking in its orientation, and centering more on the dynamic activity of the Spirit than the spiritual perception that he gives.

Third, when Edwards writes from the broad perspective of the Christian community, he often shifts into the discourse of excellency, which emphasizes the volitional and aesthetic harmonies that obtain among diverse members of a

---

6 In addition to "A Divine and Supernatural Light," (found in *Works*, 17:405-26), Edwards wrote widely on the theme of spiritual light. For representative examples see "Miscellanies" Nos. 489, 782 (yet see other entries on "conviction" and "faith" in his "Table on the 'Miscellanies'"). See also signs 1-5 in part 3 of the *Religious Affections*, in *Works*, 2:197-310. Spiritual sight and light is also featured prominently in the following sermons: "A Spiritual Understanding of Divine Things Denied to the Unregenerate," (*Works*, 14:67-96), "The Threefold Work of the Holy Ghost," (*Works*, 14:371-436), "The Pure in Heart Blessed" (*Works*, 17:57-86), and "False Light and True," (*Works*, 19:120-42).

community, whether it be the community of the church amongst their individual members or the community of the redeemed (either individually or corporately) with Christ, God, the gospel or "being in general." The terms "consent" and "harmony" frequent these discussions, as well as the metaphor of music. From this perspective, the most objective of the three, we discern the Spirit's work of union as fitting believers more into a harmonious union with the whole, so that their loving acts accords with each others' within the church and ultimately with God's purposes in redemptive history. The result is an aesthetically pleasing harmony, beautiful to the soul, and reiterative of God's inner fullness.

From each of these three perspectives, we see the Spirit working as the bond of union in the saints' sanctification. Because Edwards often shifts gears between each of these perspectives, we will not use them to frame our investigation. Rather our plan will take us on an investigation of the Spirit's work as the bond of union in the Christian's sanctification through more identifiable regions of Edwards's theology—his reflections on the nature of Christian spiritual experience, and his ecclesiology—keeping mindful of the fact that these three thematic perspectives outlined above lay behind his writings, exerting a powerful influence on his thought.

6.1 Personal Sanctification: The Holy Spirit and the Nature of Christian Experience

From the period of the Valley Awakening (1734-35) until the time he wrote the *Religious Affections* (1746), Edwards's theology and pastoral attitude concerning sanctification underwent a significant shift.[7] Prior to this period, the careful attention he gave to the topic of spiritual sight led him to emphasize personal experience of God in such a way that appears to overshadow the importance of Christian sanctification and ongoing growth in grace. To catch a glimpse of divine excellency in the gospel story is all that is truly needed to certify that salvation had dawned in one's heart. One implication of this emphasis is that the implicit connection between spiritual sight and godly living is not immediately recognizable. Such an implicit antinomianism indeed was neither Edwards's intention nor his theological opinion, but merely arose out of the strong emphasis he placed upon spiritual illumination early in his career. His perspective, however, matured greatly in the shadow of the awakenings when so many of his parishioners, whom he thought were graced with a saving

---

7 Ava Chamberlain's analysis of this shift, which I rely upon here in this paragraph, is found both in her "Editors's Introduction" to volume 18 (*Works*, 18:18-24) and her article, "Brides of Christ and Signs of Grace: Edwards's Sermons Series on the Parable of the Wise and Foolish Virgins," in *Jonathan Edwards's Writings*, 3-18. For historical background see George Marsden's analysis of the aftermath of the Awakenings in the early 1740s in *Jonathan Edwards: A Life*, 268-305.

knowledge of Christ, had disappointingly slid back into their former ways. How could a people, blessed by not one but two special visitations of the Spirit, turn their backs *en masse* upon God who had manifested his glories among their community so powerfully and so wonderfully? This turn of events was a cause of no little disillusionment for Edwards, especially in his own ability to discern a work of grace in the hearts of others:

> I once did not imagine that the heart of man had been so unsearchable as I find it is. I am less charitable, and less uncharitable than once I was. I find more things in wicked men that may counterfeit, and make a fair shew of piety, and more ways that the remaining corruption of the godly may make them appear like carnal men, formalists and dead hypocrites, than once I knew of. The longer I live, the less I wonder that God challenges it as his prerogative to try the hearts of the children of men, and has directed that this business should be let alone till the harvest. I find that God is wiser than men.[8]

Edwards addressed this issue by emphasizing the organic linkages between Christian practice and his "experimental" theology of spiritual light. His notebooks and sermons show an increased interest in how Christian perseverence relates to and is even necessary to justification. Spiritual light is necessary to salvation, assuring to the conscience, and certifies the fact that God has come to dwell with the individual and will never leave. Yet persevering Christian practice, as the necessary outgrowth of this principle of grace in the heart, is the ultimate proof that the light seen is truly of God, a conclusion that we find in its maturity in the *Religious Affections*. In this section we will examine the Spirit's role as the bond of union in Edwards's reflections on spiritual light, which serves as the foundation to his doctrine of personal sanctification.

6.1.1 Spiritual Sight: The Foundation of Christian Experience

At the heart of Edwards's theology of true Christianity lies his characteristic depiction of the Christian's spiritual vision of God. The true Christian "sees God" in a spiritual way, and knows the sweetness of having God's light shine into the soul. In reading his detailed descriptions of what it is to see God

---

[8] Jonathan Edwards, *The Distinguishing Marks of a Work of the Spirit of God*, in *The Works of Jonathan Edwards*, vol. 4, *The Great Awakening*, ed. C. C. Goen (New Haven: Yale University Press, 1972), 285 (hereafter *Distinguishing Marks*). The apparent inconsistency, observed by Stephen Holmes (*God of Grace and God of Glory*, 184-91), between Edwards's increased skepticism at being able to discern the presence of grace in others, and his quest in the 1740s to purify the church based upon his judgment of their spiritual standing (which culminated in numerous excommunications and eventually the communion controversy) may be summed up in this curious phrase: "I am less charitable, and less uncharitable than once I was."

spiritually, one gets a profound sense that we are not being led into the presence of his study, merely given access to his theological reflections, but rather into his prayer closet, given exposure to his own spiritual experiences. From an objective vantage point, Edwards's understanding of the dynamics of spiritual sight take on a trinitarian shape, as evidenced by "Miscellanies" Nos. 396-97. There he observes that when the Bible uses the word "spirit" with reference to God, it oftentimes "signifies the holy temper, or disposition or affection of God, as when we read of the Spirit of God." It is this personal affection, the third person of the Trinity, who indwells the saints, giving them the same peaceable, meek, holy disposition and temper that God himself has. "This Holy Spirit of God, the divine temper, is that divine nature spoken of, II Pet. 1:4, that we are made partakers of through the gospel." The result? The soul in conversion is altered, possessing a new "temper and disposition and spirit of the mind. . . . 'Tis this is the new nature and the divine nature; and the nature of the soul being thus changed, it admits divine light. Divine things now appear excellent, beautiful, glorious, which did not when the soul was of another spirit."[9] This shift from the objective description of the Spirit as the divine temper to the saints' subjective awareness of the excellency of divine things, illustrates the linkages he made between the Spirit's immanent nature, his *ad extra* work in the saint, and the saints' subjective experience of this work. Edwards's descriptions of the saints' spiritual sight are quite simply the flip side of his discussion on the Spirit's "principle-like" work in the heart. The main difference is that when he writes from the perspective of the saint's spiritual sight, he describes the Spirit's effects in the hearts of the saints and not so much the Spirit himself. The focus of these discussions consists in what is "seen," not the Spirit, but what He illumines to the soul, the divine excellency of God, Christ and the way of the gospel. The Holy Spirit is thus "hidden" in these discussions, and his work as the bond of union is discerned in the way the saint subjectively embraces God and Christ.

What does Edwards mean when he asserts that the true Christian "sees" God spiritually? A lengthy discussion is required to answer this question, for Edwards was fascinated with the spiritual and epistemological mechanics of spiritual vision throughout his life. By analyzing this issue we are basically exploring the Spirit's "subjectivity" in the hearts of the saints, a subjectivity that he shares with the elect.

A good place to begin our analysis is to examine one of his lesser known sermons, "The Pure in Heart Blessed."[10] Preached to his Northampton congregation in early 1730, the sermon takes its text from the beatitude found in Matthew 5:8, "Blessed are the pure in heart: for they shall see God." There Edwards argues that "It is a thing truly happifying to the soul of men to see God." Seeing God is thus the road to the soul's everlasting happiness. To

---

9 Edwards, "Miscellanies" No. 396-97, in *Works*, 13:462-63.
10 Edwards, "The Pure in Heart Blessed," in *Works*, 17:59-86.

argue this he first must establish what "seeing God" is, and typical to his method of argumentation, he begins with "negative" arguments, (i.e., showing what seeing God is *not*.) "'Tis not any sight with the bodily eyes," Edwards writes, "[True] blessedness of the soul don't enter in at that door; [this] would be to make the blessedness of the soul depend [on] the body, or the happiness of men's superior [parts] be dependent on the inferior." Scripture, he points out, teaches that God is invisible and cannot be seen with bodily eyes. Similarly, the angels, who as Christ mentioned, "*behold* the face of my Father which is in heaven" (Matt 18:10), see God without the use of bodily eyes. What, then, are we to make of the Old Testament sightings of God's form such as the glory of the Lord descending on the temple, Moses' seeing God's "back," and Isaiah's vision? These events, Edwards explains, are none other than God condescending himself "to the infant state of the church and to the childish notions that were entertained [in] those days of lesser light." They saw a physical form, not of God as he really is, but merely a natural image that God miraculously effected meant to lead his people to contemplate his spiritual reality. Moses, for instance, got his wish of seeing God's glory pass before him (Exodus 34), not in what he saw, but in God's "proclaiming his name, and giving [a clear sense] of mind of those things contained in that name"(see Exod 34:5-7). Similarly, the saints' vision of Christ's body in heaven "will be ravishing and delighting" not because of the physical glories perceived in his resurrection body, but "chiefly as it will express his spiritual glories," a logic he also applies to the disciples' vision of Christ at the transfiguration. Thus, while true spiritual vision in the Scriptures is sometimes accompanied by perceiving a miraculous form of God with bodily eyes,[1] this physical sighting does not consist in the sight that true saints have of God. Spiritual sight is something quite different.[11]

In contrast to seeing God physically, true spiritual sight is seeing God by way of spiritual perception, a way of sensing objects that is accomplished by a person's inner being and not reliant upon the physical senses. "The soul has in itself those powers whereby it is capable of apprehending of objects, and especially spiritual objects, without looking through the windows of the outward senses."[12] Edwards distinguishes many different ways the soul apprehends objects, and true spiritual sight consists in only one unique kind of intellectual perception. To distinguish spiritual sight from other ways the soul apprehends objects, Edwards again tests this general idea of spiritual perception in the crucible of his "negative" argumentation, and in doing so he leads us into

---

11 Edwards, "The Pure in Heart Blessed," in *Works*, 17:61-63. We will revisit the saint's sight of Christ in heaven and Edwards's understanding of the beatific vision in the next chapter, pages 177-82. For other discussions on the distinction between God's visible appearances in Scripture and his manifesting himself spiritually to the understanding, see his sermon "False Light and True," in *Works*, 19:136-37.

12 Edwards, "The Pure in Heart Blessed," in *Works*, 17:63.

one of the most celebrated areas of his theology, his discussion on the "sense of the heart."[13]

In "The Pure in Heart Blessed," Edwards argues that an "intellectual view by which God is seen" consists neither in having an intellectual opinion of God or his attributes, nor in the act of speculative reasoning.[14] Later in "Miscellanies" No. 782, Edwards re-categorizes these two levels of knowing (intellectual opinion and speculative reasoning) into "mere cognition" and "speculative knowledge," and recognizes them as the two most basic levels of knowledge. Yet even between these two levels there is a great difference, for only the latter type of knowing, speculative knowledge, can truly be called intellectual apprehension. "Mere cognition" by contrast is simply symbolic thinking. For instance, to hold an opinion about God whereby one is merely using the mental sign of a certain attribute, such as goodness or holiness, is merely to handle a mental emblem that possesses no substance. One may think "goodness" in the course of discussion, yet at the level of mere cognition, the mind does not really entertain its idea. Goodness is not "in" the mind, he argues, only its semantic symbol is. This, the lowest level of knowledge and reasoning, Edwards argues is a necessary part of rational thinking not only because of the "difficulty of exciting the actual ideas of things" but also because this kind of thinking is too slow: "if we must have the actual ideas of everything that came in our way in the course of our thoughts this would render our thoughts so slow as to render our powers of thinking in a great measure useless."[15]

Speculative reasoning by contrast brings mental activity into an entirely different level of reflection, which Edwards calls apprehension, "wherein the mind has a direct *ideal view* or *contemplation* of the thing thought of."[16] When the mind "apprehends" an idea, the actual idea is excited in the mind, and not merely its sign. Thus for instance, when the mind reflects upon the nature of goodness, the reality of goodness is actually repeated in the mind's presence, such that one can really say that goodness is present *in* the mind, and that the mind is viewing it or entertaining its presence.[17] Edwards distinguishes different levels of apprehension, and speculative reasoning (or mere "head

---

13 For his most extensive treatment of this topic see "Miscellanies" No. 782 (entitled "IDEAS. SENSE OF THE HEART. SPIRITUAL KNOWLEDGE OR CONVICTION") in *Works*, 18:452-66.
14 Edwards, "The Pure in Heart Blessed," in *Works*, 17:63.
15 Edwards, "Miscellanies" No. 782, in *Works*, 18:456.
16 Edwards, "Miscellanies" No. 782, in *Works*, 18:458.
17 "Those ideas which we call ideas of reflection – all ideas of the acts of the mind, such as the ideas of thought, of choice, love, fear, etc. – if we diligently attend to our own minds, we shall find they are not properly representations, but are indeed repetitions of those very things, either more fully or more faintly; they therefore are not properly ideas. Thus 'tis impossible to have an idea of [a] thought or of an idea but it will [be] that same idea repeated." "Miscellanies" No. 238, in *Works*, 13:353.

knowledge") deserves the place at the lowest level primarily because it only engages the mind and does not reach the heart. Such head knowledge includes "all ideal views of things that are merely intellectual, or appertain only to the faculty of understanding, i.e. all that understanding of things that don't consist in or imply some motion of the will, or in other words (to speak figuratively) some feeling of the heart, is mere speculative knowledge."[18] For instance, secular philosophers who reflect upon God's being, eternity and infinity may have correct knowledge of the divine being. They may penetrate with great acuity into the mysteries of eternity, divine substance, and goodness for the purposes of rational consistency and intellectual sport. But if their reflections leave their affections unchanged, if they do not reach their hearts and engross their wills, then their reflections have not engaged the entirety of their humanity. Speculative reasoning, while necessary to the rational process, is in a sense, half human. To be and to act in a fully human manner one must engage the totality of one's entire being, mind and will or affections. While speculative reasoning is an important part of human reflection, comprising "all the modes of mere discerning, judging, or speculation,"[19] it does not engage the entire person for the heart is not vitally involved in the process. To have a speculative understanding of God alone does not consist in true spiritual sight.

In contrast to speculative knowledge, Edwards discerns a higher form of apprehension which encompasses both the individual's mind and heart, a kind of apprehension he calls "sensible knowledge." When an individual perceives an object in this manner, the soul is either sensible of delight in the presence of that idea, or sensible of unpleasantness associated with it.[20] This sense, which is located in the will of the person, serves as the foundation of either love or hatred. To delight in an idea, is to love it, whereas to find it unpleasant is to hate it. It is this "sense" of the soul in the presence of the idea, which distinguishes sensible knowledge from merely speculative knowledge; "nothing is called a sensible knowledge upon any other account, but on the account of the sense, or kind of inward tasting or feeling, or sweetness or pleasure, bitterness or pains, that is implied in it, or arises from it."[21] What is immediately recognizable is that sensible knowledge, while it is characterized by the heart's activities, is based upon the object that is entertained in the mind. In other words, for there to be true sensible knowledge, the heart is dependent upon the mental idea which the "head" beholds. Mindless emotion, or a religious state that generates an "objectless" affection cannot be called sensible

---

18 Edwards, "Miscellanies" No. 782, in *Works*, 18:459.
19 Edwards, "Miscellanies" No. 782, in *Works*, 18:458.
20 "And the other [kind of knowledge] is that which consists in the sense of the heart: as when there is a sense of the beauty, amiableness, or sweetness of a thing; so that the heart is *sensible of pleasure and delight in the presence of the idea of it.*" Edwards, "Divine and Supernatural Light," in *Works*, 17:413, emphasis mine.
21 Edwards, "Miscellanies" No. 782, in *Works*, 18:459.

knowledge. "The will in all its determinations whatsoever is governed by its thoughts and apprehensions of things, with regard to those properties of the objects of its thoughts, wherein the degree of the sense of the heart has a main influence."[22] Edwards illustrates this point by the example of a person under conviction, who feels the great terror of God's displeasure against his sin. He indicates that "in a sense of the terribleness of God's displeasure, there is implied an ideal apprehension of more things than merely of that pain, or misery, or sense of God's heart, there is implied an ideal apprehension of the being of God, or of some intellectual existence, and an ideal apprehension of his greatness and of the greatness of his power."[23] Consequently, we can discern a psychological order in Edwards's understanding of sensible knowledge. While a "sense of the heart" is located in the heart, affections, and will, this sense derives its sensibleness from the properties found in the rational idea. Thus, we can say that for Edwards head and heart are equal and necessary partners in the affair of sensible knowledge, though there is an identifiable priority and order of the former over the latter.[24]

As the above example illustrates, it is possible to possess correct sensible knowledge of God and not be a true Christian. The individual under conviction by an immediate work of the Spirit, has a deep-seated apprehension of God's greatness, power, and wrath against sin, and feels the displeasure that God himself has against it. Similarly, in "The Pure in Heart Blessed," Edwards writes that

> The wicked spirits in the other world, they doubtless [have] more immediate apprehensions of the being of God, and his power and wrath, than the wicked in this world. They stand before God to be judged; they receive the sentence from him; they have a dreadful, amazing apprehension of his wrath and displeasure. But yet they are exceeding remote from seeing God in the sense of the text [of Matt 5:8].[25]

Sensible knowledge by itself, and even sensible knowledge of God does not

---

22 Edwards, "Miscellanies" No. 782, in *Works*, 18:460-61. See also "False Light and True," (*Works*, 19:134) where he writes that "Spiritual light always discovers something to the mind, something of God, or Christ, or some divine thing. There never shines any spiritual light into the mind but that there is some knowledge got by it; some understanding is gained by it. Spiritual light reveals something."
23 Edwards, "Miscellanies" No. 782, in *Works*, 18:460.
24 This "equality yet priority" formula mirrors the equality and priority of the persons of the Trinity. The Son and the Holy Spirit are equal persons with one another and with the Father based on their ontological identity. Yet the Son, as the *Logos* and reason of the Godhead, is prior in order to the Spirit who is the *Agape* and will of the Godhead. See the first section in Edwards's large "Miscellanies" essay on the Covenant of Redemption (No. 1062, in *Works*, 20:430-35).
25 Edwards, "The Pure in Heart Blessed," in *Works*, 17:64.

necessarily entail that one possesses spiritual sight. As a result, in his quest to describe what it is to see God spiritually, Edwards derives yet another distinction between two different kinds of sensible knowledge, a distinction between *natural* sensible knowledge, and *spiritual* sensible knowledge.

In the first category Edwards places all sensible knowledge that has respect to natural good or evil. "By natural good and evil I mean all that good or evil which is agreeable or disagreeable to human nature as such, without regard to the moral disposition."[26] This description may mislead us to think that natural sensible knowledge does not include ideas of a moral nature because it is "without regard to the moral disposition." This is not Edwards's intention. Rather, sensible knowledge which has respect to natural good and evil, is knowledge that solely concerns the natural sphere within which humankind was placed, and in conjunction with the natural principles with which human beings were endowed. A toddler for instance does not need the immediate help of the Holy Spirit to perceive and delight in a colorful ball or a happy children's song. These natural objects in conjunction with the natural principles of sense which the child has by creation, enables her not only to perceive these objects, but to intuit immediately their excellency, giving rise to the delight and joy associated with them. In *True Virtue*, Edwards argues in great depth that human beings are endowed with natural principles of morality which enable them to attain sensible knowledge of moral objects such as justice, evil, goodness and mercy.[27] Like the toddler with her toys, a person does not need supernatural intervention to develop a moral sense that loves justice, cherishes mercy, seeks the good of others, and hates violence. Thus when Edwards states that natural sensible knowledge is "without regard to the moral disposition," his aim is something quite different from the idea that this kind of sensible knowledge does not concern morality. As a matter of fact, Edwards believed that most of the morality found in the world and the theories of ethics found in its schools are clearly derived from the natural sensible knowledge that human beings have of moral objects. What Edwards means is that natural sensible knowledge is without regard to the *supernatural* moral disposition of grace in the heart.

The second kind of sensible knowledge Edwards identifies respects *spiritual* good or evil. "By spiritual good I mean all true moral good, all real moral beauty and excellency, and all those acts of the will, or that sense of the heart, that relates to it, and the idea of which involves it, as all sense of it, all relish and desires of it and delight in it, happiness consisting in it, etc."[28] The distinguishing factor between natural and spiritual sensible knowledge has to do with the nature of objects perceived: natural sensible knowledge relates to "natural" objects that are perceived and apprehended by our natural faculties, whereas spiritual sensible knowledge concerns divine and supernatural objects,

---

26 Edwards, "Miscellanies" No. 782, in *Works*, 18:462.
27 See chapters 3-7 in *True Virtue* (*Works* 8:561-618).
28 Edwards, "Miscellanies" No. 782, in *Works*, 18:462.

which an individual perceives intellectually via the illumination of the Spirit. While natural and spiritual sensible knowledge are both similar processes of knowing in that both are an affectionate response of the soul to an idea viewed in the mind, three points illustrate the vast difference between these two kinds of sensible apprehension.

First, to have a sensible idea of God's "real moral beauty and excellency" is, in a real sense, to entertain God's gracious and holy presence in the mind or in the soul. Because there is no ultimate distinction between God's being and his activity, real moral excellency as apprehended by the soul cannot be distinguished from God himself. Thus intellectual apprehension of divine excellency consists in a direct perception of God himself within the confines of the soul. The soul, in other words, "sees" divinity in the idea of divine excellency, not natural objects of the world or the invisible realities of natural justice and goodness, but supernatural divinity, God himself. This is the essence of spiritual sight for Edwards. The Christian "sees" God through a real spiritual apprehension of the idea of divine excellency.[29]

Second, Edwards argues that spiritual sensible knowledge is impossible to be perceived apart from the Spirit of God because "these [divine objects] don't consist in any agreeableness or disagreeableness to human nature as such, or the mere human faculties or principles."[30] Like trying to perceive infrared light, a human being in the state of nature has no built in capacity to discern or attain spiritual sensible knowledge; "it must be wholly and entirely a work of the Spirit of God, not merely as assisting and co-working with natural principles, but infusing something above nature."[31] As we examined in the last chapter, the Spirit becomes the new supernatural principle united to the soul and operating within its faculties, enabling it to perceive the excellency of divine things with the mind's eye.

Third, because the moral, spiritual, and ontological excellency of this object is so infinite, so glorious beyond comprehension, the sanctified soul, wired for excellency, immediately intuits this divine beauty as something infinitely desirable and is thus drawn to it in love. This is a fully human response of love toward the knowledge of God, one that reaches the heart and stirs the affections. The more relations of beauty the soul discerns in contemplating

---

29 When we examine precisely what is seen by the saint below, it will appear that this very epistemological description of spiritual sight, with its technical subtleties, becomes a very Christian idea of knowing the triune God.

30 Edwards, "Miscellanies" No. 782, in *Works*, 18:463. Edwards wrote earlier (fall, 1723) in "A Spiritual Understanding of Divine Things Denied to the Unregenerate," (*Works*, 14:85), that "The reason why they cannot see the excellency of spiritual things is very plain: because it is contrary to their natures. It is a contradiction to suppose that those things should appear excellent to us that are contrary to our natures and inclinations, for if they did appear excellent, they would not be contrary to us, but very agreeable."

31 Edwards, "Miscellanies" No. 782, in *Works*, 18:463.

God's excellency, the more it will love him, be more conformed to Him, and find its ultimate happiness in Him.

As a good teacher, we find Edwards in "The Pure in Heart Blessed" translating the preceding epistemological discussion into terms that his congregation could understand. "[T]o see God is this: it is to have an immediate and certain understanding of God's glorious excellency and love."[32] The immediacy which Edwards emphasizes here is his way of distinguishing spiritual sight from mere ratiocination. By an "immediate" understanding of God's excellency, the mind spiritually perceives God's excellency by a direct view of soul without any intermediary support, such as a rational syllogism arguing for the fact that God is holy or merciful. For the saint, spiritual sight does not rest upon a rational argument coming between the perceiver and the known object. "It must be a more immediate discovery, that must give the mind a real sense of the excellency and beauty of God. He that sees God, he has an immediate view of God's great and awful majesty, of his pure and beauteous holiness, of his wonderful and enduring grace and mercy."[33]

Accordingly, what the saint "sees" in spiritual vision consists not of a bare shining luminosity intuited by the soul or an excellency that is indistinguishable from non-Christian spiritual experiences. The excellency seen by the Christian, which draws the soul outside of itself in love and which enlightens the mind, is a *gospel* excellency, patterned on the scriptural witness.[34] The mind surveys the great complexity of revealed religion—God's holiness, justice and mercy, Christ's person and work, the fitness of faith as a means to salvation, the shape of salvation history as portrayed in Scripture—and it glimpses such a proportion and harmony among these various objects that the soul is overwhelmed by the beauty it sees, resulting in its consent, love, and joy in what it beholds. Because it is God and Christ who are objects of this sight, Edwards's description of spiritual experience results in more than just an

---

32 Edwards, "The Pure in Heart Blessed," in *Works*, 17:64.

33 Edwards, "The Pure in Heart Blessed," in *Works*, 17:64.

34 Edwards's comments on this are numerous. Here are two examples from his sermons: The Christian "sees things in a new appearance, in quite another view, than ever he saw before: he sees an excellency in God; he sees a sweet loveliness in Christ; he sees an amiableness in holiness and God's commandments; he sees an excellency in a Christian spirit and temper; he sees the wonderfulness of God's designs and a harmony in all his ways, a harmony, excellency and wondrousness in his Word: he sees these things by an eye of faith, and by a new light that was never before let into his mind." ("A Spiritual Understanding," *Works*, 14:79). "Spiritual light always discovers something to the mind, something of God, or Christ, or some divine thing. . . . It either discovers something of the excellency of the things of religion: the excellency of God or Christ; the excellency of the holiness of God, or truth of God, or the justice of God, or the mercy of God; or the wonderfulness of the grace of God; or [the] dying love of Christ; or the excellency of the way of salvation, or the like." ("False Light and True," *Works*, 19:134).

epistemological and aesthetic exercise. Rather, the soul is drawn out into a loving personal embrace of God. Furthermore, because many of the remaining objects of excellence ("impersonal" objects such as the harmonious plan of salvation history, and even the delight in the physical creation) reflect God's inner-trinitarian glory, a delight in them is ultimately a delight in the triune God.[35] The experience of divine excellency, in beholding Christ, or surveying the Old Testament history of Israel, thus always remains a communal affair between the saint and God as Trinity.[36]

In addition to this immediate understanding of God's excellency, Edwards affirms that there is a "certain understanding of his love as well" included in this spiritual sight. "He that has a blessed-making sight of God, he not only has a view of God's glory and excellency, but he views it as having a propriety in it. They also see God's love to them; they receive the testimonies and manifestations of that."[37] Knowing God's excellency includes in it a certainty that the love discerned in the known object (God) necessarily includes in it a love for the knower. To know God's excellency and understand his love, is to know that he loves me. Two points lie embedded in this assertion, which we find Edwards making explicit both here and elsewhere in his writings. First, seeing God carries with it an intense certainty of the existence, truth, and beauty of the object perceived. Though the saint does not behold God by any bodily sense, but strictly through the soul's Spirit-enabled apprehension, the type of certainty granted by spiritual sight is just as certain, and even more certain, than that of bodily vision.[38] In beholding God this way, the soul does not debate with itself as to the truthfulness and certainty of what it sees; rather the idea of God's excellency and love is self-authenticating. True divinity when it is known by the soul needs no apologetic helps because its own infinite

---

35 John F. Wilson notes that Edwards's prolonged reflection on the history of redemption in his many "Miscellanies" on the subject and in his sermon series on the *History of Redemption*, "demonstrate how prolonged and deep was his commitment to develop a theology based upon the theme of the redemption of the world as a consequence of the internal dynamics of the Trinity – that it, the interrelationships of Father, Son, and Spirit." See his "Editor's Introduction" to the *History of Redemption* in *Works*, 9:16.
36 Thus demonstrating that he steered his philosophical principles in the direction of the gospel.
37 Edwards, "The Pure in Heart Blessed," in *Works*, 17:64.
38 Writing about the spiritual sight that the saints in heaven will have, Edwards notes that "the view will be as immediate as when we see things with our bodily eyes. God will as immediately discover himself to their minds, so that the understanding shall as immediately behold the glory of God and his love as a man can behold the countenance of his friend that he looks in the face." This kind of spiritual sight is the same in kind with the sight the saints have of God here on earth, the only difference being the degree to which we behold and apprehend God, which is less in this world, and which is interrupted by doubts and temptation (*Works*, 17:65).

excellency is its own authentication. Edwards often called this sensible knowledge of God "intuitive" knowledge:

> The child of God doth as it were see and feel the truth of divine things even intuitively; that is, they see so much of religion, that they plainly discern that it must needs be the offspring of God. They can feel such a power and kind of omnipotency in Christianity, and taste such a sweetness, and see such wisdom, such an excellent harmony in the gospel, as carry their own light with them, and powerfully do enforce and conquer the assent and necessitates their minds to receive it as proceeding from God, and as the certain truth.[39]

The second point implied within the assertion that spiritual sight includes within it a certain understanding of God's love, consists in the fact that the saints are aware of God's personal love to them. To see God is not only to know the certainty of his glorious excellency and truth, it is also to know with relative certainty that I am included as the object of his love in my knowing of his excellent love. There is thus an experiential inconsistency between having a certain and affectionate view of God's glorious excellency, mercy, and love on the one hand, and entertaining a radical doubt of one's own salvation on the other. While Edwards did acknowledge that sin, in its infinite subtleness, and the temptations of the devil, very often prey upon the believer's personal assurance, bringing about this inconsistency, this does not nullify the fact for him that there is an organic and logical connection between affectionately beholding God's glorious excellency in the soul, and knowing that he has turned the gaze of his infinite love on *me*.

With this assertion we are led directly into his discussion on assurance, which we will briefly discuss here by analyzing one of his many reflections on the subject in the *Religious Affections*.[40] How can Christians know that God has chosen them? Edwards's interpretation of the Pauline categories of the "witness," "seal," and "earnest" of the Spirit (Rom 8; 2 Cor 1:22; Eph 1:13, and 4:13) illustrates his general approach to the doctrine, an approach that highlights the centrality of pneumatology to the Christian's assurance. Each of these terms, Edwards contends, refer to the same reality, namely the lively presence and activity of the Spirit indwelling the soul, an activity which the conscience discerns, convincing it that Spirit has taken up his abode within the heart. The Spirit's "witness" does not consist in an audible assertion or vision from heaven, which many "enthusiasts" of the Awakenings claimed. Rather, in accordance with the way Scripture uses the word, this witness is merely the

---

39 Edwards, "A Spiritual Understanding," in *Works* 14:78. See also his comment twenty two years later in the *Religious Affections*: "The gospel of the blessed God does not go abroad a begging for its evidence, so much as some think; it has its highest and most proper evidence in itself." (*Works*, 2:307).

40 Edwards, *Religious Affections*, in *Works*, 2:230-39. For a recent study on Edwards's doctrine of assurance, see Nichols, *An Absolute Sort of Certainty*, 77-153.

evidence or proof of the Spirit's indwelling presence, evidence which consists in holy affections to God, love for neighbor and obedience to all of God's commands. Likewise, both the "seal" and the "earnest" of the Spirit are none other than a divinely effected mark or deposit which the soul possesses, distinguishing it as uniquely Christian. "Therefore this earnest of the Spirit, and first fruits of the Spirit, which has been shown to be the same with the seal of the Spirit, is the vital, gracious, sanctifying communication and influence of the Spirit."[41]

Assurance thus possesses a reflexive dimension. The saints arrive at it through reflecting upon the nature and ends of their holy behavior and affections for God, and then gradually gain the confidence to conclude, to the satisfaction of their conscience's doubts, that they are indeed children of God. He needed to stress the reflexive nature of assurance over against the enthusiasts who professed to have immediate revelation of assurance supernaturally given by the Spirit through a vision or audible voice, lest he grant there to be a practical separation of Word and Spirit. Yet even though this was his position, the gravity of his thinking led him to affirm that an element of immediacy does reside in clear spiritual views of God.

> And though it be far from being true, that the soul in this case, judges only by an immediate witness, without any sign or evidence; for it judges and is assured by the greatest sign and clearest evidence; yet in this case [of strong and lively exercises of love to God] the saints stands in no need of multiplied signs, or any long reasoning upon them. And though the sight of his relative union with God, and his being in his favor, is not without a medium, because he sees it by that medium, viz. his love; yet his sight of the union of heart to God is immediate: love, the bond of union, is seen intuitively: the saint sees and feels plainly the union between his soul and God; it is so strong and lively, that he can't doubt of it.[42]

Edwards seems to want to have it both ways. While assurance is reflexive with regard to the conscience, the very medium through which we are united to God, divine love, possesses within itself its own testimony. To love God with the love which God gives, and to be in the strong exercise of it, is to know immediately of one's union with God.

As we wrap up our examination of Edwards's discussion on spiritual sight and the nature of Christian experience, one point needs to be emphasized: his discussions on spiritual sight in essence give us an added glimpse into the dynamics of the immanent Trinity. If God repeats his immanent divine life *ad extra* through the redemption of his people and the life of the church, then the experience of this repeated trinitarian life in the life of the saints serves as a finite window into the infinite, immanent Trinity. The saint's subjective

---

41 Edwards, *Religious Affections*, in *Works*, 2:237.
42 Edwards, *Religious Affections*, in *Works*, 2:239.

experience of God through spiritual sight and the affections that result, is in a real sense a repetition of the inner-trinitarian relationship that obtains between the Father and the Son. To be more precise, the saint's experience is actually a partaking of that relationship as it exists in the Spirit "externally"; the saint is caught up, as it were, as a creature in the eternal ebb and flow of the infinite communion that exists between Father and Son.

The trinitarian shape of Edwards's doctrine of spiritual sight and Christian experience is demonstrated in two important ways. First, the psychological order of spiritual experience reveals the trinitarian parallels between his theology of spiritual knowledge and the Trinity. Human beings as embodying the triad of mind, understanding, and will do not become fully human unless they fully and equally engage the world through each of their three faculties. This is especially true in human engagement with God: the mind, understanding, and will are equal partners in the affair of divine communion. Yet there is an order discernable among these three. The mind must have its understanding informed by knowledge if the will is to respond. A similar equality yet priority is to be found among the members of the Trinity.

Second, the saint's sight of God's excellencies is not trinitarian in the sense that she regards each person of the Trinity as a specific object of one's spiritual sight. True, the Christian does reflect upon the Trinity, baptize in the name of the three, and glory in the three. We saw earlier that Edwards's own meditations on the Trinity were the source of many exalting thoughts of God.[43] Yet more often than not, the core of Edwards's theology of Christian experience is trinitarian in the sense that the saint views of the excellencies of "God and Christ" *affectionately, in the atmosphere of divine love.* The saint's sight of God the Father, as glorious, holy, infinite in grace, is magnified even more through the knowledge of the fact that he has from eternity begotten an only and dearly beloved Son on whom he pours out all his love, and whom he did not spare on behalf of the church. The saints' sight of Christ, in whom many diverse excellencies reside, and for whom they were created to be his bride, is magnified even more through knowledge of the fact that he freely gave his life for the church, laying himself in the way of their due penalty, and rising again to be the first fruits of a renewed humanity. The sight of such a divine society, and of the multitudinous excellencies of their activities, engenders delight, love, and joy in the saint which draws her ever deeper into this society via love, in ever deepening discoveries of God's infinite gloriousness. Where is the third person of the Trinity in this? He is deeply and personally involved here as the gift of love for God and grace from Christ that Christians experience. He is generally not the object of sight, but is felt, experienced, known and loved in our knowing and loving of God and Christ. In other words,

---

43 "God has appeared glorious to me, on account of the Trinity," Edwards wrote in his *Personal Narrative*, (*Works*, 16:800), "It has made me have exalting thoughts of God, that he subsists in three persons; Father, Son and Holy Ghost."

the saints do not "see" the Holy Spirit; rather the Christian's seeing is *by the Spirit,* and it is due to the fact *that* they see affectionately, with all their being, in the divine love of God's excellencies, that his theology of spiritual sight is rounded out in a fully trinitarian way.[44]

6.2 Ecclesial Sanctification: The Holy Spirit as the Bond of Union in the Church

Edwards was no individualist, concerned only with personal religious experience of God. As one profoundly affected by Scripture, he believed that true religion necessarily incorporates the individual into the communal dimension, arguing that the true test of sainthood is found in the individual's actions within the church and society, not only within one's prayer closet.[45] A true vision of God will always eventuate in love to neighbor, social union, and ecclesial harmony, or at least it will always seek to promote these things. The church thus occupies a significant place in Edwards's thought. Not only is she the bride for whom Christ died, the bride whom the Father prepares for his only begotten Son, but she is also that entity whom the Spirit both sanctifies through the communication of divine love and beautifies through the bestowing of divine excellency. Thus, in her own finite way, the church loves as God loves, reflecting the inner harmonies and excellencies of the trinitarian society in their relationships. In this section we will explore the pneumatological themes that run through Edwards's writings on the church. We will see the Spirit's activity as the bond of union in the church in three distinct areas: in his discussions on the love individual Christians are to have for one another, in his discussions on prayer, and in his theology of the Lord's Supper. Yet before we turn our attention to these topics, we must first examine some of the general characteristics of his ecclesiology.

Edwards never wrote a systematic work on the church. Nevertheless, there

---

44 Edwards affirms this in numerous places. Notice the trinitarian shape to this exhortation he gives toward holiness in the following sermon extract: "We should endeavor continually to be more and more as we hope to be in heaven, in respect of holiness and conformity to God. We should endeavor to be more & more {as we hope to be in heaven}, with respect to light and knowledge, should labor to be continually growing in the knowledge *of God and Christ,* and divine things, clear views of the gloriousness and excellency of divine things that we come nearer and nearer to the beatific vision. . . . We should labor to {be continually growing} *in divine love,* that this may be an increasing flame in our hearts, till our hearts ascend wholly in this flame . . . . {We should labor to be continually growing} in comfort and spiritual joy, in sensible communion *with God and Jesus Christ.*" (Edwards, "The True Christian's Life a Journey Towards Heaven," in *Works,* 17:434-35, emphases mine). Edwards's emphasis on growth in knowledge of God and Christ, and growth in divine love, is fully trinitarian.

45 See his twelfth sign in his *Religious Affections* (*Works,* 2:383-461).

is enough information scattered throughout his "Miscellanies" entries, treatises and sermons to bring the contours of his ecclesiology into focus, a work which has been done admirably by a number of scholars.[46] For our purposes we will focus on one major aspect of his ecclesiology, the trinitarian foundations of the church.[47] From the widest possible angle, the church ultimately is the bride of Christ. Edwards takes this biblical concept and attempts a philosophical and trinitarian rationale for the church's existence in his "Miscellanies" No. 104. The key to his argument lies in the dispositional parallels between the Father's eternal inclination to beget and communicate himself in his own idea, and the Son's similar inclination to communicate his own fullness to another. The Son, as the infinite fullness of the Father's communicative disposition, himself desires to communicate his own fullness "in an image of his person that may partake of his happiness."[48] He is the perfect image of the Father, and thus naturally desires to imitate his Father even in the latter's disposition toward infinite communication.[49] The church thus becomes the object of the Son's affections; she is the fullness, joy, and delight of God the Son as the Son is the fullness, joy, and delight of God the Father.[50] The intense love and communion that the Father enjoys with the Son, the Son likewise seeks out in his own bride, the church. Following the apostle Paul's lead, Edwards goes so far as to say that the church is the "completeness of Christ (Eph. 1:23), as if Christ were not complete without the church, as having a natural inclination thereto."[51] Elsewhere he comments on the same verse that "Till [Christ] had attained [his spouse, the church], he was pleased not to look on himself as complete, but as

---

46 Thomas A. Schafer's "Jonathan Edwards' Conception of the Church," *Church History*, 24.1 (March 1955):51-66, is still an excellent starting place to get an overview of Edwards's ecclesiology. See also Fredrick W. Youngs, "The Place of Spiritual Union in Jonathan Edwards's Conception of the Church," *Fides et Historia* 28:1 (Winter/Spring 1996): 27-47; and Douglas A. Sweeney's article "The Church," in *The Princeton Companion to Jonathan Edwards* (Princeton: Princeton University Press, 2005), 167-89.

47 For a detailed study on this issue, see Krister Sairsingh, "Jonathan Edwards and the Idea of Divine Glory: His Foundational Trinitarianism and its Ecclesial Import" (Ph.D. diss., Harvard University, 1986). See also Stephen Holmes's critical appreciation of Sairsingh's thesis, *God of Grace and God of Glory*, 177, 188-90, and Steven Studebaker's appendix, "Krister Sairsingh and Edwards' Relational Trinitarianism," in his dissertation "Jonathan Edwards' Social Augustinian Trinitarianism," 358ff.

48 Edwards, "Miscellanies" No. 104, in *Works*, 13:272.

49 The Spirit cannot be the object of this communication for the reason that he is not a generated object of affection (as the Son is for the Father, and as the church shall be for the Son). Rather, as the divine love, he is the Godhead's own spirated subjective affection.

50 "The Son," writes Edwards in "Miscellanies" No. 104, "is the fullness of God, and the church is the fullness of the Son of God." (*Works*, 13:273).

51 Edwards, "Miscellanies" No. 104, in *Works*, 13:272.

Sanctification

wanting something, as Adam was not complete till he had obtained his Eve."[52] The basic strategy Edwards appears to be taking here in "Miscellanies" No. 104 is as follows: the church is an entity created primarily by the Son to be for him what he is for the Father, an "other" image of himself upon whom he can pour out his fullness and in whom he can delight. While Edwards would acknowledge significant differences between these two parallel relationships,[53] one important commonality they share is the Spirit's work as the bond of love between each party in these two relationships. As the Spirit unites Father and Son in the immanent Trinity via love, so too does he unite the Son and his bride the church in a similar union. This results, Edwards suggests, in a secondary reflection of the immanent Trinity:

> In this also there is a trinity, an image of the eternal Trinity; Christ is the everlasting father, and believers are his seed, and the Holy Spirit, or Comforter, is the third person in Christ, being his delight and love flowing out towards the church. In believers the Spirit and delight of God, being communicated unto them, flows out toward the Lord Jesus Christ.[54]

The church, through her history and ever increasing growth in grace, shall reflect back to Christ his own excellencies as he pours forth his love and grace upon her, communicating to her the Holy Spirit, in whom they may enjoy the richest love and communion. In the remainder of this section we will investigate small pieces of this grand narrative, noting the Spirit's involvement in the church's sanctification.

6.2.1 The Holy Spirit among the Ecclesial Community

In the last chapter we observed the mysterious union between the love of the true saint and the person of the Holy Spirit. In some strange way the Spirit is the personal love that believers experience in their devotion to God. If this is the case, then we would expect to see similarities between the church's love and the Spirit's, for the Spirit's *ad extra* activities are not to be too sharply distinguished from who he is and what he does within the Godhead. In this section we will briefly examine three ways that Edwards illustrates this connection between the Spirit's loving and the church's: first, through his understanding of love as being naturally effusive within the community of faith; second, through the connection he draws between the Spirit's love among the church and prayer, and the need for a visible union among Christian's

---

[52] Edwards, "Notes on Scripture," No. 235, in *Works*, 15:187.
[53] Whereas the Son is the infinite uncreated image of the Father begotten *ad intra* in eternity, the church is a finite created image of the Son begotten *ad extra* in time.
[54] Edwards, "Miscellanies" No. 104, in *Works*, 13:273-74. Notice that this "image of the Trinity" is distinctively "western" in its emphasis on the love flowing out from both Christ and the church to one another.

worldwide to unite in corporate prayer for God's blessings; and third, in his theology of the Lord's Supper.

"To be of a Christian temper is to be of a liberal bountiful disposition," Edwards wrote in a 1727 sermon entitled "True Nobleness of Mind."

> This is esteemed one great qualification of a noble mind, not to be niggardly speaking and selfish, but to be communicative and openhanded, to be ready to lay out ourselves for the benefit and comfort of others. And this is a disposition abundantly insisted upon in the gospel, to be ready to distribute, willing to communicate, not to look every man on his own things but everyone on the things of others; to love our neighbors as ourselves, to scatter abroad and cast our bread upon the waters. And Christianity does not only require this, but it also disposes to it everyone that truly embraces Christianity; it fills the heart with a noble diffusive love and benevolence to mankind, and makes to love not only in work and in tongue but in deed and in truth.[55]

The natural inclination of Christian love is not just toward God alone, but also toward all that he has made. Christian love is "a noble diffusive love and benevolence to mankind." It is "communicative and openhanded" and is of a "liberal bountiful disposition." This language echoes the themes we find in his *Two Dissertations*, and for good reason. There he describes God as naturally diffusive, similar to the sun and a fountain (*End of Creation*), and there he portrays the ethical shape of the universe in agapeic terms (*True Virtue*). True virtue is none other than love to Being in general, or being favorably disposed toward the universality of existence. The picture Edwards is trying to paint is that the church's love is not merely imitative of God, but participative. Her members love each other and the world because somehow she participates in God's very own life, for she is united to Christ and is indwelt with the Holy Spirit. Her activity will thus shadow forth God's own loving ways.

Edwards illustrates the nature of the church's diffusive love in his occasional sermons on the duty of charity that Christians are to show to the poor.[56] While excessive poverty did not inhabit Edwards's Northampton, Mark Valeri has shown that he did live in a time of increasing economic tension.[57] The political and economic climate of the early 1730s in Massachusetts was marked by fractional politics and instability, due in part to the disputes between the royally appointed governor of the colony and the elected legislature. Such tensions not only threatened the Massachusetts colony charter, on which its religious

---

55 Edwards, "True Nobleness of Mind," in *Works*, 14:238.
56 See "The Duty of Charity to the Poor," in *Works*, 17:369-404, and "Much in Deeds of Charity," in *The Sermons of Jonathan Edwards: A Reader*, ed. Wilson H. Kimnach, Kenneth P. Minkema, and Douglas A. Sweeney (New Haven: Yale, 1999) 197-211; hereafter *Sermons Reader*.
57 Valeri's analysis, which I rely upon here, can be found in his introductory essay in *Works*, 17:17-28.

institutions depended, but also added to the colony's deepening fiscal problems. These economic woes coupled with both an increase in social stratification and the limitation of land available for purchase led to a rise in debt, social tensions between the rich and poor, and an increase in poverty.

It is against this background that we must read these sermons. Doing deeds of charity, Edwards argued, is not only one way to live out the gospel, it is a means to spiritual discovery. "It is revealed that to live in love is the way to have much of the presence of God," Edwards wrote in "Much in Deeds of Charity," a sermon he delivered to his congregation in 1741. "But one thing wherein living in love does principally consist is living in deeds and fruit of love and charity."[58] Integral to a life of charity is providing for the needs of the poor and destitute. In arguing for the necessity of charity for the attainment of spiritual discoveries, Edwards again employs the language of diffusive love: "If we would obtain any great benefits at the hand of God for what we do in deeds of charity, we must not only do something but we must be liberal and bountiful, free-hearted and open-handed."[59] The hand which God regards in its giving, gives with a heart full of benevolence, joy, and liberality in her giving, a state that rises well above the obligation of duty and strengthens one's sense of assurance: "But a freeness to give away of our worldly possessions to the poor is an expression of our weanedness from the world and the looseness of our affections to these things and, therefore, fits persons for spiritual discoveries and comforts."[60] It is the Spirit, Edwards makes clear at the end of this sermon, who has effected this abundant liberality throughout the history of the church. In the past, God's Spirit blessed those who possessed this effusive temper, like Cornelius (Acts 10:1-2). In the present, Edwards draws our attention to the fact that the orphanage ministries of George Whitfield and August Francke have been wonderfully accompanied by remarkable outpourings of spiritual blessing. And in the future, "in that great outpouring of the Spirit of God that shall be in the latter days," God's Spirit shall bring about an abundance of deeds of charity in those who profess Christ, a point that Isaiah prophesied (Isa 31:1, 5, 8).[61] It is clear in these passages that the shape of divine love in the community of the faithful naturally mirrors the effusive nature of God's own love, precisely because that love which the church spreads abroad to the world and returns back to God is mysteriously none other than the Spirit himself, existing, working, and loving *ad extra* in the same way he does within the Godhead.

The Spirit is also observed within the church in and through their praying, a fact which Edwards observes in scattered places throughout his writings. In contrast to the theme of diffusion which we just observed in the church's love toward one another, we see in this context that the Spirit engenders a harmony,

---

58 Edwards, "Much in Deeds of Charity," in *Sermons Reader*, 200.
59 Edwards, "Much in Deeds of Charity," in *Sermons Reader*, 198.
60 Edwards, "Much in Deeds of Charity," in *Sermons Reader*, 205.
61 Edwards, "Much in Deeds of Charity," in *Sermons Reader*, 209-11.

excellency, and unity among the members of the church. Individually the Spirit engenders a holy temper within the believer, a temper that naturally leads the Christian to converse with God in prayer. "The spirit of prayer is a holy spirit, a gracious spirit. . . . The true spirit of prayer is no other than God's own Spirit dwelling in the hearts of the saints. And as this spirit comes from God, so doth it naturally tend to God in holy breathing and pantings. It naturally leads to God to converse with him by prayer."[62] As Edwards explains elsewhere, minds make their thoughts known to one another through the medium of conversation, and word and prayer are the main modes of conversation between human beings and God. "Conversation between God and mankind in this world, is maintained by God's *word* on his part, and by *prayer* on ours. By the former, he speaks and expresses his mind to us; by the latter, we speak and express our minds to him."[63] Both word and prayer are intimately associated with the Spirit in Edwards's theology. The Spirit inspires the written word through which Christians are illuminated to the things of God, and he draws them forth in returning the conversation as they seek out God's presence in prayer.

As the Spirit is the source of prayer for the Christian, so too is he the greatest good and reward that the church can seek after in their praying. Through prayer, the Spirit draws Christians into fellowship, communion, and union with God the Father as they are united to the Son. Yet he is also the reward of prayer, for he replicates the excellency of his immanent trinitarian being in the life of the church by uniting their hearts in love. Edwards makes this point explicit in his 1747 treatise *An Humble Attempt to Promote Explicit Agreement and Visible Union of God's People in Extraordinary Prayer*, a work he wrote to drum up support for the nascent concert of prayer movement where Christians would covenant to gather together at the same time in diverse points around the globe to beseech God for revivalistic blessings.[64] Drawing exegetical support from Zech 8:20-22, he argues that Scripture indicates that in the "latter days" there will be an extraordinary advancement of God's church across the face of the earth, a time that will be accompanied by many different peoples going "speedily to pray before the Lord, and to seek the Lord of Hosts" (Zech 8:21). This pilgrimage of the nations to seek out the Lord in prayer is evidence to Edwards that the church today should seek the Lord in a visible demonstration of united prayer for his gifts, blessings, and revival. Written in

---

62 Jonathan Edwards, "Hypocrites Deficient in the Duty of Prayer," in *The Works of President Edwards*, ed. Sereno E. Dwight (New York, 1830), vol. 6, 72-73. Hereafter, citations from this edition will be noted as "*Works (Dwight)*" followed by the volume and page numbers.

63 Edwards, "On the Medium of Moral Government," in *Works (Dwight)*, 7:282.

64 Jonathan Edwards, *An Humble Attempt to Promote Explicit Agreement and Visible Union of God's People in Extraordinary Prayer*, in *The Works of Jonathan Edwards*, vol. 5, *Apocalyptic Writings*, ed. Stephen J. Stein (New Haven: Yale University Press, 1977), 5:309-436 (hereafter *An Humble Attempt*).

the sad shadow of the Awakening's passing (from his vantage point), Edwards encouraged the New England church to join the concerted prayer effort that had been practiced by the church in Scotland in the ultimate hopes of hastening the latter days. Among his many reasons for encouraging the church toward this kind of prayer appear themes concerning the Spirit which by now ought to be familiar to us.

The Spirit, for Edwards, is the highest reward and greatest blessing that the church should seek after in prayer because he is the grace that Christ purchased on behalf of the church. "The Holy Spirit, in his indwelling, his influences and fruits, is the sum of all grace, holiness, comfort and joy, or in one word, of all the spiritual good Christ purchased for men in this world and is also the sum of all perfection glory and eternal joy, that he purchased for them in another world."[65] The fruits of such a visible united effort for the outpouring of the Spirit, Edwards argues, consists in the greater harmony and love among the members of the body of Christ. "Such an union in prayer for the general outpouring of the Spirit . . . . would tend very much to promote union and charity between distant members of the church of Christ, and a public spirit, and love to the church of God. . . . Union in religious duties, especially in the duty of prayer, in praying one with and for another, and jointly for their common welfare, above almost all other things, tends to promote mutual affection and endearment."[66] This harmony which obtains within the church community in the Spirit's outpouring is but a faint glimpse of his own internal glory externalized in creation. It is thus through the church that one can catch a faint glimpse of the Spirit's immanent workings.

Lastly, we may examine the Spirit's activity in Edwards's theology of the Lord's Supper. It has been observed that Edwards's theology of this sacrament has still not been fully examined due to the fact that in assessing his views, scholars have relied primarily upon his polemical works which he wrote to defend his rejection of his grandfather's position of open communion, a rejection that ultimately cost him his pulpit.[67] The half dozen sacramental

---

65 Edwards, *An Humble Attempt*, in *Works*, 5:341.
66 Edwards, *An Humble Attempt*, in *Works*, 5:366.
67 Both Kenneth P. Minkema and William J. Danaher Jr. make this observation. See Minkema's introductory essay, "Preface to the Period," (*Works* 14:38-9) and Danaher's article "By Sensible Signs Represented: Jonathan Edwards' Sermons on the Lord's Supper," *Pro Ecclesia* 7 (1998): 261-87. See also Walter V. L. Eversley's essay "The Pastor as Revivalist," in *Edwards in our Time: Jonathan Edwards and the Shaping of American Religion*, ed. Sang Hyun Lee and Allen C. Guelzo (Grand Rapids: Eerdmans, 1999), 113-30; and R. David Rightmire's "The Sacramental Theology of Jonathan Edwards in the Context of Controversy," in *Fides et Historia* 21.1 (Jan. 1989): 50-60. Edwards's two polemical writings on the Lord's Supper are *An Humble Inquiry into the Rules of the Word of God, Concerning the Qualifications Requisite to a Complete Standing and Full Communion in the Visible Christian Church*, (1749; hereafter, *An Humble Inquiry*) and his *Misrepresentations Corrected*,

sermons, which he wrote specifically to be preached on the observance of the Lord's Supper, and which have never been published (with the recent exception of one),[68] were written in the course of his pastoral ministry, not in the highly charged atmosphere of theological and ecclesiastical controversy. These sermons contain the marrow of his theology of the Supper. They reveal a more deeply sacramental view of the ordinance than has been recognized, and are significantly contrasted with the view found in his polemical writings, which are not so much concerned with sacramental theology *per se*, but more so with the delicate question of who should participate.[69] While it is beyond the scope of this study to adjudicate these discussions, two points can be made which faithfully represent his mature views on the Lord's Supper and which serve our purpose of illuminating the Spirit's part in the church's sacramental observance.

First, Edwards understands the observance of the Lord's Supper to be a visible reenacting of what has spiritually transacted between Christ and the members of the church in the covenant of grace, a point he makes clear in one section of *An Humble Inquiry*. Through the words and actions of the minister, Christ presents himself to believing communicants by exhibiting the sacrifice of his "body broken and his blood shed." Also through the offering of the sacramental elements to the communicants, "Christ presents himself... as their propitiation and bread of life; and by these outwards signs confirms and seals his sincere engagements to be their Savior and food, and to impart to them all the benefits of his propitiation and salvation."[70] Likewise, the communicants profess their adherence to Christ in the covenant of grace through receiving the elements. "[T]hey profess to embrace the promises and lay hold of the hope set before them, to receive the atonement, to receive Christ as their spiritual food, and to feed upon him in their hearts by faith."[71] This profession by Christ and his church in the sacrament, is a mutual profession of heart—"indeed what is professed on both sides is the heart." Through this mutual profession the invisible spiritual relation between Christ and the church is made visible. Both Christ and his people openly profess their union to each other through the signs woven into the ceremony of the Supper.[72]

---

and Truth Vindicated (1752; hereafter *Misrepresentations Corrected*). Both of these works are found in *The Works of Jonathan Edwards*, vol. 12, *Ecclesiastical Writings*, ed. David D. Hall (New Haven: Yale University Press, 1994), 165-348 and 349-504, respectively.

68 "The Spiritual Blessings of the Gospel Represented by a Feast," published in *Works*, 14:280-97, and believed to have been delivered between late 1728 and early 1729.

69 See Danaher's "By Sensible Signs Represented," 261-63.

70 Edwards, *An Humble Inquiry*, in *Works*, 12:256.

71 Edwards, *An Humble Inquiry*, in *Works*, 12:256.

72 "The established signs in the Lord's Supper are fully equivalent to words; they are a renewing and reiterating the same thing which was done before; only with this difference, that now it is done by speaking signs, whereas before it was by speaking

This emphasis on mutuality is linked to pneumatological themes which we find elsewhere in Edwards's theology. As Edwards illustrates in his sacramental sermons, this mutuality which Christ and the church enjoy in the observance of the Supper consists in a communing of a common good.[73] Communion for Edwards "is a common partaking of benefit, or of good, in union or society."[74] The common good which members partake of in union and society is none other than the Spirit himself; he is the common good which is enjoyed between Christ and his church,[75] and thus he is that common Spirit from which they drink in the Supper. Edwards deftly mixes all of these themes in an early sacramental sermon:

> The word "communion," as it is used in Scripture, signifies a common partaking of some good. Thus we read of the communion of the body of Christ and the communion of the blood of Christ, that is, the common partaking of his body and blood. Therefore, as in a feast they all have communion in the same fare with the those and with the other guests, so Christians have communion with Jesus: they partake of the same Spirit, of the same holiness and the same happiness; they are members of Christ's body and partake of the same life with the head; the are branches in him and partake of the same sap and nourishment with the vine. Christ and believers are partakers of the same Spirit. Christ has the Spirit not by measure, and they have of the same Spirit by measure [John 3:34]. Christ has all fullness of grace in him, and believers have grace for grace [John 1:16].[76]

Because they drink from one ocean of divine love, the church thus is unified. "And by this sacrament is well signified the union, love and communion of the saints. They feast together, friends and brethren, members of the same Lord, and those that drink of the same Spirit. They are of the same family and eat of the same spiritual meat and drink."[77] The Supper thus also signifies the invisible spiritual union that Christians themselves possess as one body, and like we observed with prayer above, promotes and confirms that union.

> sounds. Our taking the bread and wine is as much a professing to accept of Christ, at least as a woman's taking a ring of the bridegroom in her marriage is a profession and seal of her taking him for her husband." Edwards, *An Humble Inquiry*, in *Works*, 12:257.

73 See Danaher's analysis of this theme in his unpublished sermons in "By Sensible Signs Represented," 263-65.
74 Edwards, "Miscellanies" No. 404, in *Works*, 13:468.
75 "Hence our communion with God the Father and God the Son consists in our possessing of the Holy Ghost, which is their Spirit: for to have communion or fellowship with another, is to partake with them in their good in their fullness, in union and society with them." Edwards, *Treatise on Grace*, in *Works*, 21:188.
76 Edwards, "The Spiritual Blessings of the Gospel Represented by a Feast," in *Works*, 14:286-87.
77 Edwards, "The Spiritual Blessings of the Gospel Represented by a Feast," in *Works*, 14:289.

Second, we may observe the Spirit's activity in the Supper through the way Christ is present in its observance. Edwards frequently repeats the fact that Christ is present in the Lord's Supper: "Christ was not only with his disciples at the first sacrament, but he sits with his people in every sacrament."[78] This is not merely a symbolic presence simulated in the union of hearts of the communicants; as we saw above Christ *himself* is offering himself to them in the words and actions of the officiating minister. For Edwards, Christ is spiritually present by the Holy Spirit, or in other words, it is the Spirit who mediates the presence of Christ to the believer in the experience of the gospel and in the observance of the Lord's Supper. In a sermon on Psalm 72:6, Edwards lists the different ways that Christ "comes down from heaven," including his incarnation, his acts of providence and "in his saving influences of his Spirit on the hearts of men."[79] It is through this latter mode, he makes clear, that Christ is present in the Lord's Supper: as the Spirit fills the hearts of believers in their observance of the Lord's Supper, Christ "comes down" and communes with his people through the "saving influences of his Spirit," which presumably entails a spiritual sight of the glory of the gospel, a great love for God, communion with his people, and a deeply felt feeling of dependence upon God for their every need. The Spirit's work in communion in the hearts of believers is thus a concentration of what normally occurs in the course of the Christian's spiritual experiences. He fills them with the glorious knowledge of Christ their Savior, mediates the latter's spiritual presence to them so that they may enjoy the communion that is fitting between a bridegroom and bride, and illumines them to the unity they share as the bride of Christ. The Lord's Supper for Edwards, thus powerfully weaves together and makes visible everything that is spiritually transacted in the Christian life.

In all of these ways, either in his being the divine love which the church enjoys in God and in one another, in his engendering a spirit of prayer and unity among the church through their prayers, or by powerfully making visible to the saints and the world the invisible spiritual realities that obtain among the members of the church in their relation to Christ, the Spirit is reiterating his immanent trinitarian life *ad extra* in the church. In Edwards's theology of the church, we can view the Spirit's activity as the bond of union objectively through the way love fills the community of Christ, and through the excellent and harmonious society that the church reflects.

It is this love and this excellency that the church shall exemplify with greater

---

78 Edwards, "The Spiritual Blessings of the Gospel Represented by a Feast," in *Works*, 14:289.

79 Jonathan Edwards, unpublished sermon on Psalm 72:6, as quoted by Danaher, "By Sensible Signs Represented," 268. As Danaher rightly observes here, Edwards "did not go as far as Calvin himself did concerning the mode of Christ's communicating presence in the Lord's Supper. Like [the seventeenth-century Puritans], he tempered his thought on communion with key Zwinglian concepts."

intensity in the life to come. Heaven is a world of love and of divine excellency. It will be the place where the elect will be filled with divine love, where the saints dwell with one another and with God in perfect harmony, and where they shall "see" God all the more clearly in the beatific vision. To these issues we now turn.

Part IV

Finale

The Spirit and the Christian's Glorification

CHAPTER 7

Glorification: The Holy Spirit as the Bond of Union in Heaven[1]

[The saints in heaven] shall have the beatific vision of God because they will be full of God, filled with the Holy Spirit of God.[2]

In the spring of 1723, Jonathan Edwards came to a deeper appreciation of the value of heavenly mindedness. Having just completed his first stint as a pastor, an eight month ministry serving a small Presbyterian congregation in New York City, he came to the sober realization that "in every different state of life, I have hitherto been in, [I have always] thought the troubles and difficulties of that state, to be greater than those of any other, that I proposed to be in." Furthermore, even after efforts of personal reformation to better his condition and circumstances, "I have still thought the same; yea, that the difficulties of that state, are greater than those of that I left last." As it gradually dawns upon him that happiness, richness, and fullness in this life are fleeting dreams, and that all he can expect are difficulties and trouble, he shifts into prayer mode, asking for God's assistance to set his mind fully upon heaven.

> Lord, grant that from hence I may learn to withdraw my thoughts, affections, desires and expectations, entirely from the world, and may fix them upon the heavenly state; where there is fullness of joy; where reigns heavenly, sweet, calm and delightful love without alloy; where there are continually the dearest expressions of their love: where there is the enjoyment of the persons loved, without ever parting: where those persons, who appear so lovely in this world, will really be inexpressibly more lovely, and full of love to us. How sweetly will the mutual lovers join together to sing the praises of God and the Lamb! How full

---

1 A significant portion of this chapter can also found in my essay "A Brief History of Heaven in the Writings of Jonathan Edwards," to be published in the forthcoming book on the proceedings from the Northampton-Stockbridge Tercentenary Celebration of the Birth of Jonathan Edwards, October 2003, published by Edwin Mellen Press and edited by Richard Hall.
2 Jonathan Edwards, "Sermon VIII" (on Rom 2.10), in *Works (Dwight)*, 8:268.

will it fill us with joy to think, this enjoyment, these sweet exercises, will never cease or come to an end, but will last to all eternity.[3]

If the record of his notebooks and sermons on heaven are any indication, it seems that God did indeed answer this prayer. In them we find dozens of theological meditations on the nature of heaven, passages which comprise some of the most wonderfully written texts in all of his writings.

In this chapter we shall examine the Holy Spirit's activity found in Edwards's theology of glorification. Because the saints' ultimate glorification represents the culmination of all the currents of redemptive history, we will discover that the pneumatological themes covered in this chapter are merely amplifications of themes we have analyzed in previous chapters. The delight of holiness, joy of happiness, and divine love that fills the saints of heaven is none other than the Spirit himself, united to their souls. The love by which they love God is not distinct from God's own self-love communicated *ad extra*. Furthermore, the Spirit's union to the saint's soul is christologically oriented, drawing her further into union with Christ and, by implication, into a participation of Christ's sonship under God the Father. This christocentrism that the Spirit effects in the lives of the elect is also evident in the powerful vision they have of God. The spiritual sight by which the saints see God in this lifetime is immensely magnified in heaven as the beatific vision, which the saints shall forever enjoy with increasing clarity unto eternity. Edwards is also fond of articulating the final state of the heavenly church as one of increasing union and communion with God. He does not envision the perfection of the saints' union with God in static categories. Rather, it is a state that admits degrees and growth. The more the saint's capacity is filled with divine knowledge and love, the more she will be drawn further into union with God.

7.1 A Brief History of Heaven

Before we discuss the nature of the Spirit's work in the saints' glorification, it is necessary to paint the proper background of the nature and history of heaven in order to place our analysis in its proper context. Two major dimensions are helpful to keep in mind when investigating Edwards's fascinating "Miscellanies" entries on heaven: namely, the spacial and temporal dimensions. The former deals with the "place" of heaven and its creation. The latter deals with the history of heaven and is thus concerned more with redemption.

7.1.1 Heaven's Creation: Imagining Heaven's Place and Original Inhabitants

Spatially, Edwards affirms that "The creation consists in two parts, [the] upper

---

3 Edwards, "Diary," in *Works*, 16:768.

and lower [worlds]."[4] He has little difficulty establishing this distinction for he argues that Scripture plainly presents us with this view of the created order: (1) the Bible makes a clear contrast between this world and the world to come (Eph 1:21; Heb 2:5), (2) it portrays heaven as God's throne whereas earth is portrayed as his footstool (Is 66:1), and (3) it represents God as "looking down" or "coming down" out of heaven (Ps 33:13-14; Exod 19:11, 18, 20).[5] Accordingly, God created two types of intelligent creatures to inhabit each of these worlds: human beings for the lower world, earth, and angels for the upper world, heaven.[6] While neither world is incorruptible by nature (only God himself holds this privilege), God has granted a measure of incorruptibility to heaven *by grace*,[7] for the apparent reason that it is this part of creation where God dwells most fully,[8] and it was built specifically to be a "habitation for Christ, his dear Son," whom the angels were created to serve.[9] This grace, however, did not always render heaven's occupants incorruptible. "[T]he highest heavens in their own nature are capable of ruin," Edwards argues, "in the highest and most excellent part of it, in the head of all that part of the creation, and so of the whole creation, viz. Lucifer."[10] Consequently, Edwards argues that the faithful and loyal angels of heaven did not receive their "confirmation," or the reward of a "security of perseverance," until Christ's ascension to heaven.[11] Prior to this period, falling away was a real possibility for all angels. Thus while heaven is the place of God's dwelling in creation, its creatures are not so far removed from the lower world to be out of the reaches of sin, corruptibility, and decay. Heaven, like the lower world, is thus a place of drama in Edwards's theology, and as such it possesses a history that is linked to the cosmic redemption which God sovereignly orchestrates through all things.

Before we turn our attention to this history, a few words about Edwards's view of angels are appropriate. According to Edwards, angels are sentient, intelligent beings who possess no body and were created to serve Christ in heaven. He describes them as "a superior order of beings and of a more exalted nature and faculties by far than men."[12] As they were created for the upper world, so they possess a nature that is greater than humankind. He writes that

---

4 Edwards, "Miscellanies" No. 952, in *Works* 20:210.
5 See Edwards's exegesis of these and many more passages not only in "Miscellanies" No. 952 (*Works*, 20:210-11), but also more extensively in "Miscellanies" No. 743 (*Works*, 18: 376-83).
6 Edwards, "Miscellanies" No. 952, in *Works*, 20:210-11.
7 "[H]eaven is incorruptible . . . by the divine will and grace, and not necessarily from the nature of heaven." See "Miscellanies" No. 952, in *Works*, 20:211.
8 Edwards, "Miscellanies" No. 743, in *Works*, 18:376-78.
9 Edwards, "Miscellanies" No. 952, in *Works*, 20:212.
10 Edwards, "Miscellanies" No. 952, in *Works*, 20:211.
11 See "Miscellanies" No. 744, in *Works*, 18:383-90.
12 Edwards, "Miscellanies" No. 681, in *Works*, 18:239.

they "will indeed evermore excel the saints in strength and wisdom,"[13] thereby reflecting God's natural attributes with greater clarity than the saints shall ever attain.

If it is the case that angels are higher than humankind in the order of nature, then why does God assign them the task of serving the church (Heb 1:14)? Furthermore, why would God, in the course of redemption, choose human nature to unite himself with rather than angelic nature? Does not the order of nature render it fit, beautiful, and excellent to respect the scale of being and the superiority of angelic nature when initiating the cosmic work of redemption? Edwards answers these questions by pointing to the logic of the gospel. In the grand scheme of things, angels, the superior beings, are to serve the church, the inferior, because by this service the wisdom and depths of God's grace shine more brightly in the universe. It is a central pillar of the gospel that God, the greatest of all beings, humbled himself, united himself to humanity by taking on the form of the servant, and endured the shame of death on a cross. In doing so, he disarmed the powers and authorities by procuring eternal life for his own people just at the very point when it seemed that he had been defeated. Edwards notes that this logic is applied by the apostles to other relationships within the church: between and among church members (1 Cor 12:23-24; "upon [the less honorable members] we bestow more abundant honor"), and between church leaders and the flock (Matt 20:25-27; "whosoever will be chief among you, let him be your servant").[14] Given this economy in God's gracious kingdom, Edwards reasons that the angels are "sent forth to minister to them that shall be the heirs of salvation, and so in some respect are made inferior to the saints in honor," precisely because they are superior to the church in both nature and order of being.

> God's ways are all analogous, and his dispensations harmonize one with another. As 'tis between the saints that are of an inferior order of beings [sic], and the angels who are of more exalted nature and degree, and also between those Christians on earth that are of inferior order, and those who are of superior, being ministers of Christ; so without doubt it also is in some respect in heaven between those that are of lower, and those that are of higher degrees of glory.[15]

The result of this is that humanity, though lower in the order of nature than angels, shall enjoy a greater honor in heaven than the angels. In other words, they shall outshine the angles in reflecting God's moral attributes. "[T]he angles will indeed evermore excel the saints in strength and wisdom, for their office requires [them] to be universal ministers of God in the universe, but [they shall not excel the saints] in grace and sweet holiness and love to God;

---

13 Edwards, "Miscellanies" No. 103, in *Works*, 13:271.
14 Edwards, "Miscellanies" No. 681, in *Works*, 18:239-40.
15 Edwards, "Miscellanies" No. 681, in *Works*, 18:240.

which excellencies are the highest."[16] Another result of this divine design is that it allows no one, neither angel nor human, any room for boasting. The angel, while exalted in nature over humanity, is evermore to serve Christ and his people, a service which in heaven shall be performed in gladness and out of sweet love and admiration for God. The saint, while exalted to the heights of trinitarian communion, ever remembers in her salvation the depths of sin from which she was redeemed, and the condescension of God in assuming human nature unto himself. "Thus wisely hath God ordered all things for his own glory, that however great and marvelous the exercises of his grace and love and condescension are to the creature, yet he alone may be exalted, that he may be all in all."[17]

7.1.2 Heaven and the History of Redemption

As we turn our attention to heaven's history, or to the temporal aspects of Edwards's understanding of heaven, we are first confronted with the fact that while angels are heaven's inhabitants originally by creation, God designs heaven to be the final abode of all his elect creatures by redemption. "The one of these worlds [i.e., the lower world, earth] is to fall and be ruined, and is to be the eternal seat of those creatures that fall and are ruined; the other [the upper world, heaven] is to stand and to be exalted, and brought to higher excellency, perfection and glory, and is to be the seat of those creatures that stand and are brought to higher excellency."[18] This history is fascinating, yet it is difficult to outline from the tangle of his many different meditations on heaven. We know, from a letter written to the trustees of the College of New Jersey in October, 1757, that toward the end of his life he was preparing to write a "great work" entitled *A History of the Work of Redemption*, "a body of divinity in an entire new method, being thrown into the form of an history." In it, he expresses his wish to write a history that "will be carried on with regard to all three worlds, heaven, earth and hell: considering the connected, successive events and alterations, in each so far as the Scriptures give any light."[19] It is beyond the scope of this chapter to detail the entirety of this tripartite history. For our purposes a brief history of heaven will suffice, a history which Edwards notes is demarcated by two major events: Christ's ascension, and the final resurrection and judgment.[20] These two events thus divide the history of

---

16 Edwards, "Miscellanies" No. 103, in *Works*, 13:271.
17 Edwards, "Miscellanies" No. 681, in *Works*, 18:242.
18 Edwards, "Miscellanies" No. 952, in *Works*, 20:211.
19 Edwards, Letter No. 230, "To the Trustees of the College of New Jersey," October 19, 1757, in *Works*, 16:727-28.
20 For entries on the effect of the ascension of Christ on heaven and the confirmation of the angels, see "Miscellanies" Nos. 442, 515, 570, 591, 593, 664b, 702 corollary 4, 744, and 939. For the effect of the consummation of all things upon heaven, see

heaven up into three periods.

7.1.3 Heaven's First Period: From Creation to Christ's Ascension

The first age of heaven Edwards does not name, but we may call it an age of probation for the angels. As noted above, Edwards does not hold even the highest heavens to be immune from rebellion against God. The angels had an ability to sin similar to pre-lapsarian Adam, yet they were by "divine will and grace" blessed with a substantial capacity for obedience to God. Nonetheless, some of the angels fell away, even the greatest of all of them, Lucifer, whom Edwards holds to have been the "head of all that part of creation."[21] Edwards describes the fall of the angels in "Miscellanies" No. 702 by means of a fascinating exegesis of Psalm 2. There the Psalmist portrays the divine declaration to the kings of the earth that God has established his own king as messiah and sovereign over the earth (v. 6: "I set my king upon my holy hill of Zion"). This king, Edwards writes, was "begotten out of the earthly chaos" and "exalted to the honor of sonship." The rest of earth's kings, however, despised this divine declaration, "and could not bear to submit to this person that God had *anointed* to be king over them, and therefore entered into conspiracy to oppose and resist this design, and deliver themselves from such subjection (vv. 2-3)."[22]

What does this have to do with the fall of Satan and his angels? One important point to remember about Edwards's theological reflections on heaven is that he places a great deal of importance on symmetry, proportionality, and balance between the parallel histories of earth and heaven: "God's ways are all analogous, and his dispensations harmonize one with another."[23] Thus, what is portrayed by Psalm 2 in the earth's history mirrors an event that took place in the highest of heavens before the creation of humankind. When God was about to create the human race, Edwards notes, he declared to the thrones and powers of heaven his plan of redemption to unite all things under Christ, as well as his intention for the angels to be servants of the church. Not wanting to submit to this service of a lower race, and to a God-man who is destined to rule over heaven, there arose "a conspiracy amongst the thrones and principalities in heaven," and a host of angels fell.[24]

The remaining angels, Edwards continues, were assigned the task of serving the "church," which at this time consisted of the Old Testament saints who remained faithful to Yahweh. Upon the death of these saints, they were

---

"Miscellanies" No. 664b corollary 9, his lengthy entry No. 952, and Nos. 1122 and 1126.
21 Edwards, "Miscellanies" No. 952, in *Works*, 20:211.
22 Edwards, "Miscellanies" No. 702 corollary 3, in *Works*, 18:301.
23 Edwards, "Miscellanies" No. 681, in *Works*, 18:240.
24 Edwards, "Miscellanies" No. 702 corollary 3, in *Works*, 18:301-2.

escorted to heaven by angels where they remained awaiting the final resurrection. Their time in heaven did not consist of a waiting game or of a static state. Rather, Edwards argued that the Old Testament saints viewed with great delight the slow progression of God's kingdom in the centuries prior to Christ's coming. "It seems to be probable that that part of the church that is in heaven have been, from the beginning of the world, progressive in their light and in their happiness, as the church on earth has; and that much of their happiness has consisted in seeing the progressive wonderful doings of God with respect to his church here in his world."[25] Thus Moses saw Israel's entrance into the promised land from heaven with greater joy than he could have on earth.[26] This also explains the reason how Abraham rejoiced to see Christ's day (John 8:56),[27] and why the angels of heaven rejoiced greatly (Luke 2:13-14) over the birth of Christ, because their "salvation," in the form of their confirmation, was tied to him, a point we shall examine in the next stage in heaven's history.

7.1.4 Heaven's Second Period: From Christ's Ascension to the Consummation

The second age of heaven begins at the point of Christ's ascension. For Edwards, a fundamental dynamic which courses through the history of heaven consists in the growth of its inhabitant's happiness, a growth which takes place visually through beholding new "accession[s] of [God's] glory and blessedness."[28] To see more of God's glory increases the blessed happiness of the heavenly church and angels. One of the greatest of these new "accessions" occurred at the time of Christ's ascension to heaven, an event that brought a remarkable transformation to the angelic community. At the ascension, the angels received their "confirmation," or the reward of "eternal life," which rendered them unable to fall away from God. Edwards offers two arguments to prove this point. His first is based upon a detailed exegesis of Eph 4:10 ("He that descended is the same also that ascended up far above all heavens, that he might fill all things"), which seems to indicate that Christ "fills all things" at his ascension.[29] Drawing upon other Pauline parallels (Eph 1:10, 20-22; Phil 2:9-10; Col 1:20), Edwards concludes that "all things" refers to the totality of elect creatures, including both the church and angels. When Paul mentions that Christ "fills" all things, here and in Eph 1:22 ("the fullness of him that *filleth all in all*"), Edwards interprets this idea as follows: "The Apostle here has a special respect to his filling the angels, and particularly their being subjected to him, to receive their fullness from him as their head and as their Lord at his

---

25 Edwards, "Miscellanies" No. 421, in *Works*, 13:478.
26 Edwards, "Miscellanies" No. 421, in *Works*, 13:478.
27 Edwards, "Miscellanies" No. 777 corollary 3, in *Works*, 18:432.
28 Edwards, "Miscellanies" No. 777 corollary 3, in *Works*, 18:431.
29 See his extended argument in "Miscellanies" No. 744 (*Works*, 18:383-90).

ascension."[30] These observations are strong evidence to Edwards that Eph 4:10 refers to a greater fullness that the angels receive from Christ at his ascension.

A second argument, based upon John 6:33 ("the bread of God is he which cometh down and giveth life unto the world"), illustrates that this fullness which the angels receive from Christ is literally "eternal life."[31] Edwards notes that the discussion between Jesus and the Jewish rulers in John's text makes reference to Ps 78:25, which speaks of manna as the "angels' food" given to humankind ("Man did eat angels' food"). Edwards's point is simple: Jesus Christ is not only the bread of life given for the eternal life of the human world, but also "angels' food" by which they too eat unto eternal life. By uniting these two arguments, Edwards concludes that upon Christ's ascension to heaven, the angels received eternal life as a reward for their persevering obedience. Consequently, he discerns a grand symmetry between the two worlds, and how all are united in Christ:

> Here we may take occasion to observe the sweet harmony that there is between God's dispensations, and particularly the analogy and agreement there is between his dealings with the angels and his dealings with mankind: that though one is innocent and the other guilty, the one having eternal life by a covenant of grace, the other by a covenant of works, yet both have eternal life by his Son Jesus Christ God-man; and both, though different ways, by the humiliation and sufferings of Christ, the one as the price of life, the other as the greatest and last trial of their steadfast and persevering obedience.[32]

This concern of Edwards's for symmetry and proportion between the upper and lower worlds occupies a key role in his reflections on heaven, allowing him to bring clarity to the glimpses of heaven found in the biblical witness. Of even greater significance to his theology, however, is his emphasis on the progressive nature of the heavenly state. Edwards has numerous lengthy "Miscellanies" entries treating this topic, showing that heaven's happiness, joy, and holiness consist in a continual increase from glory to glory.[33] "'Tis God's manner to keep things always progressive, in a preparatory state, as long as there is another change to a more perfect state yet behind [i.e., beyond]."[34] The theological bedrock of this idea lies in God's infinitely communicative disposition; heaven *must* be progressive because God designs to communicate his infinite fullness to a finite creation. Since the finite cannot receive the infinite, this goal is never realized in time and space. Yet this does not stop God from aiming at this end in pouring out his love and joy upon his elect

---

30 Edwards, "Miscellanies" No. 744, in *Works*, 18:385.
31 Found in "Miscellanies" No. 744, in *Works*, 18:387.
32 Edwards, "Miscellanies" No. 744 corollary 1, in *Works*, 18:387-88.
33 For an excellent overview on this theme, see Paul Ramsey's essay, "Heaven is a Progressive State," in *Works*, 8:706-38.
34 Edwards, "Miscellanies" No. 435, in *Works*, 13:483.

creatures. "Let the most perfect union with God be represented by something at an infinite height above us; and the eternally increasing union of the saints with God, by something that is ascending constantly towards that infinite height, moving upwards with a given velocity; and that is to continue thus to move to all eternity."[35] It is because of this basic dynamic in his theology that Edwards has a great interest in preserving the elements of drama, hope, and increase throughout the entire history of heaven.

It is at this point where Edwards appears to have run into a difficulty. Does the church which now resides in heaven partake of this increase before the resurrection, and if so how? Edwards could biblically defend the idea that the heavenly church before the advent of Christ progressed in their understanding and joy as they learned of plan of salvation and of Jesus Christ (i.e. John 8:56; "Your father Abraham rejoiced to see my day: and he saw it, and was glad"). Likewise, he could affirm that the angels grew in their joy both before and after their confirmation, for at all times they rejoice at the repentance of sinners (Luke 15:7), and after Pentecost they learn more about the wisdom and glory of God through the church (Eph 3:10). Edwards also had little difficulty arguing for the eternal increase of the heavenly community after the day of judgment.[36] Could he say the same thing about the church as it now exists in heaven during this second stage of heaven's history? With this we turn our attention more specifically to the church triumphant and the Spirit's role in their pre-resurrection state.

7.1.5 The Church Triumphant and the Beatific Vision

Edwards divides the church this side of the day of judgment into two parts: the earthly church, or church militant, which resides in the lower world; and the heavenly church, or the church triumphant, which has triumphed in Christ and now resides in heaven. He notes that the saints who make up the church triumphant are called "the spirits of just men, made perfect" (Heb 12:23). If the church triumphant consists of "spirits . . . made perfect," then can one biblically affirm a progression in their holiness and happiness? How can perfection be improved upon? The key to his argument lies in the nature of perfection. Perfection for Edwards admits degrees, and if so then there can be a progression of greater and greater perfection in heaven. "Indeed, the spirits of just men made perfect will be perfectly free from sin and sorrow, [and] will have inexpressible, inconceivable happiness and perfect contentment; but yet part of their happiness will consist in hope of what is to come."[37] Present

---

35 Edwards, *End of Creation*, in *Works*, 8:534.
36 "That the glorified spirits shall grow in holiness and happiness to eternity, I argue from this foundation, that their number of ideas shall increase to eternity." Edwards, "Miscellanies" No. 105, in *Works*, 13:275; see also No. 198 (*Works*, 13:336-37).
37 Edwards, "Miscellanies" No. 371, in *Works*, 13:443.

perfection is not inconsistent with a hope of greater things to come, in this case the biblical hope of the future resurrection. Scripture's own categories, Edwards surmises, seem to indicate that the present perfection of the saints in heaven admits to a future increase. Taking this scriptural lead, he develops two arguments which confirm that the current church in heaven is progressive in its nature.

First, Edwards argues that the church triumphant is progressive in its sense of anticipation of the glorious events to come in redemptive history. While they are already redeemed and enjoy the presence of Christ in heaven, there is still a greater and more perfect state of events that they hope for. In "Miscellanies" No. 371, Edwards lists five ways in which the saints will be more perfect after the resurrection and day of judgment, ways which occupy the current hopes of the church triumphant. The saints first "will be in the natural state of union with bodies" after the resurrection, "bodies perfectly fitted for the uses of a holy glorified soul." Second, the church of Christ shall be perfect and complete, no more parts of it shall be under sin, affliction or in the militant state. Third, Christ's work shall be fully completed, his reward obtained, and his joy truly made complete at this time; "and his members must needs rejoice with him." Fourth, all of God's "deep designs" will have unfolded, and "then the wisdom of his marvelous contrivances in his hidden, intricate and inexplicable works appear, the end being obtained." And lastly, that great wedding feast of the Lamb shall commence, the "day of Christ's triumph, and this day will last forever. This will be the wedding day between Christ and the church, and this wedding day will last forever."[38] Currently, the saints in heaven eagerly anticipate these events with great joy and hope, in spite of the fact that they are perfect and now reside with Christ in glory. Their happiness, while perfect, anticipates a greater happiness dawning on the horizon of the consummation. Edwards likens this happiness to that of a bride-to-be on the eve of her wedding day: "The happiness the church in heaven now has in Christ, compared with their ultimate happiness, is like that of lovers in mutual conversation and manifestation of love, after they are betrothed, and that are in hope and expectation of nearer union and more full enjoyment."[39]

Yet the joy of the church triumphant is not only based upon the anticipation of what will be, it also is fueled by what is now taking place in the redemption of sinners on earth. The main reason Edwards argues for the progressive nature of the saints in heaven has to do with (1) their sight of God, commonly known as the beatific vision, and (2) how this sight is connected with their awareness of God's work in the lower world. Edwards links these two ideas in "Miscellanies" No. 777. A true sight of God, Edwards argues, is both a christological and a redemptive-historical affair. The two are inseparable.

---

38 Edwards, "Miscellanies" No. 371, in *Works*, 13:443-44.
39 Edwards, "Miscellanies" No. 435, in *Works*, 13:484.

> 'Tis God's pleasure that Christ should be the light, the Sun of heaven, by which God should be seen and known there, for it pleases the Father that in him all fullness should dwell. And again they see and know God in heaven in his works, which are the effects of the glorious perfections there are in him; and this also is in Christ, of all the works of God are wrought in him by whom all things are made. . . . So far as they see God and know him in his works (which is the principle way in which God manifests himself . . .) they see and know [him] as he manifests himself in the work of redemption, which [is] the greatest and most glorious of all God's works, the work of works to which all God's works are reduced.[40]

Knowledge of Christ is inseparable from a knowledge of redemptive history. Therefore, a true sight of God necessarily entails an understanding of his redemptive dealings with his creatures, a narrative that is intimately bound to Christ. The saints in heaven do not know a God who is divorced from history, or an ethereal beatific luminosity that has limited concern for time and space. Rather they know the God of Abraham, Isaac, and Jacob, the God who led his people out of Egypt and into the promised land, the God who spoke through the prophets, the God who ultimately manifested himself through his only Son who takes away the sins of the world, and the God who is now orchestrating the events of redemptive history to sum up all things under Christ. It is through the medium of this christologically-oriented, redemptive-historical visage that the heavenly saints "see" God. They do not see him directly (only Christ does); they rather see him in his works, for here is where he reveals himself to the creature. "[T]hat beatifical vision that the saints have of God heaven, is in beholding the manifestations that he makes of himself in the work of redemption."[41]

In his sermon on Rom 2:10, Edwards expands with great detail upon the nature of the beatific vision. This vision substantially coincides with the spiritual sight that Christians today enjoy on earth. The main difference between the two is that the beatific vision is not mixed with the darkness of sin and doubt. "It will be an Intuitive view of God," he writes, "it shall be perfect in its kind, it shall be perfectly certain, without any doubt or possibility of doubt." Here the saints see God by a reflexive light refracted through the lenses of Scripture, the ordinances, and nature. There the saints shall see God directly as in the noonday sun: "There shall be a view of God in his being, and in his power, and wisdom, and holiness, and goodness, and love, and all-sufficiency, that shall be attended with intuitive certainty. . . . They shall behold

---

40 Edwards, "Miscellanies" No. 777, in *Works*, 18:430.
41 Edwards, "Miscellanies" No. 777 corollary 1, in *Works*, 18:431. By contrast, Ramsey notes that medieval theologians, such as Aquinas, emphasized a vision of God's spiritual glory that is apprehended by bodily eyes. See his essay, "Heaven is a Progressive State," in *Works*, 8:719-23.

the infinite excellency and glory of God."[42] They do not see his attributes, nor do they see God with physical eyes. Rather through the contemplation of Christ, his person, his love, his conversation, and his work of redemption which he orchestrates on earth, the saints perceive, with ever increasing amazement and wonder, the manifold glories of God. Such a sight reveals God to them, and is of such excellency and divine beauty that they are drawn further and further outside of themselves in love.

> This very manifestation that God will make of himself that will cause the beatific vision, will be an act of love in God . . . . When they see God so glorious, and at the same time see how greatly this God loves them, what delight will it not cause in the soul! Love desires union. They shall therefore see this glorious God united to them, and see themselves united to him. They shall see that he is their Father, and that they are his children. They shall see God gloriously present with them; God with them; and God in them; and they in God.[43]

As we might expect, Edwards identifies the Holy Spirit as the agent of the beatific vision. "As it is by the Holy Spirit that a spiritual sight of God is given in this world, so it is the same Holy Spirit by whom the beatific vision is given of God in heaven."[44] Immersed in the Spirit, with no contrary impulse to sin, the saint discerns the manifestations of divine glory which are sighted in the excellent progression of the history of redemption, from the answer of a prayer of deliverance, to the great outpouring of the Spirit of revival on earth. The more God manifests himself gloriously on behalf of the church militant, the more the church triumphant discerns his infinite excellency and responds in love. All this is by the Spirit.

Edwards concludes from his understanding of the beatific vision that "the saints in heaven see what comes to pass in the church on earth."[45] If God is the final object of their affectionate vision, and if they can view his glories in Christ himself and through the progress of redemption, then it must be the case that they are somehow spectators of the redemptive historical events on earth. "Shall the royal family be kept in ignorance of the success of the affairs of the kingdom?"[46] Edwards explains this in two ways. Earlier in his theological development, he supposes that the heavenly saints learn about earthly redemptive-historical events through their interaction with the angels who are eyewitnesses to God's work on earth. "One end of the creation of angels, and

---

42 Jonathan Edwards, "Sermon VIII" (on Rom 2:10), in *Works (Dwight)*, 8:266-67.
43 Edwards, "Sermon VIII" (on Rom 2:10), in *Works (Dwight)*, 8:267. In this portion of the sermon, Edwards is addressing the beatific vision from the vantage point of the consummate state, after the resurrection and day of judgment. These reflections, however, can apply to the heavenly church prior to this final state.
44 Edwards, "Sermon VIII" (on Rom 2:10), in *Works (Dwight)*, 8:268.
45 Edwards, "Miscellanies" No. 777 corollary 2, in *Works*, 18:431.
46 Edwards, "Miscellanies" No. 529, in *Works*, 18:71.

giving them such great understanding," he writes in "Miscellanies" No. 555, "was that they might be fit witnesses and spectators of God's works here below, and might behold all parts of the divine scheme." Human beings by contrast "see but very little" of this scheme, and live such short lives to take in any correct view of it on earth (even with divine revelation!). Given the fact that Scripture indicates that there is one society in heaven (Heb 12:22-23), it would be a remarkable thing if there were no conversations on this subject between the saints and angels in heaven.[47]

Later, however, Edwards became increasingly convinced that the saints' vision of the earthly church was intimately connected with their union with Christ. "Christ is the head of the glorified saints in heaven," which entitles them to be with him in all things, "being partakers with him in all the exaltation and glory, all his reward, all his enjoyment of God the Father." As the head, Christ is "the sight of the eyes that are in the head for the information of the whole body." Thus, "What he sees of the church of God on earth, and of the flourishing of religion here, they see according to their capacity. What he sees of the punishment of his enemies in hell, they see in him."[48] Edwards does not explain the details as to how exactly the saints see things "in him," though he does indicate that they have a direct view of the church militant's activities, likening their view to a mountaintop experience where one can see the vast panorama of the valley below.

> And ascending to a pinnacle in the very center of light, where everything appears in clear view, the saints that are ascended to heaven have advantage to view the state of Christ's kingdom in this world, and the works of the new creation here, as much greater than they had before; as a man that ascends to the top of an high mountain has greater advantage to view the face of the earth than he had while he was below.[49]

From this heavenly overlook they see the great advancements of God's kingdom on earth, which reveals the divine glory more and more fully as the ages progress. Before the advent of Christ, "the church in heaven had a new accession of glory when the church on earth was redeemed out of Egypt." Later "they had another happy period of glorious advancement in the time the establishment of the throne of David and Solomon; and again had another happy period of new accession of glory at the redemption of the church on earth out of Babylon."[50] In the current age of heaven, the church triumphant has advanced ever higher in their knowledge of God's glory through viewing the ascension of Christ, the day of Pentecost, and onward "in Constantine's

---

47 Edwards, "Miscellanies" No. 555, in *Works*, 18:99-100. See also "Miscellanies" No. 529 for similar arguments (*Works*, 18:71-3).
48 Edwards, "Miscellanies" No. 1089, in *Works*, 20:469-70.
49 Edwards, "Miscellanies" No. 1089, in *Works*, 20:471-72.
50 Edwards, "Miscellanies" No. 777 corollary 3, in *Works*, 18:432.

time, and at the Reformation; and again, far above all that has been hitherto, in the fall of Antichrist, and the beginning of the millennium."[51] Not only shall they see these events, but they shall interpret them with a wisdom and knowledge that enables them to "understand the marvelous steps that divine wisdom takes in all that is done, and the glorious ends he accomplishes, and what opposition Satan makes, and how he is baffled and overthrown. They can see the wise connection of one event with another and the beautiful order of all things that come to pass in the church in different ages, that to us appear like confusion."[52] The combined effect of these sightings of God's redemptive work on the earth only increases the joy and happiness of the heavenly saints. Thus he was able to affirm, to his own satisfaction, that the current state of heaven is a progressive state.

7.2 Heaven is a World of Union: Heaven's Third Period from the Consummation to Eternity

As glorious as this portrait is of heaven populated by the glorified spirits of the redeemed, there remains still an even greater glory to come, a state of divine joy which renders the current state of heaven as a "night" in comparison to the "day" of the consummated state of the church. This state comprises the third great period in the history of heaven. "It looks to me probable that the glory of the state of the church after the resurrection will as much exceed the present glory of the just men made perfect, as the glory of the gospel dispensation exceeds the Mosaic dispensation." Edwards argues this in "Miscellanies" No. 710. The Old Testament "church" saw God's redemptive design "very darkly" and by "reflex light." They "saw gospel things in dark types and shadows, and in dark sayings that were as it were riddles and enigmas."[53] In the gospel dispensation, the church enjoys the "daylight" of Christ; the veil is removed enabling the church to see Christ and gospel things "with open face" (2 Cor 3:18). Yet even in the light of this day, they still see by a reflexive light, "through a glass dimly" (1 Cor 13:12), enough so that Paul was not permitted to speak of the things he saw there (2 Cor 12:4).[54] When the saints are absent from the body and present with the Lord in heaven, their vision into the things of God and the gospel increases immensely for then they shall see "face to face" (1 Cor 13:10, 12). "And therefore, when the soul of the saint leaves the body and goes to heaven, it will be like coming out of the dim light of the night into daylight."[55]

---

51 Edwards, "Miscellanies" No. 777 corollary 3, in *Works*, 18:432. See No. 529 (*Works*, 18:71) for his reference to Pentecost.
52 Edwards, "Miscellanies" No. 529, in *Works*, 18:72.
53 Edwards, "Miscellanies" No. 710, in *Works*, 18:335.
54 Edwards, "Miscellanies" No. 710, in *Works*, 18:335-36.
55 Edwards, "Miscellanies" No. 710, in *Works*, 18:336.

Edwards applies this logic of successive degrees of glory to the relationship between the glorified spirits and the resurrected glorified saints. Though the glorified souls in heaven "can't be said properly to see as in an enigma, yet 'tis but darkly in comparison of what they will see after the resurrection." Biblically, Edwards supports this position with 1 John 3:2, which states that when Christ appears at his second coming (after the millennium, in Edwards's eschatology), "we shall be like him; for we shall see him as he is." He notes that this sight of Christ at his appearing seems to be depicted by the Apostle as containing a new element that was never before discerned by the church triumphant: "the sight that the saints shall have at the resurrection is spoken as if it were the first sight, wherein they should see him as he is. . . . The glory of Christ is what will as it were then first appear to all the church, to all that shall then lift up their heads out of their graves to behold it, as well as those that will then be alive."[56] Edwards does not specify what this new element of glory is in their sight of Christ, yet he does liken it to the dawning of a new day.

Heaven in its final state commences with the resurrection and day of judgment. Afterwards, heaven shall ascend to a new level of happiness, glory, and joy as the following realities obtain: individuals in the church are finally united to their resurrection bodies, the church is no more divided between the upper and lower worlds, all receive their heavenly rewards, and Christ's bride, the church, enters into the eternal marriage-day feast of the Lamb. Heaven itself is transformed because Christ, whose glory is the light of heaven, receives greater glory at the final triumph and judgment over all his enemies. "It seems impossible that it should be otherwise than that all heaven should put on new glory at the same time that Christ puts on new glory. All must be altered [in] proportion, for Christ is the glory of heaven, the beauty and ornament, life and soul of all; and there is no glory there, but only the reflection of his glory, and the emanation of his brightness and life."[57] Edwards's reflections on the "stuff" of heaven and the nature of the saints' glorified bodies remain some of the most fascinating, if not the most speculative, reflections in his theology. Heaven will be a place where light and sound shall be conveyed with much more accuracy, and the saints' senses shall be so fine tuned that "aught we know they may distinctly see the beauty of one another's countenances and smiles, and hold a delightful and most intimate conversation, at a thousand miles' distance."[58] New proportionalities may exist there in the medium of creation which shall effect exceedingly great joys in the elect.[59] In contrast to

---

56 Edwards, "Miscellanies" No. 710, in *Works*, 18:337.
57 Edwards, "Miscellanies" No. 952, in *Works*, 20:216.
58 Edwards, "Miscellanies" No. 263, in *Works*, 13:369.
59 "And in all probability, the abode of the saints after the resurrection will be so contrived by God, that there shall be external beauties and harmonies altogether of another kind from what we perceive here, and probably those beauties will appear

the current state of earth where decay and corruption prevail, "by length of time things become more and more youthful [in heaven], that is more vigorous, active, tender and beautiful."[60] Because the light there shall be provided by the Lord's glorified body, it shall prove to be "a perfectly different sort of light" from what we are used to, "exciting a sensation or idea in the beholders perfectly different – of which we can no more conceive than we can conceive of a color we never saw, or than a blind man can conceive of light and colors – a sort of light immensely more pleasant and glorious, in comparison of which the sun is a shade, and his light but darkness."[61] The saints' glorified bodies shall be attuned to every physical pleasure, in a way that shall not inhibit but only add to their spiritual pleasures.[62] "Every perceptive faculty shall be an inlet of delight."[63] They shall shine with the glory of the Lord's light.[64] Edwards even went so far as to speculate that they may be able to discern the excellencies of each other's mind by an immediate intellectual view of each other's soul.[65]

It is in these settings that the church as the bride of Christ unites with her bridegroom in an everlasting wedding day. And it is also here where the saints enjoy the pneumatological fullness of God, primarily as He is poured out on them as the mutual love between the Father and Son. In the remaining pages of this section we will analyze three facets of his doctrine of glorification which relate to the Spirit's activity as the bond of union in the elect: (1) the nature of the divine love which the saints partake of, (2) the saints union with Christ, and (3) the eternal progression of the saints' union with God.

7.2.1 Heaven: The Place of Love

Heaven, as Edwards writes in his well-known sermon, is a world of love. As such, it is a world of union, communion with the eternal Trinity and partaking of the delights of his glorious attributes. As it is the place of love, so too is it the place where the Spirit's presence is most fully felt, primarily as the mutual love of the Father and the Son. "There [in heaven] dwells God the Father, and so the Son, who are united in infinitely dear and incomprehensible mutual

---

    chiefly on the bodies of the man Christ Jesus and of the saints." Edwards, "Miscellanies" No. 182, in *Works*, 13:328.
60 Edwards, "Miscellanies" No. 206, in *Works*, 13:341.
61 Edwards, "Miscellanies" No. 721, in *Works*, 18:350-51.
62 Edwards, "Miscellanies" No. 233, in *Works*, 13:350-51.
63 Edwards, "Miscellanies" No. 721, in *Works*, 18:350.
64 Edwards, "Miscellanies" No. 263, in *Works*, 13:369-70.
65 "It is out of doubt with me, that there will [be] immediate intellectual views of minds, one of another and of the supreme mind, more immediate, clear and sensible than our views of bodily things with bodily eyes." Edwards, "Miscellanies" No. 182, in *Works*, 13:329.

love."[66] Edwards's trinitarian logic centering on the Father's and Son's infinite mutual love for one another, surfaces again in Edwards's portrayals of heavenly love. In a section of "Heaven is a World of Love," where he addresses the "the subjects of [divine love]," he analyzes the logical direction of this love as it unfolds and fills all the heavens. This love is primarily toward Christ the Son, and secondarily toward all those who are united to him. What is important to note is that this love shared by all is the same inner-trinitarian love which he describes in his *Discourse on the Trinity*. He writes in his sermon: "The infinite essential love of God is, as it were, an infinite and eternal mutual holy energy between the Father and the Son, a pure holy act whereby the Deity becomes nothing but an infinite and unchangeable act of love, which proceeds from both the Father and the Son." It is this love which is shared "secondarily" by all those in heaven; "it flows out in innumerable streams towards all the created inhabitants of heaven; he loves all the angels and saints there. The love of God flows out towards Christ the Head, and through him to all his members."[67] While this is the same love enjoyed by both Christ and his members (for it is the same Spirit), it is not enjoyed in exactly the same way. "[T]he saints and angels are secondarily the subjects of holy love, not as in whom love is as in an original seat, as light is in the sun which shines by its own light, but as it is in the planets which shine by reflecting the light of the sun."[68] Whereas Christ is the infinite object and subject of divine love, the elect creatures, united to him, enjoy this love in only a participatory fashion.

Because the Spirit is identified as the "sacred energy" of divine love, we find him hidden in Edwards's discussions of the communion that takes place in heaven. The interpersonal interactions he describes are between the Father and the Son, between the church, angels and God, and between and among the church and angels together. The Holy Spirit is the "context" of their communion, the subjectivity of their love for one another, not the object of a participating communicant. Edwards's formula runs like this: communion *with* God and each other, *in* the Holy Spirit. By applying this formula to heavenly communion, Edwards's prose at times appears to overlook the Spirit. In these passages, the Spirit is not neglected, he rather is present in the communion, fellowship, joy, holiness, and divine love that personally subsists among the divine and created persons in holy communion. These points are highlighted in a "Miscellanies" entry (No. 571), entitled "Heaven. Wisdom and Gloriousness of the Work of Redemption."

> Christ has brought it to pass, that those that the Father has given him should be brought into the household of God, that he and his Father and they should be as it were one society, one family; that his people should be in a sort admitted into that

---

66 Edwards, "Heaven is a World of Love," *Charity and Its Fruits*, in *Works* 8:369.
67 Edwards, "Heaven is a World of Love," *Charity and Its Fruits*, in *Works* 8:373.
68 Edwards, "Heaven is a World of Love," *Charity and Its Fruits*, in *Works*, 8:373-74.

society of the three persons in the Godhead. In this family or household, God [is] the Father, Jesus Christ is his own natural and eternally begotten Son. The saints, they also are children in the family; the church is the daughter of God, being the spouse of his Son. They all have communion in the same spirit, the Holy Ghost.[69]

The only way for created beings to participate in this divine love is by virtue of the Spirit's union to their souls. It is who the Spirit is as the divine affection of the Godhead that admits the participation of created beings into the rich fellowship of the Trinity. Without his work of mysteriously uniting himself to the souls of creatures, Edwards's theology of Christian experience would not possess the rich themes of divine communion and fellowship he is known for. It is because the Spirit is the bond of union between the Father and the Son that this rich spirituality is generated in his theology.

7.2.2 Heaven, Union with Christ, and the Object of Love

The object of heaven's love, Christ, also reflects pneumatological themes in Edwards's theology of glorification. The very fact that it is Christ who is both the object of the saints' love and the person through whom they know the Father, mirrors the priority and order found in the trinitarian relationships. The Father loves his own infinite excellencies by means of the perfect substantial image he has eternally begotten of himself in the Son. The Son, who sees God the Father, returns the love with equal intensity to him who is the divine original, of whom he is the image. All this transacts within the affection of the Spirit who is their mutual love breathed forth between Father and Son. In a similar way, the church and angels of heaven participate in the knowledge and love of God in a christologically mediated fashion, that is in and through Christ, a transaction which all occurs in the Spirit. A central effect of this pneumatological operation in the lives of the glorified is an increase in their union with Christ. As they participate more in divine knowledge and love, they grow in union with Christ, a theme that Edwards frequently visits in his reflections on heaven from various angles.

We may wonder how it is that the angels are "in Christ," since they neither have been redeemed from sin nor share the same human nature with him. While they do not share a relationship with Christ as the saints do, in that they are not related to Christ as a branch is to the vine, or as a bride is to her groom, they do have "eternal life" in him in that it is through him that they have their confirmation and know God. Edwards writes that God's design from all eternity was to communicate himself to his creatures by uniting himself to one

---

69 Edwards, "Miscellanies" No. 571, in *Works*, 18:110. Edwards drew much material from this entry when composing the closing section of his sermon "The Excellency of Christ." The first half of this quote is copied almost verbatim as the closing words to the sermon (see *Works*, 19:594).

of their natures, gather all the elect creatures into one heavenly society under him, and relate to them all through him. "Christ is not the Mediator of the angels in the same sense that he is of men, yet he is a middle person between God and them, through whom is all their intercourse with God and derivations from him."[70]

It is the saints who are most properly united to Christ. By virtue of the Spirit they see him, love him, and commune with both him and God the Father through him. Edwards is captivated by the biblical metaphor of marriage as illustrating the special nature of this union. The saints are Christ's "fullness" (Eph 1:23) in the sense that they are his "good" and his happiness, without which he would be "wanting" something. "He, who supplies angels and men with all that good in which they are perfect and happy, receives the church as that in which he himself is happy."[71] Their salvation and final glorification are the highest end in the creation of the entire universe (angels included),[72] and once that end is secured, they both enjoy the fruits of an eternal wedding day. While the angels enjoy God in and through Christ, and possess greater wisdom and strength than do the saints, they do not partake of this marriage union, but are forever joyful spectators of it, like witnesses to a wedding.

Edwards illuminates numerous benefits that attend the saints in their final "most perfect" union with Christ, benefits which help bring some more clarity to the mysterious nature of this union. All of these benefits highlight the importance of the incarnation and christology within Edwards's theology of glorification. It is by virtue of Christ as the God-man, that entitles the church to a more special and greater relationship with God then they could have enjoyed apart from the incarnation. By his incarnation, the infinite distance between the divine and human natures is bridged, enabling the saints who are united to Christ to partake of the divine nature as glorified human beings. Apart from this, "The divine nature has that infinite majesty and greatness, whereby 'tis impossible that we should immediately approach to that, and converse with that intimacy as we might do one that is in our own nature." Job wished for such a possibility (Job 9:32-35), and so too did the ancient church of the Old Testament, as Edwards saw evidenced by the Song of Solomon 8:1: "O that thou wert my brother, that sucked the breasts of my mother! when I should find thee without, I would kiss thee; yea. I should not be despised." Yet in Christ this whole set of circumstances changed: "Christ, descending so low in uniting himself to our nature, tends to invite and encourage us to ascend to the most

---

70 Edwards, "Miscellanies" No. 744 corollary 3, in *Works*, 18:389.
71 Edwards, "Notes on Scripture," No. 235, in *Works*, 15:186.
72 "This seems to be the good that Christ sought in the creation of the world, who is the beginning of the creation of God, when all things were created by him and for him, viz. that he might obtain a spouse that he might give himself to and give himself for, on whom he might pour forth his love, and in whom his soul might eternally be delighted." See "Notes on Scripture," No. 235, in *Works*, 15:187.

intimate converse with him, and encourages us that we shall be accepted and not despised therein."[73]

Because of this, Edwards concludes that there is no limit to the degree in which the saints can participate in the activity, experience, and knowledge in which Jesus Christ himself participates. In him they have the capacity to ascend to ever greater and greater heights of happiness in heaven.[74] "Christ their head is as it were their organ of enjoyment," Edwards writes in "Miscellanies" No. 1072,

> But the capacity of enjoyment that this organ hath is of infinitely greater extent than the capacity of any of Christ's members, taken separately or by themselves, as the head of the natural body, by reason of the extensive and noble senses, has a much greater capacity of enjoyment than the inferior members of the body by themselves. Were not the saints united to Christ, they could never enjoy God the Father in so excellent a manner as now they will in heaven, partaking with Christ of in his enjoyment of him.[75]

In him they inherit all things and sit on the throne with Christ to reign over heaven.[76] In him they have the perfect wisdom and strength for this kingly office, which they share with Christ.[77] And if these benefits were not good enough, they are also enabled by their union with Christ to participate in Christ's own sonship under the Father; "they are partakers of his relation to the Father, or of his sonship," Edwards writes in "Miscellanies" No. 571. As a result, they partake of the Father in the same communion and intimacy that the

---

73 Edwards, "Miscellanies" No. 741, in *Works*, 18:367.
74 "We have all reason to conclude that no degree of intimacy will be too much for the manhood of Christ, seeing that the divine Logos has been pleased to assume him into his very person; and therefore, we may conclude that no degree of intimacy will be too great for others to be admitted to, of whom Christ is the head or chief, according to their capacity." Edwards, "Miscellanies" No. 741, in *Works*, 18:368.
75 Edwards, "Miscellanies" No. 1072, in *Works*, 20:455.
76 "The members of Christ will have the communion with Christ in his dominion, for they shall sit with him in his throne. And as Christ is Lord of the angels, so the saints shall in some sort reign over angels in heaven. . . . Whatsoever they shall inherit as joint heirs with Christ, they shall in some respect reign over as kings with Christ." It is for this reason, he argues, that the saints shall judge all angels at the end of this age (1 Cor 6:3). Edwards, "Miscellanies" No. 702 corollary 2, in *Works*, 18:300
77 "If the whole universe were given to a saint separately, he could not fully possess it: his capacity would be too narrow. He would not know how to dispose of it for the his own good, as the inferior members of the natural body would not know [how] to dispose of things that the body possesses for their good without the eyes of their head; and if the saints did know, they would not have strength sufficient. But in Christ their head they have perfect knowledge and infinite strength." Edwards, "Miscellanies" No. 1072, in *Works*, 20:455-56.

Son does, an intimacy which is the Holy Spirit:

> So they are in their measure partakers of the Son's enjoyment of his Father: they have his joy fulfilled in themselves, and by this means they come to a more familiar and intimate conversing with God the Father, than otherwise ever would have been. For there is doubtless an infinte intimacy between the Father and the Son; and the saints being in him shall partake with him in it, and of the blessedness of it.[78]

The angels, while they delight and enjoy God supremely to the limit of their capacities, do not partake of this intimacy with the Father and the Son in the same way. They are filled with the Spirit and possess an eternal blessedness that will increase forever. By virtue of the Son's personal union to human nature, the saints through their union with Christ are allowed, in some finite way, to partake of the trinitarian union that the three members of the Trinity have forever enjoyed. This appears to be what Edwards is saying when he speaks of the church as "partaking of Christ's sonship." They are admitted into the "inmost fellowship of the deity. There was [as] it were an eternal society or family in the Godhead in the Trinity of persons. It seems to be God's design to admit the church into the divine family as his son's wife, so that which Satan made use [of] as a temptation to our first parents, '*Ye shall be as gods,*' shall be fulfilled contrary to his design."[79]

7.2.3 Heaven and the Eternal Progress of Love and Union

The final state of heaven is not only a world of love, it is also a place where the saints grow in an eternal progress of love and union with God. "There are many reasons to think that what God has in view, in an increasing communication of himself throughout eternity, is an increasing knowledge of God, love to him, and joy in him. And 'tis to be considered that the more those divine communications increase in the creature, the more it becomes one with God."[80] We have seen that Edwards ties this idea to the fact that once God has determined to communicate his fullness *ad extra* to finite creatures, he aims at the infinite communication of his internal glory to the creature. Because creatures are finite and time bound, they can never ultimately finish receiving these divine communications.[81] Edwards surveys the dimensions of this eternal

---

78 Edwards, "Miscellanies" No. 571, in *Works*, 18:109.
79 Edwards, "Miscellanies" No. 741, in *Works*, 18:367.
80 See the last part of chapter 1, section 3 in *End of Creation*, (*Works*, 8:443-44) for numerous observations on this progression.
81 "If God has respect to something in the creature, which he views as of everlasting duration, and as rising higher and higher through that infinite duration, and that not with constantly diminishing (but perhaps an increasing) celerity: then he has respect to it as, in the whole, of infinite height; though there never will be any particular time

progression at two points in *End of Creation*, dimensions which enable us to understand more clearly what he intends by the phrases "union with Christ" and "union with God."

As we saw in chapter three, the process of this eternal progression of union with God unfolds along the lines of a two-fold communication of the divine fullness to the creature. "God's internal glory, as it is in God, is either in his understanding or will," Edwards writes. "The glory or fullness of his understanding is in his knowledge. The internal glory and fullness of God, which we must conceive of as having its special seat in his will, is his holiness and happiness."[82] The more God communicates these aspects of his fullness to the saint, the more she is united to God in Christ. In the *End of Creation* Edwards does not make the trinitarian connections of this communication explicit, but they are not hard to discern given our knowledge of his trinitarianism. God is in the business of communicating both his divine knowledge and divine will to the creature, a knowledge and will which he identifies in other places as the Son and Spirit respectively.[83] By participating in God's two-fold fullness of his own self-knowledge and self-love, the saint is drawn by love ever deeper into the trinitarian community.

What, may we ask, is the nature of this two-fold divine communication? To attempt to answer this question again leads us to the issue of divinization and whether or not Edwards blurs the lines between the Creator and the creature. Edwards's choice of words fascinate, impressing the reader with the powerful insights of his theological vision, yet at the same time they leave us puzzled over his true meaning. "[T]he communication itself, or thing communicated," Edwards notes, "is something divine, something of God, something of his internal fullness; as the water in the stream is something of the fountain; and as the beams are of the sun."[84] Edwards apparently wants to stress the indistinguishability between God's own knowledge and will and that same knowledge and will existing *ad extra* in the creature. We see this faintly in his choice of metaphors that illustrate this communication. As seen in the previous quote, Edwards often likens divine grace and knowledge in the creature to a rivulet or stream with relation to a fountain, or to the beams of sunlight with

---

when it can be said already to have come to such an height." Edwards, *End of Creation*, in *Works*, 8:534.

82 Edwards, *End of Creation*, in *Works*, 8:528. In this dissertation Edwards splits the communicated fullness of the divine will into two parts, divine holiness and divine happiness. Thus while he structures his discussion around the communication of these three aspects of divinity that the saints partake in (knowledge, holiness and happiness), we must not forget that the latter two are two sides of the divine will, which helps us keep the trinitarian connections to his discussion in greater focus.

83 Edwards makes these trinitarian connections more explicit in several "Miscellanies" entries; see "Miscellanies" Nos. 1082, 1084, 1094. See also our discussion in chapter three, pages 68-71.

84 Edwards, *End of Creation*, in *Works*, 8:531.

relation to the sun itself. Also telling are his descriptions of divine knowledge, holiness, and happiness in the creature:

> this [communicated] knowledge is most properly a communication of God's infinite knowledge which primarily consists in the knowledge of himself. . . . This knowledge in the creature is but a conformity to God. 'Tis the image of God's own knowledge of himself. 'Tis a participation of the same: 'tis as much the same as 'tis possible for that to be, which is infinitely less in degree: as particular beams of the sun communicated, are the light and glory of the sun in part.[85]

Likewise, the holiness that the saints partake of is literally God's own holiness, "as truly as the brightness of a jewel, held in the sun's beams, is participation, or derivation of the sun's brightness, though immensely less in degree."[86] And the happiness and divine joy that they experience is not to be too sharply distinguished from God's own joy in his own infinite excellencies. This is all consistent with our findings in chapter five, where we observed that in Edwards's view of regeneration the saint's own holiness and love for God are mysteriously identical with the third person of Trinity indwelling the soul, acting in and through her faculties as a new principle of nature. "What is communicated is divine, or something of God: and each communication is of that nature, that the creature to whom it is made, is thereby conformed to God, and united to him."[87]

When Edwards adds to this argument the fact that there is an eternal progression and increase in this divine communication to the creature, he again uses language that would raise many eyebrows. The more God communicates his knowledge, love, and joy to the saint, "the more it becomes one with God: for so much the more is it united to God in love. . . . The image is more and more perfect, and so the good that is in the creature comes forever nearer and nearer to an identity with that which is in God."[88] He notes that from God's eternal perspective, from he who sees the entire infinite increase of the creature's union with himself, there is truly an "eminent fulfillment" of Jesus' prayer in John 17:21 and 23 ("That they all be one; as thou, Father, art in me, and I in thee, that they also may be one in us . . . . I in them, and thou in me, that they may be made perfect in one"). Commenting on these verses, he writes:

> In this view, those elect creatures . . . considered with respect to the whole of their eternal duration, . . . must be viewed as being, as it were, one with God. They were respected as brought home by him, united with him, centering most perfectly

---

85 Edwards, *End of Creation*, in *Works*, 8:441.
86 Edwards, *End of Creation*, in *Works*, 8:442.
87 Edwards, *End of Creation*, in *Works*, 8:442.
88 Edwards, *End of Creation*, in *Works*, 8:443.

in him, and as it were swallowed up in him: so that his respect to them finally coincides and becomes one and the same with respect to himself.[89]

The question again confronts us: Is Edwards teaching something akin to the divinization of the creature?

We must keep in mind that Edwards here is pushing boundaries in his language to show the staggering realities of the Christian's eternal salvation. That they should be brought into a union of fellowship with the almighty triune God, and that this union shall grow to ever increasing oneness throughout all eternity is intended, no doubt, to lead the Christian reader into the realms of praise. The line between theology and doxology is scarcely discernible in these sections of *End of Creation*. Yet we must remember that Edwards always places limits on this pushing-of-the-boundaries, especially with regard to the greatest theological and ontological distinction of all: the distinction between Creator and creature. He never crosses this line. We see clear evidence of this in his word choice as he describes the saint's union with God. Qualifiers such as "as it were," "to the degree of their capacities," "in some sense" pepper his discussions and reveal that in the back of his mind he is conscious and respectful of this boundary.

Elsewhere, Edwards consistently affirms three positions that serve as theological limits to this merging of the creature with the Creator. First, the saints always remain finite beings. No matter how far they grow in union with God they shall forever participate in the divine nature as finite beings. Their participation in the divine knowledge is "infinitely less in degree; as particular beams of the sun communicated, are the light and glory of the sun *in part*."[90] Because they are finite, there shall always be room for increase and change. Throughout the history of heaven only God is unchangeable.[91] Even though God aims at bridging the vast distance between the finite and infinite in his communicative overflow, "the time will never come when it can be said it has already arrived at this infinite height."[92]

Second, the saints shall always remain *personally* distinct from God. Writing in the context of spiritual sight, Edwards states in "Miscellanies" No. 777 that if God were to create two minds and one viewed all the same ideas immediately as the other, and as *in* the mind of the other, then the two would be the same person for all intents and purposes. There would be, in other words, a "union of personality" existing between the two.[93] He concludes from this that only Christ has an immediate sight of God, presumably based on the fact that there exists a union of personality between God the Son and the man Jesus

---

89 Edwards, *End of Creation*, in *Works*, 8:443.
90 Edwards, *End of Creation*, in *Works*, 8:441, emphasis mine.
91 See "Miscellanies" Nos. 796 (*Works*, 18:497-98) and 952 (*Works*, 20:211).
92 Edwards, *End of Creation*, in *Works*, 8:534.
93 Edwards, "Miscellanies" No. 777, in *Works*, 18:427-28.

Christ. Christ by virtue of the personal union with God the Son sees and knows God, for he is God and communes with the Father and Spirit in a perichoretic union. The saints, who are united to Christ, and in whom God's own knowledge and love dwell *ad extra*, do not partake in the union of the personality that exists in the personal union, nor do they partake in the perichoretic union. Rather, they approximate these unions as they forever grow in their union with Christ. Thus, no matter how we are to understand the ontological mechanics of Edwards's sometimes surprising statements on the nature of union with God, the saints shall always remain personally distinct from God. Their knowledge and sight of him remains, to a degree, qualitatively different from that of Christ.

Third, according to Edwards the saints shall forever remain creatures who participate in the divine nature *ad extra*. For all his statements highlighting the fact that they shall be drawn into the inmost fellowship of the Trinity, Edwards never declares that the saints are drawn into the Godhead *ad intra*, for to do so would be to dissolve the barrier between God and creature. It is this fact which underscores his characteristic vocabulary of participation and communication: while creatures *participate in* the divine fullness and have that fullness *communicated to* their created natures, Deity *is* the divine fullness. This distinction remains forever.

These three theological barriers that Edwards maintained throughout his life do not only confirm that he respected the boundary between God and creature, they also ensure that heaven shall forever remain a society of saints and angels communing with the triune God. They shall never merge with divinity, but shall ever grow closer in their fellowship and love to one another and to God and Christ in the Holy Spirit.

Chapter 8

Conclusion

Neither pray I for these alone, but for them also which shall believe on me through their word; *That they all may be one; as thou, Father, art in me, and I in thee, that they also may be one in us*: that the world may believe that thou has sent me. And the glory which thou gavest me I have given them; *that they may be one, even as we are one: I in them, and thou in me*, that they may know that thou hast sent me, and hast loved them, as thou has loved me. Father, I will that they also, whom thou has given me, be with me where I am; *that they may behold my glory*, which thou has given me: for thou lovedst me before the foundation of the world. O righteous Father, the world hath not known thee: but I have known thee, and these have known that thou hast sent me. And I have declared unto them thy name, and will declare it: *that the love wherewith thou hast loved me may be in them, and I in them.* John 17:20-26

Edwards's deep fascination with spiritual union and its theological articulation derived from his love for the Scriptures. Passages such as this one where Jesus prays for his disciples and their future followers fueled both his spiritual life and his theological imagination. Several issues we have covered in our study are mirrored in this text: the mutual indwelling of the Father and the Son representing a paradigm for the unity of the church (*"that they may be one, even as we are one: I in them, and thou in me"*); spiritual sight and the beatific vision (*"that they may behold my glory"*); and the close association between the Father's love for Christ (i.e., the Spirit) being in the saints on the one hand, and Christ himself being in them (i.e., their collective union with Christ) on the other (*"that the love wherewith thou hast loved me may be in them, and I in them"*). While we may not agree with all the conclusions of Edwards's theological exegesis, we should appreciate the degree to which he attempted to anchor his theology in the bedrock of Scripture. Indeed Edwards explicitly sought to stay close to the scriptural categories when writing on this topic of union. In a letter responding to the question of whether he taught that the Spirit communicates his essence to the saint or not, Edwards writes

> I don't know [i.e., think] that I have exceeded the due bounds of a writer in divinity, in expressing that communication that God makes to his saints of his holiness in the very forms that God himself does in his Word, in calling it their being made partakers of the divine nature; and I think the representations I have

made of the matter is such as the Scriptures do abundantly warrant in innumerable texts that might be mentioned.[1]

It is perhaps this characteristic of his theology of union which has the potential to lead to confusion. Scripture does not present us with a systematic theology detailing the intricacies of the saints' union with God. It speaks of "partaking in the divine nature," of being "in Christ," and of both God's love and Christ himself dwelling in the saints, and does not present a complete picture of these staggering realities. By sticking close to Scripture's categories and refraining from excessive speculation, Edwards's thought on spiritual union evinces a similar trait: we glimpse the wonderful reality of spiritual union in his writings, while questions remain regarding the exact nature of this union. Such is the nature of pneumatology and spiritual union: no matter how much theological precision we bring to these issues, new questions arise and great mysteries remain.

Yet despite this our study has demonstrated that there are identifiable themes that run throughout his writings on pneumatology and spiritual union, themes which provide us some clarity for understanding his pneumatology. The Holy Spirit is the central agent in Edwards's discussions on union. He is the divine love of the Godhead, who unites the Father and the Son together in an infinite union of fellowship and communion. Yet he repeats this divine reality externally in the creature's union with God. What George Hunsinger writes about Karl Barth can also be said of Edwards: "The person (*hypostasis*) of the Spirit is no different – no different in being, essence, or identity – in relation to us than he is antecedently in himself, and what he is antecedently in himself he discloses and confirms in relation to us. His saving work in our midst reiterates in temporal form the prior mode of existence that is his to all eternity."[2] The pneumatological dynamic discerned in the immanent Trinity we see repeated in the economic unions of Edwards's theology. The Spirit is the bond of union of the God-man Jesus Christ; he effects the *hypostatic* union between the two natures of Christ. In the lives of the elect, he also repeats the inner-trinitarian life in their hearts by communicating divine love to their souls, so that they share in the communion that obtains in the Trinity. The Spirit in Edwards's theology operates *ad extra* in very much the same way as he does *ad intra*. In our concluding remarks we will summarize Edwards's concept of union, and ask what our study of Edwards's pneumatology reveals about his theology.

---

1 Edwards, Letter No. 66, "To an Unknown Correspondent," after March 13, 1745/6, in *Works*, 16:203.
2 George Hunsinger, "The Mediator of Communion: Karl Barth's Doctrine of the Holy Spirit," in *Disruptive Grace: Studies in the Theology of Karl Barth* (Grand Rapids: Eerdmans, 2000), 152.

8.1 The Spirit and Spiritual Union in Edwards's Theology

In summarizing Edwards's understanding of the nature of spiritual union, we may remember from the introduction that in an early "Miscellanies" entry (No. 184, entitled "Union, Spiritual") Edwards writes that he is convinced, based upon his "insight into the nature of minds," that "there is no guessing what kind of union and mixation, by consciousness or otherwise, there may be between [different minds]."[3] He does not specify his meaning, and leaves us hanging as to what he intends. Given what we have studied, a good case can be made that the fundamental concept of spiritual union for Edwards consists in a sharing of divine knowledge and divine affection. To be more precise, the common denominator of the inner-trinitarian union, the *hypostatic* union, and the saints' union with Christ appears to be the shared possession of divine knowledge *within* the affection or love that is the divine will. Experiencing this affection for the knowledge of God is to be brought in a relation of union with God. Edwards closely identifies this divine affection with the third person of the Trinity, the Holy Spirit.

We see this understanding of union obtain within the immanent Trinity, a union that is not only infinitely complete, essential, and necessary, but one which serves as the paradigm for the external unions in Edwards's theology. Through an infinite regard for himself, God has eternally begotten a substantial image of himself, who is God the Son. The mutual affection that Father and Son enjoy together is "a most pure act and an infinitely holy and sacred energy" which stands forth as another personal subsistence within the deity, the Holy Spirit. The Spirit joins the Father and the Son in an infinite and eternal bond of union; he is their communion and fellowship. Human language and concepts strain in vain to make sense of this mysterious divine reality. How can a union of two infinite consubstantial persons *be* another infinite consubstantial person? How can the infinite mutual affection between the Father and the Son *be* the Spirit? For Edwards, it is not *how* this can be, but merely *that* it is the case. The fact that he makes this connection between the personal Spirit and the seemingly impersonal divine affection, allows him to modulate with ease between these two linguistic and conceptual worlds within his theology: on the one hand he speaks of God, his knowledge and his love; on the other, he writes of Father, Son, and Holy Spirit. These are not two different models of the Trinity or separate spheres of his theology, but rather two different modes of speaking about the same reality in his thought. To say that God infinitely delights in the knowledge of himself is simply another way of saying that the Father and the Son commune together in the Holy Spirit, for the self-knowledge whom the Father delights is the Son himself, and the infinite delight by which the Father enjoys the Son (and by which the Son loves the Father) is the Holy Spirit.

---

3 Edwards, "Miscellanies" No. 184, in *Works*, 13:330.

Externally, God has structured the universe in such a way that this same divine knowledge and affection is said to exist *really* and *externally* in the minds and hearts of his creatures. By creation, God has granted a triadic nature to sentient creatures: they are personal minds that possess understanding and will, and thus have a capacity for union with God by partaking in his own divine knowledge and love. With regard to the mediator, there is a complete communication of the *hypostasis* of the divine Son to the man Jesus Christ, so that a "union of personality" exists between Christ's two natures. This communication is by the Spirit, for it is the Son's love (i.e., the Spirit) for the man Jesus Christ which eternally effects a personal union between Christ's divine and human nature. The Spirit, in Edwards's reading of John 3:34, is given "without measure" to Jesus Christ.

In redemption, when a saint knows God, she knows him with God's very own self-knowledge, not with a created image of divine knowledge. Likewise, when she loves God, she loves with God's own holy affection, by virtue of the Spirit's union to her faculties. Her knowledge and love of God is divine self-knowledge and divine self-love communicated. In a way that Edwards does not fully explain, she participates finitely in these divine realities whereby her knowledge and love are "something divine, something of God." It appears that Edwards wants to have it both ways in these discussions. On the one hand, he labors greatly to portray the intense intimacy the saints have with God: they truly participate in the divine trinitarian life in their love of God's image, Jesus Christ. This participation should not be too sharply distinguished from God's own self-knowledge and self-love. On the other hand, he is explicit in his affirmation of the distinction between the creature and God. The saints are finite creatures who forever remain personally distinct from God and who forever partake of the divine life in its *communicated* form *ad extra*, not in its eternal, essential, and infinite form *ad intra*. Edwards does not fully explain the ontological and metaphysical components to this union, he merely "clarifies the mystery" in a way that he feels is faithful to the witness of Scripture.

From another angle, this shared possession of divine knowledge and love is really the creature's communion with the persons of the Godhead. The divine knowledge and divine love in which the saint participates are not to be distinguished from the second and third persons of the Trinity. To know and love God is to commune with Christ in the Spirit. It is to have the Father's own love for Christ (i.e., the Spirit) dwelling in them, and to have Christ dwell in them. It is to be brought into the fellowship of the eternal Trinity. A powerful spirituality of communion with the Father and with Christ in the Spirit results from his reflections. Furthermore, this spirituality of communion is not to be distinguished from his philosophical portrayal of union with God as if he is modulating into in a more personalist mode of discourse, funded by a distinct social model of the Trinity. To commune with the Father and Son in the Spirit is to participate in the divine knowledge and love that God communicates to the creature. They are two different ways of describing one vision of the

Christian's union with God.

To summarize our observation on the nature of union and the role the Spirit plays in it in Edwards's theology, we may reiterate the point that the fundamental concept of spiritual union consists in a sharing of divine knowledge and divine affection. The common denominator of the inner-trinitarian union, the *hypostatic* union, and the saints' union with Christ appears to be the shared possession of divine knowledge *within* the affection or love that is the divine will.

8.2 The Spirit as the Bond of Union and the Structure of Edwards's Theology

What does our study reveal about the shape of Edwards's theology? We might group our observations around two headings: (1) the broadly Augustinian shape of his trinitarianism and the pneumatological themes that arise from it and (2) the strong continuity between the immanent and economic Trinities in his theology.

First, our study has demonstrated that Edwards developed the major themes of his pneumatology within the context of an Augustinian trinitarianism. Throughout his life, whenever he wrote on the Trinity, we find him consistently articulating it in Augustinian categories: the Father eternally begetting an infinitely perfect and substantial image of himself in the Son, whom he loves (and to whom the Son reciprocates in love) in the personal love who is the Holy Spirit. The Spirit is the bond of love, the communion, or the bond of union between Father and Son. Social trinitarian themes which are sometimes discerned in Edwards's trinitarianism emerge not from Edwards's modulation between two different models of the Trinity. Rather, they emerge from the two different perspectives from which Edwards wrote about the same Trinity; on the one hand, speaking about the "Trinity" of God-understanding-love, and conversely, speaking about the Father, Son, and Holy Spirit as three persons. In each of these contexts, the Trinity he describes possesses the same Augustinian trinitarian shape: the Father and the Son communing *in* the love or union of the Holy Spirit. Because these two perspectives on the Trinity were one and the same in his mind, Edwards never felt there was any incompatibility between them. Thus he never thought that to speak of the Holy Spirit as divine love threatened the personhood of the Spirit.

The fact that he attempts to address the pneumatological deficiency that he discerned in the theology of his day by amplifying the themes of divine love in his own theology confirms this very point. We have seen that Edwards desired to restore a greater sense of balance in theology by granting "equal honor" to the Holy Spirit in both his immanent and economic work. Because the Spirit is fully God along with the Father and the Son, Edwards felt that he too deserves "equal time" in our theological reflection. His strategy to achieve this was not to turn the attention of our theological eyes onto the person of the Spirit, but rather to amplify the themes of divine love throughout his theology. If Edwards thought that equating the Spirit with divine love depersonalized the Spirit in any way then he certainly would have not proceeded in this manner to grant him this "equal honor" due him. Thus, our study confirms that not only did Edwards adhere to an Augustinian trinitarianism, he also sought to extend a fundamental insight of Augustine to remedy the pneumatological neglect he discerned in the theology of his day. By amplifying the themes of divine love in his theology he felt he was supremely honoring the Holy Ghost.

The fact that the Spirit is the bond of union in Edwards's theology also reveals the "hidden" presence of the Spirit throughout Edwards's theology. Much of the theology Edwards is known for is "pneumatology in disguise." While the Spirit is the bond of union, the gaze of our spiritual eyes turn most frequently to that which is unified—the Father and the Son, the two natures of Jesus Christ, believers "in Christ," and Christians united in one holy and happy society—not to the Spirit himself. He is "hidden" in Edwards's theology, yet his presence is felt throughout. The theology of spiritual sight, union with Christ, the nature of true virtue, the discernment of religious affections in the heart, and the love that we experience between believers are all saturated with pneumatological themes. Furthermore, this hiddenness of the Spirit in Edwards's theology, whereby he is identified with the bond of love between persons, does not contribute to a bankrupt spirituality in Edwards's thought. For Edwards, the Spirit need not constantly be conceived of as a communing person in order to effect a powerful triune spirituality. While Edwards affirmed the full personhood of the Spirit, much of the time he thought it best to conceive of the Spirit as the personal communion of the Father and the Son which the saint partakes of rather than as a separate communing person alongside of the Father and the Son. The saints honor the Spirit by partaking of him as the personal communion of the Father and the Son. This he felt coincided best with the Scripture's explicit teaching, which he felt turns the gaze of the soul to Christ and to God the Father.

Together these observations on the Augustinian contours of Edwards's trinitarianism and pneumatology enable us to discern the shape of Edwards's theology more clearly. They also call into question the current critique of Augustinian trinitarianism, a critique based upon the fact this type of trinitarianism tends to depersonalize the Spirit by portraying him as an impersonal love. We have seen this does not have to be the case if we take Edwards's lead and firmly hold in view the mystery that the personal Holy Spirit is the divine communion and love of the Godhead. Edwards's profound spirituality grew from this soil.

Our study not only reveals the Augustinian themes that run throughout Edwards's pneumatology, it also demonstrates the strong continuity he saw between the immanent and economic Trinities. Edwards's theology of redemption opens the door wide to God's inner life. Yet it is perhaps more accurate to say that his theology of the Spirit opens the doors of the Godhead wide to the elect for the Spirit communicates his immanent trinitarian life *ad extra* in the life of the saints by filling them with the divine love for the Son, or for God's own self-understanding. Through this the saints are united to God by participating in his divine life. Because God's dispositional being communicates his inner divine fullness *ad extra*, there will necessarily be a close correspondence in Edwards's thought between the way in which the triune God reveals himself in history and the way he is in his internal fullness. Also, because Edwards saw no fundamental distinction between the God-understanding-love Trinity, and the Trinity of Father, Son, and Holy Spirit, this participation in God, while it is a communion of minds sharing a common understanding and love, is truly a communion of divine and human persons: the redeemed united to Christ in the Holy Spirit, sharing in Christ's sonship under God the Father, and growing forevermore in the glorious knowledge and love of God. Furthermore, this communion neither absorbs history into the Godhead nor dissolves it for even the saints in heaven learn and grow in their knowledge of God only through the contemplation of Christ as the mediator and great wonder worker of redemption.

> [The] beatifical vision that the saints have of God in heaven, is in beholding the manifestations that he makes of himself in the work of redemption. . . by [the] manifestations God makes of himself in his Son. . . . And so we may infer that [the] business and employment of the saints, so far as it consists in contemplation, praise, and conversation, is mainly in contemplating the wonders of this work, in praising God for the displays of his glory and love therein, and in conversing about things appertaining to it.[4]

This history of praise shall never end.

8.3 Postscript: Sarah Edwards on Being "Lost in God"

Jonathan Edwards's theological reflections on the Holy Spirit and spiritual union were not only meant to be masterful feats of the mind that mine the magnificent mysteries of divinity. Rather he intended them to be wings that give flight to the soul. His teachings undoubtedly found good soil in his wife Sarah's heart over the years as he laced his sermons with these reflections. It was during the height of the great revivals of the early 1740s, however, where Sarah reaped the full harvest of these teachings, experiencing a great awakening in her own spiritual life. Edwards published her experiences (anonymously) in *Some Thoughts Concerning the Revival* (1742) as an example of true piety and correct religious affections. Similar to the apostrophe he wrote about young Sarah two decades earlier, his account represents another example of the love he had for the woman whom he enjoyed such an "uncommon union" of happiness with for over thirty years. We close with a

---

4 Edwards, "Miscellanies" No. 777 corollary 1, in *Works*, 18:431.

segment of this glorious portrait Edwards painted of his wife's encounter with the Holy Spirit:

> I have been particularly acquainted with many persons that have been the subjects of the high and extraordinary transports of the present day; and in the highest transports of any of the instances that I have been acquainted with, and where the affection of admiration, love and joy, so far as another could judge, have been raised to a higher pitch than in any other instances I have observed or been informed of, the following things have been united: viz. a very frequent dwelling, for some considerable time together, in such views of the glory of the divine perfections, and Christ's excellencies, that the soul in the meantime has been as it were perfectly overwhelmed, and swallowed up with light and love and a sweet solace, rest and joy of soul, that was altogether unspeakable; and more than once continuing for five or six hours together, without any interruption, in that clear and lively view or sense of the infinite beauty and amiableness of Christ's person, and the heavenly sweetness of his excellent and transcendent love; so that (to use the person's own expressions) the soul remained in a kind of heavenly Elysium, and did as it were swim in the rays of Christ's love, like a little mote swimming in the beams of the sun, or streams of his light that come in at a window; and the heart was swallowed up in a kind of glow of Christ's love, coming down from Christ's heart in heaven, as a constant stream of sweet light, at the same time the soul all flowing out in love to him; so that there seemed to be a constant flowing and reflowing from heart to heart. The soul dwelt on high, and was lost in God.[5]

---

5 Jonathan Edwards, *Some Thoughts Concerning the Revival*, in *The Works of Jonathan Edwards*, vol. 4, *The Great Awakening*, ed. C. C. Goen (New Haven: Yale University Press, 1972), 331-32.

Bibliography

Aquinas, T., *Summa Theologica*, in *Nature and Grace: Selections from the Summa Theologica of Thomas Aquinas*, ed. and trans. A. M. Fairweather, Library of Christian Classics, vol. 11 (Philadelphia: Westminster, 1954).

Augustine, *Faith and the Creed*, in *Augustine: Earlier Writings*, trans. John H. S. Burleigh, Library of Christian Classics, Ichthus Edition (Philadelphia: Westminster, 1953).

- *The Trinity*, in *The Works of Saint Augustine: A Translation for the 21st Century*, part I, Vol. 5, ed. John E. Rotelle, trans. Edmund Hill (Brooklyn: New City Press, 1991).

Ayers, L., 'The Fundamental Grammar of Augustine's Trinitarian Theology', *Augustine and His Critics: Essays in Honour of Gerald Bonner*, ed. Robert Dodaro and George Lawless (London: Routledge, 2000), 51-76.

Badcock, G.D., *Light of Truth and Fire of Love: A Theology of the Holy Spirit* (Grand Rapids: Eerdmans, 1997).

Barnes, M.R., 'De Regnon Reconsidered', *Augustinian Studies* 26 (1995), 51-79.

- 'Rereading Augustine on the Trinity', *The Trinity: An Interdisciplinary Symposium on the Trinity*, ed. Stephen T. Davis, Daniel Kendall, and Gerald O'Collins (New York: Oxford, 1999), 145-76.

Brown, R., *Jonathan Edwards and the Bible* (Bloomington: Indiana, 2002).

Bombaro, J.J., 'Dispositional Peculiarity, History, and Edwards's Evangelistic Appeal to Self-Love', *Westminster Theological Journal* 66 (2004), 121-57.

Calvin, J., *Institutes of the Christian Religion*, ed. John T. McNeill, trans. Ford Lewis Battles, 2 vols. (Philadelphia: Westminster, 1960).

Cherry, C., *The Theology of Jonathan Edwards: A Reappraisal* (Garden City, N.Y.: Doubleday Anchor, 1966).

- 'Symbols of Spiritual Truth: Jonathan Edwards as Biblical Interpreter', *Interpretation* 39 (1985), 263-71.

Conforti, J., *Jonathan Edwards, Tradition, and American Culture* (Chapel Hill: University of North Carolina Press, 1995).

Daley, B.E., 'Revisiting the 'Filioque': Roots and Branches of an Old Debate', *Pro Ecclesia* 10 (2001), 31-62.

Danaher, W.J. Jr., 'By Sensible Signs Represented: Jonathan Edwards' Sermons on the Lord's Supper', *Pro Ecclesia* 7 (1998), 261-87.

- *The Trinitarian Ethics of Jonathan Edwards* (Louisville: Westminster John Knox, 2004).

Delattre, R.A., *Beauty and Sensibility in the Thought of Jonathan Edwards* (New Haven: Yale University Press, 1968).

Dorner, J. A. *History of the Development of the Doctrine of the Person of Christ*, trans. D. W. Simon. Edinburgh: T. & T. Clark, 1880.

Edwards, J. *The Works of Jonathan Edwards* ed. Paul Ramsey, Vol. 1, *The Freedom of the Will* (New Haven: Yale, 1957).

- *The Works of Jonathan Edwards*, ed. John E. Smith, Vol. 2, *Treatise on the Religious Affections* (New Haven: Yale, 1959).

- *The Works of Jonathan Edwards*, ed. Clyde A. Holbrook, Vol. 3, *The Great Christian Doctrine of Original Sin Defended* (New Haven: Yale, 1970).

- *The Works of Jonathan Edwards*, ed. C. C. Goen, Vol. 4, *The Great Awakening* (New Haven: Yale, 1972).
- *The Works of Jonathan Edwards*, ed. Stephen J. Stein, Vol. 5, *The Apocalyptic Writings* (New Haven: Yale, 1977).
- *The Works of Jonathan Edwards*, ed. Wallace Anderson, Vol. 6, *Scientific and Philosophical Writings* (New Haven: Yale, 1980).
- *The Works of Jonathan Edwards*, ed. Norman Pettit, Vol. 7, *The Life of David Brainerd* (New Haven: Yale, 1985).
- *The Works of Jonathan Edwards*, ed. Paul Ramsey, Vol. 8, *Ethical Writings* (New Haven: Yale, 1989).
- *The Works of Jonathan Edwards*, ed. John F. Wilson, Vol. 9, *A History of the Work of Redemption* (New Haven: Yale, 1989).
- *The Works of Jonathan Edwards*, ed. Wilson H. Kimnach, Vol. 10, *Sermons and Discourses, 1720-1723* (New Haven: Yale, 1992).
- *The Works of Jonathan Edwards*, ed. Wallace E. Anderson, Vol. 11, *Typological Writings* (New Haven: Yale, 1993).
- *The Works of Jonathan Edwards*, ed. David D. Hall, Vol. 12, *Ecclesiastical Writings* (New Haven: Yale, 1994).
- *The Works of Jonathan Edwards*, ed. Thomas A. Schafer, Vol. 13, *The "Miscellanies," Entry nos. a-z, aa-zz, 1-500* (New Haven: Yale, 1994).
- *The Works of Jonathan Edwards*, ed. Kenneth P. Minkema, Vol. 14, *Sermons and Discourses, 1723-1729* (New Haven: Yale, 1997).
- *The Works of Jonathan Edwards*, ed. Stephen J. Stein, Vol. 15, *Notes on Scripture* (New Haven: Yale, 1998).
- *The Works of Jonathan Edwards*, ed. George S. Claghorn, Vol. 16, *Letters and Personal Writings* (New Haven: Yale, 1998).
- *The Works of Jonathan Edwards*, ed. Mark Valeri, Vol. 17, *Sermons and Discourses, 1730-1733* (New Haven: Yale, 1999).
- *The Works of Jonathan Edwards*, ed. Ava Chamberlain, Vol. 18, *The "Miscellanies," Entry nos. 501-832* (New Haven: Yale, 2000).
- *The Works of Jonathan Edwards*, ed. M. X. Lesser, Vol. 19, *Sermons and Discourses, 1734-1738* (New Haven: Yale, 2001).
- *The Works of Jonathan Edwards*, ed. Amy Plantinga Pauw, Vol. 20, *The "Miscellanies," Entry Nos. 833-1152* (New Haven: Yale, 2002).
- *The Works of Jonathan Edwards*, ed. Sang Hyun Lee, Vol. 21, *Writings on the Trinity, Grace, and Faith* (New Haven: Yale, 2003).
- *The Works of Jonathan Edwards*, ed. Harry S. Stout, Nathan O. Hatch, with Kyle P. Farley, Vol. 22, *Sermons and Discourses, 1739-1742* (New Haven, Yale, 2003).
- *The Works of Jonathan Edwards*, ed. Douglas A. Sweeney, Vol. 23, *The Miscellanies," Entry Nos. 1153-1360* (New Haven: Yale, 2004).
- *Works of President Edwards*, ed. Sereno E. Dwight, 10 vols. (New York: 1830).
- *The Sermons of Jonathan Edwards: A Reader*, ed. Wilson H. Kimnach, Kenneth P. Minkema, and Douglas A. Sweeney (New Haven: Yale, 1999).

Elwood, D.J., *The Philosophical Theology of Jonathan Edwards* (New York: Columbia University Press, 1960).

Eversley, W.V.L., 'The Pastor as Revivalist', *Edwards in our Time: Jonathan Edwards and the Shaping of American Religion*, ed. Sang Hyun Lee and Allen C. Guelzo (Grand Rapids: Eerdmans, 1999), 113-30.

Fiering, N., *Jonathan Edwards's Moral Thought and Its British Context* (Chapel Hill: University of North Carolina, 1981).
- 'The Rationalist Foundations of Jonathan Edwards's Metaphysics', *Jonathan Edwards and the American Experience*, ed. Nathan O. Hatch and Harry S. Stout (New York: Oxford, 1988), 73-101.

Gerstner, J.H., *Rational Biblical Theology of Jonathan Edwards*, 3 vols. (Powhatan, Va.: Berea Publications, 1991-93).

Heppe, H., *Reformed Dogmatics*, ed. Ernst Bizer, trans. G. T. Thomson (London: George Allen & Unwin Ltd. Ruskin House, 1950).

Hilberath, B.J., 'Identity through Self-Transcendence: the Holy Spirit and the Communio of Free Persons', *Advent of the Spirit: Orientations in Pneumatology*, Conference Papers from a Symposium at Marquette University, 17-19, April 1998 (unpublished).

Holmes, S.R., *God of Grace and God of Glory: An Account of the Theology of Jonathan Edwards* (Grand Rapids: Eerdmans, 2001).
- 'Does Jonathan Edwards Use a Dispositional Ontology? A Response to Sang Hyun Lee', *Jonathan Edwards: Philosophical Theologian*, ed. Paul Helm and Oliver D. Crisp (Burlington, VT: Ashgate, 2003), 99-114.

Hunsinger, G., 'The Mediator of Communion: Karl Barth's Doctrine of the Holy Spirit', *Disruptive Grace: Studies in the Theology of Karl Barth* (Grand Rapids: Eerdmans, 2000).
- 'Dispositional Soteriology: Jonathan Edwards on Justification by Faith Alone', *Westminster Theological Journal* 66 (2004), 107-20.

Jenson, R.W., *America's Theologian: A Recommendation of Jonathan Edwards* (New York: Oxford, 1988).

Jones, R.T., 'Union With Christ: The Existential Nerve of Puritan Piety', *Tyndale Bulletin* 41 (1990), 186-208.

Karkkainen, V., *Pneumatology: The Holy Spirit in Ecumenical, International, and Contextual Perspective* (Grand Rapids: Baker Academic, 2002).

Lee, S.H., 'Jonathan Edwards's Dispositional Conception of the Trinity: A Resource for Contemporary Theology', *Toward the Future of Reformed Theology: Tasks, Topics, Traditions*, ed. David Willis and Michael Welker (Grand Rapids: Eerdmans, 1999), 444-55.
- *The Philosophical Theology of Jonathan Edwards*, expanded ed. (Princeton: Princeton University Press, 2000).
- "Edwards on God and Nature: Resources for Contemporary Theology', *Edwards in Our Time: Jonathan Edwards and the Shaping of American Religion*, ed. Sang Hyun Lee and Allen Guelzo (Grand Rapids: Eerdmans, 1999), 15-44.

Lee, S.H., ed. *The Princeton Companion to Jonathan Edwards* (Princeton: Princeton University Press, 2003).

Lee, S.H. and A.C. Guelzo, eds. *Edwards in Our Time: Jonathan Edwards and the Shaping of American Religion* (Grand Rapids: Eerdmans, 1999).

Lesser, M.X., *Jonathan Edwards: A Reference Guide* (Boston: G. K. Hall, 1981).
- *Jonathan Edwards: An Annotated Bibliography, 1979-1993*, Bibliographies and Indexes in Religious Studies, number 30 (Westport, Conn.: Greenwood Press, 1994).

Letham, R., *The Holy Trinity: In Scripture, History, Theology, and Worship* (Phillipsburg, NJ: Presbyterian and Reformed, 2004).

Logan, S.T. Jr., 'The Hermeneutics of Jonathan Edwards', *Westminster Theological Journal* 43 (1981), 79-96.
- 'The Doctrine of Justification in the Theology of Jonathan Edwards", *Westminster Theological Journal* 46 (1984), 26-52.
Lucas, S.M., 'Jonathan Edwards Between Church and Academy', *The Legacy of Jonathan Edwards*, ed. D.G. Hart, Sean Michael Lucas, and Stephen J. Nichols (Grand Rapids: Baker Academic, 2003).
Macleod, D., *The Person of Christ* (Downers Grove, Ill.: InterVarsity Press, 1998).
Marsden, G., *Jonathan Edwards: A Life* (New Haven: Yale University Press, 2003).
Mastricht, P. van., *Theoretico-practica Theologia* (Utrecht and Amsterdam: 1714; new edition 1725).
McClymond, M.J., 'God the Measure: Toward an Understanding of Jonathan Edwards' Theocentric Metaphysics', *Scottish Journal of Theology* 47 (1994), 53.
- *Encounters with God: An Approach to the Theology of Jonathan Edwards* (New York: Oxford, 1998).
- 'Salvation as Divinization: Jonathan Edwards, Gregory Palamas and the Theological Uses of Neoplatonism', *Jonathan Edwards: Philosophical Theologian*, ed. Paul Helm and Oliver D. Crisp (Burlington, VT: Ashgate, 2003), 139-60.
McDermott, G.R., *Jonathan Edwards Confronts the Gods: Christian Theology, Enlightenment Religion, and Non-Christian Faiths* (New York: Oxford, 2000).
Miller, P., *Jonathan Edwards* (New York: William Sloan Associates, 1949).
- 'The Rhetoric of Sensation', *Errand Into the Wilderness* (Cambridge, Mass.: Belknap, 1964), 168-83.
Minkema, K.P., 'The Other Unfinished 'Great Work': Jonathan Edwards, Messianic Prophecy, and 'The Harmony of the Old and New Testament'', *Jonathan Edwards's Writings*, ed. Stephen J. Stein (Bloomington: Indiana University Press, 1996), 52-65.
Morimoto, A., *Jonathan Edwards and the Catholic Vision of Salvation* (University Park, Pa.: Penn State Press, 1995).
Muller, R.A., *Dictionary of Latin and Greek Theological Terms* (Grand Rapids: Baker, 1985).
Murray, I.H., *Jonathan Edwards: A New Biography* (Carlisle, Pa.: Banner of Truth, 1987).
Nichols, S.J., *An Absolute Sort of Certainty: The Holy Spirit and the Apologetics of Jonathan Edwards* (Phillipsburg, NJ: Presbyterian and Reformed, 2003).
Olson, R.E. and C.A. Hall., *The Trinity* (Grand Rapids: Eerdmans, 2002).
Owen, J., *Pneumatologia or A Discourse Concerning the Holy Spirit* (Carlisle, Pa.: Banner of Truth, 1965).
Pauw, A.P., "The Supreme Harmony of All': Jonathan Edwards and the Trinity', Ph.D. diss., Yale University, 1990.
- *The Supreme Harmony of All: The Trinitarian Theology of Jonathan Edwards* (Grand Rapids: Eerdmans, 2002).
Pfizenmaier, T.C., *The Trinitarian Theology of Dr. Samuel Clarke (1675-1729): Context, Sources, and Controversy Studies in the History of Christian Thought* (New York: Brill, 1997).
Pinnock, C. *Flame of Love: A Theology of the Holy Spirit* (Downers Grove, Ill.: InterVarsity Press, 1996).
Riley, I.W., *American Philosophy: The Early Schools* (New York: Dodd, Mead & Company, 1907).

Rightmire, R.D., 'The Sacramental Theology of Jonathan Edwards in the Context of Controversy', *Fides et Historia* 21 (January 1989), 50-60.
Sairsingh, K., 'Jonathan Edwards and the Idea of Divine Glory: His Foundational Trinitarianism and its Ecclesial Import', Ph.D. diss., Harvard University, 1986.
Schafer, T.A., 'Jonathan Edwards and Justification by Faith', *Church History* 20.4 (Dec. 1951): 55-67.
Spence, A., 'Christ's Humanity and Ours: John Owen', *Persons Divine and Human*, ed. Christoph Schwoebel and Colin E. Gunton (Edinburgh: T. & T. Clark, 1991), 74-97.
Stein, S.J., 'Jonathan Edwards and the Rainbow: Biblical Exegesis and Poetic Imagination', *New England Quarterly* 47 (1974), 440-56.
– 'The Quest for the Spiritual Sense: The Biblical Hermeneutics of Jonathan Edwards', *Harvard Theological Review* 70 (1977), 99-113.
– "Like Apples of Gold in Pictures of Silver': The Portrait of Wisdom in Jonathan Edwards's Commentary on the Book of Proverbs', *Church History* 54 (1985), 324-37.
– 'The Spirit and the Word: Jonathan Edwards and Scriptural Exegesis', *Jonathan Edwards and the American Experience*, ed. Nathan O. Hatch and Harry S. Stout (New York: Oxford, 1988), 118-30.
Stein, S.J., ed., *Jonathan Edwards's Writings: Text, Context, Interpretation* (Bloomington: Indiana University Press, 1996).
Stephens, B.M., 'Changing Conceptions of the Holy Spirit in American Protestant Theology from Jonathan Edwards to Charles G. Finney', *St. Luke's Journal of Theology* 33:3 (June 1990), 209-223.
– *The Holy Spirit in American Protestant Thought, 1750-1850* (Lewiston, N.Y.: Edwin Mellen Press, 1992).
– *The Prism of Time and Eternity: Images of Christ in American Protestant Thought from Jonathan Edwards to Horace Bushnell* (Lanham, Md.: American Theological Library Association and The Scarecrow Press, 1996).
Studebaker, S.M., 'Jonathan Edwards's Social Augustinian Trinitarianism: A Criticism of an Alternative to Recent Interpretations', Ph.D. diss., Marquette University, 2003.
– 'Jonathan Edwards's Social Augustinian Trinitarianism: An Alternative to a Recent Trend', *Scottish Journal of Theology* 56.3 (2003), 268-85.
– 'Jonathan Edwards' Pneumatological Concept of Grace and Dispositional Soteriology: Resources for an Evangelical Inclusivism', *Pro Ecclesia* 14.3 (2005), 324-39.
Studer, B., *The Grace of Christ and the Grace of God in Augustine of Hippo: Christocentrism or Theocentrism?* (Collegeville, MN: Liturgical Press, 1997).
Sweeney, D.A., 'Jonathan Edwards', *Historical Handbook of Major Biblical Interpreters*, ed. Donald K. McKim (Downers Grove, Ill.: InterVarsity Press, 1998), 309-12.
– 'The Church', *The Princeton Companion to Jonathan Edwards*, ed. Sang Hyun Lee (Princeton: University Press, 2003).
– *Nathaniel Taylor, New Haven Theology and the Legacy of Jonathan Edwards* (New York: Oxford, 2003).
– "Longing for More and More of It'? The Strange Career of Jonathan Edwards's Exegetical Exertions', *Jonathan Edwards at 300: Essays on the Tercentenary of His Birth*, ed. Harry S. Stout, Kenneth P. Minkema, and Caleb J. D. Maskell (Lanham: University Press of America, 2005), 25-37.

Tracy, P.J., *Jonathan Edwards, Pastor: Religion and Society in Eighteenth-Century Northampton* (New York: Hill and Wang, 1979).

Turretin, F., *Institutes of Elenctic Theology*, ed. James T. Dennison Jr., trans. George Musgrave Giger, 3 vols (Phillipsburg, N.J.: Presbyterian and Reformed Publishing, 1994).

Van den Berg, J., 'The Idea of the Pre-Existence of the Soul of Christ: An Argument in the Controversy Between Arian and Orthodox in the Eighteenth Century', *Tradition and Re-Interpretation in Jewish and Early Christian Literature: Essays in Honour of Jurgen C. H. Lebram*, ed. J.W. Van Henten, et. al. (Leiden: Brill, 1986), 284-95.

Waddington, J.C., 'Jonathan Edwards's 'Ambiguous and Somewhat Precarious' Doctrine of Justification', *Westminster Theological Journal* 66 (2004), 357-72.

Warfield, B.B., 'John Calvin the Theologian', *Calvin and Augustine*, ed. Samuel G. Craig (Philadelphia: Presbyterian and Reformed, 1956), 481-507.

Watts, I., *The Glory of Christ as God-Man Displayed*, in *Works of the Rev. Isaac Watts, D. D. In Seven Volumes* (Leeds, 1813), volume 5.

Wiles, M., *Archetypal Heresy: Arianism through the Centuries* (Oxford: Clarendon Press, 1996).

Wilson-Kastner, P., *Coherence in a Fragmented World: Jonathan Edwards's Theology of the Holy Spirit* (Washington, D.C.: University Press of America, 1978).

Youngs, F.W., 'The Place of Spiritual Union in the Thought of Jonathan Edwards', Ph.D. diss., Drew University, 1986.

— 'The Place of Spiritual Union in Trinity Jonathan Edwards's Conception of the Church', *Fides et Historia* 28:1 (Winter/Spring 1996), 27-47.

Name and Subject Index

Agape, 42, 45, 147
Angels,
    age of probation, 174-175
    confirmation of, 175-176
    how "in Christ," 186-187
    relation to humankind, 171-173
Aquinas, Thomas, 47, 109, 110, 179, 203
Arianism, 20, 77, 80, 82, 208
Arminianism, 105-110, 114, 119
Arminius, Jacob, 105
Assurance of Salvation, 152-153
Augustine, 11, 12, 13, 20, 35, 36, 37, 38, 41, 47, 199, 203, 207, 208
Ayers, Lewis, 38, 203
Badcock, Gary, 13, 203
Barnes, Michel R., 38, 203
Beatific Vision, 15, 144, 155, 165, 169, 17, 178-182, 194, 200
Bombaro, John, 111, 122, 203
Brown, Robert, 2, 203
Calvin, John, 41, 131, 164, 203, 208
Charity, Deeds of, 159
Cherry, Conrad, 2, 9, 30, 104, 106, 131, 203
Christ, Jesus,
    baptism of, 43-44
    knowledge, human and divine, 93-96
Christology
    Alexandrian, 75-76, 93, 97
    Antiochene, 75-76, 76n12, 93, 97
    communication of divine consciousness to human, 90-91
    Isaac Watts's Christology, 80-82
    Lutheran, 75
    Owenite, 76
    persons, definition of, 89-90
    Reformed, 75
Church,
    and the Trinity, 156-157
    as bride of Christ, 156
Clarke, Samuel, 20, 206
Conforti, Joseph, 2, 203
Consent, 24, 26, 27, 28, 36, 37, 39, 50, 54, 67, 86, 124, 131, 141, 150
Covenant of Redemption, 14, 29, 60, 64, 65, 67, 71, 77, 82, 94
    Holy Spirit's role in, 66-67
Created Grace, 109-111
Creation
    Logical 'moments' of, 60-67
Cyril of Alexandria, 75
Daley, Brian, 46, 203
Danaher, William, 3, 12, 22, 37, 38, 117, 161, 162, 163, 164, 203
de Regnon, Theodore, 38
Delattre, Roland, 2, 24, 136, 203
Dispositional Ontology, 25, 28, 37, 61
    and H. S. Lee's thesis, 25-26
Dispositional Soteriology, 122-126
Divinization, 113, 116, 117, 118, 119, 120, 190, 192
Doddridge, Phillip, 77, 80
Dorner, J. A., 82, 203
Edwards, Jonathan
    conversion, 19
    "unorthodox" conversion, 123
Edwards, Sarah, 200-201
Edwards's exegesis of significant passages,
    Exod 33:14, 31
    Exod 34:5, 144
    Psalm 2, 174-175
    Prov 8:30, 31-47
    Zech 3:8-9, 88-89
    Zech 8:20-22, 160-161
    John 3:34, 86
    John 6:33, 176
    John 10:36, 87-88, 89
    John 17:26, 37, 70
    Gal 5:13-16, 43
    Eph 4:10, 175-176
    Col 2:9, 85-86
    2 Pet 1:4, 32-33, 86, 143
    1 Jn 4:8 & 16, 32
    1 Jn 4:12-13, 43
Edwards's Writings discussed in detail
    Discourse on the Trinity, 28-35
    End of Creation, 60-63

"Sense of the Heart," Misc. 782, 145-150
Treatise on Grace, 42-49
Elwood, Douglas, 61, 115, 116, 204
Eversley, Walter, 161, 204
Excellency, 21, 23, 24, 26, 27, 28, 34, 36, 37, 42, 49, 50, 51, 54, 64, 65, 70, 72, 104, 109, 131, 133, 135, 137, 140, 141, 143, 148, 149, 150, 151, 152, 155, 160, 164, 173, 180
and the Trinity, 23-24
Extra Calvinisticum, 94, 96
Faith,
and conscious embrace of Christ, 122
as an act of union with Christ, 130-133
definition of, 126-130
justifying faith, 128
relation to love, 126-130
Fiering, Norman, 105, 205
Filioque, 11, 13, 14, 36, 42, 46, 47
controversy, 46
Edwards's affirmation of, 46-47
Finitum non Capax Infiniti, 94, 96
Fitness, Natural and Moral, 135-137
Fullness, 7, 14, 21, 22, 31, 32, 42, 49, 51, 52, 54, 55, 59, 60, 61, 62, 63, 64, 68, 69, 70, 73, 85, 86, 121, 138, 140, 141, 156, 163, 169, 175, 176, 179, 184, 187, 189, 190, 193, 200
Gerstner, John, 76, 139, 205
Glorified Bodies, 183
God
as diamond, 15
as sun, 15, 21
classical theism and Edwards, 61n6
communicative/diffusive being, 21, 22, 60-63
nature of verses essence, 15
relational ontology, 26-27
two "real" attributes, 29, 42
Grace,
as a "principle of nature," 111-118
as Holy Spirit, 52-54
Great Schism, 46
Heaven,
beatific vision, 178-182, 200

history of, 170-189
progressive nature of, 176-177, 189-193
Heppe, Heinrich, 21, 86, 131, 205
Hilberath, Bernd J., 12, 13, 205
Hobbes, Thomas, 23
Holmes, Stephen, 2, 9, 21, 35, 36, 62, 76, 91, 92, 142, 156, 205
Holy Spirit
and 'binitarian' NT texts, 48
and the covenant of redemption, 66-67
as a "principle of nature," 111-118
as dove, 43
as excellency, 50-51
as fullness, 51-52
as grace, 52-54
as happiness, 51
as holiness, 32, 50
as love/affection of Godhead, 3, 32, 42-49, 196
common agent of unions, 6, 8
communicated without measure to Jesus Christ, 85
communication to the saints, 7, 54-55, 197
continuity *ad intra, ad extra*, 7-8, 47, 102, 121, 195
deficiency in theological reflection, 9-11, 12-13, 35
hiddenness of, 14, 41, 47-48, 84, 185, 199
immanent Spirit, 42-49
personhood of, 12-13, 33-34, 109, 114, 196
purchase of redemption, 35
relation to soul: as created grace, 109-111
relation to soul: as external coach, 108
relation to soul: compatiblist model, 118-120
"repeatable" *ad extra*, 4, 6
Hunsinger, George, 136, 195, 205
Hypostatic Union (see also Personal Union) 4, 14, 83, 86, 91, 195, 196, 198
Idealism, 21, 22, 28, 29, 37, 91, 126

Name and Subject Index

and the Trinity, 22-23
Illumination, 104, 105, 141, 149
Image of God, *Imago Dei*, 14, 68, 69, 70, 71, 72, 118, 191, 197
   natural and moral image, 71-73
Incarnation, 4, 5, 71, 75, 77, 78, 79, 80, 81, 82, 83, 84, 88, 89, 93, 94, 164, 187
   after creation, 80-83
   necessity of, 77-80
Infusion, 104, 105, 108
Jenson, Robert, 2, 12, 75, 91, 205
Jones, R. Tudur, 131, 205
Justification, 14, 41, 102, 105, 108, 121, 126, 128, 131, 133-137, 138, 142
Karkkainen, V., 13, 205
Knowledge, Human,
   mere cognition, 145
   sensible knowledge, 146-150
   speculative knowledge, 145-146
   spiritual sensible knowledge, 148-150
Lee, Sang Hyun, 2, 3, 6, 10, 21, 25, 26, 28, 61, 62, 75, 76, 106, 117, 118, 126, 136, 161, 204, 205, 207
Lesser, M. X., 3, 74, 204, 205
Letham, Robert, 4, 205
Logan, Samuel, 30, 135, 206
Logos, 1, 6, 31, 42, 80, 81, 82, 84, 85, 86, 88, 89, 90, 91, 92, 93, 94, 96, 97, 147, 188
Lombard, Peter, 109
Lord's Supper, 161-165
Lucas, Sean M., 3, 206
Lucifer, 171, 174
Luther, Martin, 75
Macleod, Donald, 5, 80, 206
Marsden, George, 1, 141, 206
Mastricht, Peter van, 21, 26, 206
McClymond, Michael, 2, 23, 206
McDermott, Gerald, 2, 20, 122, 206
Miller, Perry, 2, 206
Minkema, Kenneth, 3, 8, 30, 122, 138, 158, 161, 204, 206, 207
Morimoto, Anri, 2, 104, 110, 111, 126, 206
Muller, Richard, 95, 206
Murray, Iain, 1, 206
Mystical Union (see also Union with Christ) 5, 8, 86
Nature,
   and the Holy Spirit, 111-112
Newton, Isaac, 20
Nichols, Stephen, 3, 152, 206
Olson, Roger, 13, 206
Owen, John, 83, 92, 206, 207
Panentheism, 115
Pantheism, Pantheist, 61, 113, 115, 116, 119, 120
Participation in the Divine Nature, 3, 32, 54-55
Pauw, Amy P., 2, 9, 12, 26, 27, 28, 29, 37, 69, 75, 76, 91, 92, 204, 206
Pepperrell, Lady Mary, 39
Perichoresis, 4, 34, 53
Personal Union (see also Hypostatic Union) 8, 81, 83, 85, 86, 88, 89, 92, 97, 189, 192, 197
   Holy Spirit bond of, 83-93
Pfizenmaier, Thomas, 20, 206
Pinnock, Clark, 13, 206
Prayer, 159-161
Regeneration, 14, 102, 103, 108, 118, 119, 121, 122, 123, 126, 132, 133, 191
Religious Pluralism, 2, 122
Rightmire, R. David, 161, 207
Riley, I. Woodbridge, 61, 115, 206
Sairsingh, Krister, 156, 207
Salvation,
   a secret disposition to love Christ, 124
   assurance of, 152-153
   not knowing the reality of it, 122-126
   of infants, 125n72
   Old Testament saints and Christ, 124-125
Sanctification,
   as consent to "being in general," 140-141
   as overflowing dispositions, 140
   as spiritual sight, 139-140
Schafer, Thomas, 1, 2, 7, 20, 69, 122, 156, 204, 207

Spence, Alan, 92, 207
Spiritual Sight, 142-155
Stein, Stephen, 2, 8, 30, 53, 160, 204, 206, 207
Stephens, Bruce, 9, 46, 76, 207
Stoddard, Solomon, 122, 124, 125
Stogdon, Hubert, 20
Studebaker, Stephen, 27, 38, 40, 122, 156, 207
Studer, Basil, 38, 207
Sweeney, Douglas, 2, 22, 30, 75, 156, 158, 204, 207
Theosis, 7, 117
Tracy, Patricia, 1, 208
Trinitarian Controversy, 20
Trinitarianism,
    Augustinian and Edwards's 11n28, 12-13, 33-40, 198-200
    Eastern Orthodox and Edwards's, 12
    Eastern verses Western, 38n73
    Social and Edwards's, 27, 28, 37
Trinity
    and Edwards's idealism, 22-23
    and excellency, 23-24
    continuity *ad intra, ad extra*, 4, 63-64, 68-71, 121, 186
    created analogies, 11
    Edwards's confidence in reason, 21
    Edwards on the Father, 29
    Edwards on the Holy Spirit, 32-33
    Edwards on the Son, 29-32

equality of the three, 34-35, 198-199
love presupposes knowledge, 48-49
persons, definition of, 33-34, 89-90
"repeatable" *ad extra*, 29-30, 102
social trinitarianism and Edwards, 27-28
unity of divine operations *ad extra*, 36
Turretin, Francis, 26, 75, 86, 95, 208
Union, similarity between theological unions, 5-6
Union with Christ (see also Mystical Union) 5, 14, 102, 121, 126, 130, 131-133, 135, 137, 170, 181, 184, 186, 187-189, 190, 193, 194, 196, 198, 199
and justification, 133-137
increasing throughout eternity, 190-192
Valeri, Mark, 28, 158, 204
Van den Berg, J., 208
Waddington, Jeffrey, 137, 208
Warfield, B. B., 41, 208
Watts, Isaac, 1, 20, 77, 80, 81, 82, 95, 208
Wesley, John, 105
Whiston, William, 20
Wiles, Maurice, 20, 208
Wilson-Kastner, Patricia, 9, 208
Youngs, Fredrick, 9, 156, 208

Studies in Evangelical History and Thought
(All titles uniform with this volume)
Dates in bold are of projected publication

Andrew Atherstone
Oxford's Protestant Spy
The Controversial Career of Charles Golightly
Charles Golightly (1807–85) was a notorious Protestant polemicist. His life was dedicated to resisting the spread of ritualism and liberalism within the Church of England and the University of Oxford. For half a century he led many memorable campaigns, such as building a martyr's memorial and attempting to close a theological college. John Henry Newman, Samuel Wilberforce and Benjamin Jowett were among his adversaries. This is the first study of Golightly's controversial career.
***2006* / 1-84227-364-7 / approx. 324pp**

Clyde Binfield
Victorian Nonconformity in Eastern England
Studies of Victorian religion and society often concentrate on cities, suburbs, and industrialisation. This study provides a contrast. Victorian Eastern England—Essex, Suffolk, Norfolk, Cambridgeshire, and Huntingdonshire—was rural, traditional, relatively unchanging. That is nonetheless a caricature which discounts the industry in Norwich and Ipswich (as well as in Haverhill, Stowmarket and Leiston) and ignores the impact of London on Essex, of railways throughout the region, and of an ancient but changing university (Cambridge) on the county town which housed it. It also entirely ignores the political implications of such changes in a region noted for the variety of its religious Dissent since the seventeenth century. This book explores Victorian Eastern England and its Nonconformity. It brings to a wider readership a pioneering thesis which has made a major contribution to a fresh evolution of English religion and society.
***2006* / 1-84227-216-0 / approx. 274pp**

John Brencher
Martyn Lloyd-Jones (1899–1981) and Twentieth-Century Evangelicalism
This study critically demonstrates the significance of the life and ministry of Martyn Lloyd-Jones for post-war British evangelicalism and demonstrates that his preaching was his greatest influence on twentieth-century Christianity. The factors which shaped his view of the church are examined, as is the way his reformed evangelicalism led to a separatist ecclesiology which divided evangelicals.
2002 / 1-84227-051-6 / xvi + 268pp

Jonathan D. Burnham
A Story of Conflict
The Controversial Relationship between Benjamin Wills Newton and John Nelson Darby

Burnham explores the controversial relationship between the two principal leaders of the early Brethren movement. In many ways Newton and Darby were products of their times, and this study of their relationship provides insight not only into the dynamics of early Brethrenism, but also into the progress of nineteenth-century English and Irish evangelicalism.

2004 / 1-84227-191-1 / xxiv + 268pp

Grayson Carter
Anglican Evangelicals
Protestant Secessions from the Via Media, c.1800–1850

This study examines, within a chronological framework, the major themes and personalities which influenced the outbreak of a number of Evangelical clerical and lay secessions from the Church of England and Ireland during the first half of the nineteenth century. Though the number of secessions was relatively small—between a hundred and two hundred of the 'Gospel' clergy abandoned the Church during this period—their influence was considerable, especially in highlighting in embarrassing fashion the tensions between the evangelical conversionist imperative and the principles of a national religious establishment. Moreover, through much of this period there remained, just beneath the surface, the potential threat of a large Evangelical disruption similar to that which occurred in Scotland in 1843. Consequently, these secessions provoked great consternation within the Church and within Evangelicalism itself, they contributed to the outbreak of millennial speculation following the 'constitutional revolution' of 1828–32, they led to the formation of several new denominations, and they sparked off a major Church–State crisis over the legal right of a clergyman to secede and begin a new ministry within Protestant Dissent.

2007 / 1-84227-401-5 / xvi + 470pp

J.N. Ian Dickson
Beyond Religious Discourse
Sermons, Preaching and Evangelical Protestants in Nineteenth-Century Irish Society

Drawing extensively on primary sources, this pioneer work in modern religious history explores the training of preachers, the construction of sermons and how Irish evangelicalism and the wider movement in Great Britain and the United States shaped the preaching event. Evangelical preaching and politics, sectarianism, denominations, education, class, social reform, gender, and revival are examined to advance the argument that evangelical sermons and preaching went significantly beyond religious discourse. The result is a book for those with interests in Irish history, culture and belief, popular religion and society, evangelicalism, preaching and communication.

2005 / 1-84227-217-9 / approx. 324pp

Neil T.R. Dickson
Brethren in Scotland 1838–2000
A Social Study of an Evangelical Movement

The Brethren were remarkably pervasive throughout Scottish society. This study of the Open Brethren in Scotland places them in their social context and examines their growth, development and relationship to society.

2003 / 1-84227-113-X / xxviii + 510pp

Crawford Gribben and Timothy C.F. Stunt (eds)
Prisoners of Hope?
Aspects of Evangelical Millennialism in Britain and Ireland, 1800–1880

This volume of essays offers a comprehensive account of the impact of evangelical millennialism in nineteenth-century Britain and Ireland.

2004 / 1-84227-224-1 / xiv + 208pp

Khim Harris
Evangelicals and Education
Evangelical Anglicans and Middle-Class Education in Nineteenth-Century England

This ground breaking study investigates the history of English public schools founded by nineteenth-century Evangelicals. It documents the rise of middle-class education and Evangelical societies such as the influential Church Association, and includes a useful biographical survey of prominent Evangelicals of the period.

2004 / 1-84227-250-0 / xviii + 422pp

Mark Hopkins
Nonconformity's Romantic Generation
Evangelical and Liberal Theologies in Victorian England

A study of the theological development of key leaders of the Baptist and Congregational denominations at their period of greatest influence, including C.H. Spurgeon and R.W. Dale, and of the controversies in which those among them who embraced and rejected the liberal transformation of their evangelical heritage opposed each other.

2004 / 1-84227-150-4 / xvi + 284pp

Don Horrocks
Laws of the Spiritual Order
Innovation and Reconstruction in the Soteriology of Thomas Erskine of Linlathen

Don Horrocks argues that Thomas Erskine's unique historical and theological significance as a soteriological innovator has been neglected. This timely reassessment reveals Erskine as a creative, radical theologian of central and enduring importance in Scottish nineteenth-century theology, perhaps equivalent in significance to that of S.T. Coleridge in England.

2004 / 1-84227-192-X / xx + 362pp

Kenneth S. Jeffrey
When the Lord Walked the Land
The 1858–62 Revival in the North East of Scotland

Previous studies of revivals have tended to approach religious movements from either a broad, national or a strictly local level. This study of the multifaceted nature of the 1859 revival as it appeared in three distinct social contexts within a single region reveals the heterogeneous nature of simultaneous religious movements in the same vicinity.

2002 / 1-84227-057-5 / xxiv + 304pp

John Kenneth Lander
Itinerant Temples
Tent Methodism, 1814–1832

Tent preaching began in 1814 and the Tent Methodist sect resulted from disputes with Bristol Wesleyan Methodists in 1820. The movement spread to parts of Gloucestershire, Wiltshire, London and Liverpool, among other places. Its demise started in 1826 after which one leader returned to the Wesleyans and others became ministers in the Congregational and Baptist denominations.

2003 / 1-84227-151-2 / xx + 268pp

Donald M. Lewis
Lighten Their Darkness
The Evangelical Mission to Working-Class London, 1828–1860
This is a comprehensive and compelling study of the Church and the complexities of nineteenth-century London. Challenging our understanding of the culture in working London at this time, Lewis presents a well-structured and illustrated work that contributes substantially to the study of evangelicalism and mission in nineteenth-century Britain.

2001 / 1-84227-074-5 / xviii + 372pp

Herbert McGonigle
'Sufficient Saving Grace'
John Wesley's Evangelical Arminianism
A thorough investigation of the theological roots of John Wesley's evangelical Arminianism and how these convictions were hammered out in controversies on predestination, limited atonement and the perseverance of the saints.

2001 / 1-84227-045-1 / xvi + 350pp

Lisa S. Nolland
A Victorian Feminist Christian
Josephine Butler, the Prostitutes and God
Josephine Butler was an unlikely candidate for taking up the cause of prostitutes, as she did, with a fierce and self-disregarding passion. This book explores the particular mix of perspectives and experiences that came together to envision and empower her remarkable achievements. It highlights the vital role of her spirituality and the tragic loss of her daughter.

2004 / 1-84227-225-X / xxiv + 328pp

Don J. Payne
The Theology of the Christian Life in J.I. Packer's Thought
Theological Anthropology, Theological Method, and the Doctrine of Sanctification
J.I. Packer has wielded widespread influence on evangelicalism for more than three decades. This study pursues a nuanced understanding of Packer's theology of sanctification by tracing the development of his thought, showing how he reflects a particular version of Reformed theology, and examining the unique influence of theological anthropology and theological method on this area of his theology.

2005 / 1-84227-397-3 / approx. 374pp

Ian M. Randall
Evangelical Experiences
A Study in the Spirituality of English Evangelicalism 1918–1939
This book makes a detailed historical examination of evangelical spirituality between the First and Second World Wars. It shows how patterns of devotion led to tensions and divisions. In a wide-ranging study, Anglican, Wesleyan, Reformed and Pentecostal-charismatic spiritualities are analysed.
1999 / 0-85364-919-7 / xii + 310pp

Ian M. Randall
Spirituality and Social Change
The Contribution of F.B. Meyer (1847–1929)
This is a fresh appraisal of F.B. Meyer (1847–1929), a leading Free Church minister. Having been deeply affected by holiness spirituality, Meyer became the Keswick Convention's foremost international speaker. He combined spirituality with effective evangelism and socio-political activity. This study shows Meyer's significant contribution to spiritual renewal and social change.
2003 / 1-84227-195-4 / xx + 184pp

James Robinson
Pentecostal Origins
Early Pentecostalism in Ireland in the Context of the British Isles
Harvey Cox describes Pentecostalism as 'the fascinating spiritual child of our time' that has the potential, at the global scale, to contribute to the 'reshaping of religion in the twenty-first century'. This study grounds such sentiments by examining at the local scale the origin, development and nature of Pentecostalism in Ireland in its first twenty years. Illustrative, in a paradigmatic way, of how Pentecostalism became established within one region of the British Isles, it sets the story within the wider context of formative influences emanating from America, Europe and, in particular, other parts of the British Isles. As a synoptic regional study in Pentecostal history it is the first survey of its kind.
2005 / 1-84227-329-1 / xxviii + 378pp

Geoffrey Robson
Dark Satanic Mills?
Religion and Irreligion in Birmingham and the Black Country
This book analyses and interprets the nature and extent of popular Christian belief and practice in Birmingham and the Black Country during the first half of the nineteenth century, with particular reference to the impact of cholera epidemics and evangelism on church extension programmes.
2002 / 1-84227-102-4 / xiv + 294pp

Roger Shuff
Searching for the True Church
Brethren and Evangelicals in Mid-Twentieth-Century England

Roger Shuff holds that the influence of the Brethren movement on wider evangelical life in England in the twentieth century is often underrated. This book records and accounts for the fact that Brethren reached the peak of their strength at the time when evangelicalism was at it lowest ebb, immediately before World War II. However, the movement then moved into persistent decline as evangelicalism regained ground in the post war period. Accompanying this downward trend has been a sharp accentuation of the contrast between Brethren congregations who engage constructively with the non-Brethren scene and, at the other end of the spectrum, the isolationist group commonly referred to as 'Exclusive Brethren'.

2005 / 1-84227-254-3 / xviii+ 296pp

James H.S. Steven
Worship in the Spirit
Charismatic Worship in the Church of England

This book explores the nature and function of worship in six Church of England churches influenced by the Charismatic Movement, focusing on congregational singing and public prayer ministry. The theological adequacy of such ritual is discussed in relation to pneumatological and christological understandings in Christian worship.

2002 / 1-84227-103-2 / xvi + 238pp

Peter K. Stevenson
God in Our Nature
The Incarnational Theology of John McLeod Campbell

This radical reassessment of Campbell's thought arises from a comprehensive study of his preaching and theology. Previous accounts have overlooked both his sermons and his Christology. This study examines the distinctive Christology evident in his sermons and shows that it sheds new light on Campbell's much debated views about atonement.

2004 / 1-84227-218-7 / xxiv + 458pp

Kenneth J. Stewart
Restoring the Reformation
British Evangelicalism and the Réveil at Geneva 1816–1849
Restoring the Reformation traces British missionary initiative in post-Revolutionary Francophone Europe from the genesis of the London Missionary Society, the visits of Robert Haldane and Henry Drummond, and the founding of the Continental Society. While British Evangelicals aimed at the reviving of a foreign Protestant cause of momentous legend, they received unforeseen reciprocating emphases from the Continent which forced self-reflection on Evangelicalism's own relationship to the Reformation.
2006 / 1-84227-392-2 / approx. 190pp

Martin Wellings
Evangelicals Embattled
Responses of Evangelicals in the Church of England to Ritualism, Darwinism and Theological Liberalism 1890–1930
In the closing years of the nineteenth century and the first decades of the twentieth century Anglican Evangelicals faced a series of challenges. In responding to Anglo-Catholicism, liberal theology, Darwinism and biblical criticism, the unity and identity of the Evangelical school were severely tested.
2003 / 1-84227-049-4 / xviii + 352pp

James Whisenant
A Fragile Unity
Anti-Ritualism and the Division of Anglican Evangelicalism in the Nineteenth Century
This book deals with the ritualist controversy (approximately 1850–1900) from the perspective of its evangelical participants and considers the divisive effects it had on the party.
2003 / 1-84227-105-9 / xvi + 530pp

Haddon Willmer
Evangelicalism 1785–1835: An Essay (1962) and Reflections (2004)
Awarded the Hulsean Prize in the University of Cambridge in 1962, this interpretation of a classic period of English Evangelicalism, by a young church historian, is now supplemented by reflections on Evangelicalism from the vantage point of a retired Professor of Theology.
2006 / 1-84227-219-5 / approx. 350pp

July 2005

Linda Wilson
Constrained by Zeal
Female Spirituality amongst Nonconformists 1825–1875

Constrained by Zeal investigates the neglected area of Nonconformist female spirituality. Against the background of separate spheres, it analyses the experience of women from four denominations, and argues that the churches provided a 'third sphere' in which they could find opportunities for participation.

2000 / 0-85364-972-3 / xvi + 294pp

Paternoster
9 Holdom Avenue,
Bletchley,
Milton Keynes MK1 1QR,
United Kingdom
Web: www.authenticmedia.co.uk/paternoster

July 2005

www.ingramcontent.com/pod-product-compliance
Lightning Source LLC
Chambersburg PA
CBHW062019220426
43662CB00010B/1392